Property Law II
Workbook

A Behavioral Approach to Learning

Kim O'Leary and Nelson P. Miller

Property Law II Workbook–

A Behavioral Approach to Learning

Kim O'Leary and Nelson P. Miller

Publisher:
Crown Management LLC – April 2020
1527 Pineridge Drive
Grand Haven, MI 49417
USA

ISBN-13: 978-1-64871-129-9

Table of Contents

Introduction

This workbook is for the three-credit course Property Law II, comprised of thirteen weeks of new studies, identified as Week 1, Week 2, etc., followed by a Review Week and a Final Exam Week.

The exercises in this workbook provide the most benefit when you complete them with other students, in pairs or small groups. The exercises' value is not only in you thinking and writing but also talking and listening, getting and giving feedback. The more that you can see, hear, and interact with others, and that others can see and hear you, providing you with feedback, the better these exercises are likely to serve you.

This workbook provides answers to its exercises, questions, and problems, generally on the back of the page from which you work or below the exercises that you complete, on the same page. Immediate feedback enables you to confirm or correct your thought and expression. To use the answers for their best effect, try to complete the exercise first before referring to the answer. The value is in part in striving.

The exercises vary somewhat from week to week to increase your interest and so that you learn in different ways and practice different skills. The exercises help you start with discrete knowledge components that you gradually build into complex sequences involving applying law and solving problems. The exercises generally build from one to another.

Use this workbook to push yourself deeper into grasping, recalling, and applying the fundamental concepts of property law. The more active that your studies are, and the more that you strive at the boundaries of your capabilities, the better you should acquire knowledge and skills for their practical use and benefit, to you, clients, and others. Best wishes for good studies.

Week 1
Leasehold Estates

QUESTIONS FOR THE ASSIGNED READING:

The law of property incorporates the law of contracts and torts in some respects but not others. Contracts law generally governs contracts for property, although those contracts may have special rules. Same with tort law: it usually governs torts involving property, although torts involving property may also have special rules. Now that you have studied property law for a semester, what does property law add that contract and tort law do not provide?

What bundle of rights come with a leasehold estate? For the landlord? For the tenant?

What are the different types of leasehold estates? For each, how can they be terminated without cause? What is the difference between terminating for cause and without cause?

Once a leasehold estate exists, whose duty is it to evict any wrongful possessor of the property? Can you define the American rule and the English rule? Which rule is the majority in most U.S. jurisdictions?

What is a unilateral right of termination of a tenancy? Why does such a right create problems? How does common law interpret the right? Does it matter if the unilateral right lies with the tenant or the landlord? Why or why not?

What are the three main sources of law for claims of housing discrimination? How are those laws the same, and how are they different? What must landlords not do because of these laws? What is a retaliation claim, as it relates to anti-discrimination?

Name something you do not understand about this week's material.

SHORT OUTLINE:

The law of landlord and tenant involves the right of an owner to lease the real property.

A non-freehold estate under **leasehold** or **lease** makes the occupant a **tenant** and the owner a **landlord**.

Types of holdings depend on **creation** and determine rights on **termination**.

Landlords and tenants typically create the type of tenancy initially by forming a lease.

Conditions for terminating a lease depend on type of tenancy that the lease and other circumstances create.

A terms of years is a leasehold that conveys the right to occupy and use the land *for a specific period*.

Landlord and tenant may provide for a period of days, weeks, months, years, or any other specific period.

Landlord and tenant need only know when the term will end.

A term of years may be **determinable**, occurrence of a condition shortening and terminating the lease.

A term of years terminates automatically, *without notice*, at the end of its term.

A tenancy at will is a leasehold that either party may terminate at any time, with or without reason.

The common law does not require notice to terminate, but the modern rule/ statutes require *reasonable notice*.

Landlords must not terminate in violation of **anti-discrimination laws** protecting many classes.

Protected classes include race, color, national origin, sex, religion, age, disability, & family & marital status.

A holdover is a tenant who stays beyond lease termination by term of years or end of periodic tenancy.

A holdover tenant has only a **tenancy at sufferance** where the landlord may evict or hold to a renewed term.

The renewed term equals the original lease period, except some states make it monthly for residential leases.
If the original lease was for more than one year, many states limit renewal term to one month or one year.
The landlord must make the decision within a reasonable time whether to hold over or to evict.
Periodic tenancies renew automatically for the initial lease period or other renewal period that the lease provides.
A *month-to-month* lease is a periodic tenancy renewing for one month at a time while both agree.
Landlord and tenant can have year-to-year periods or longer periods such as five years.
Landlord or tenant may only terminate a periodic tenancy at the end of one of the periods.
The lease may require notice a certain number of days before the end of a period.

LONG OUTLINE:
The law of landlord and tenant

Owners of real property have rights to lease interests in the land. Those who wish to occupy land without an ownership interest may have the opportunity to form a non-freehold estate that the law recognizes as a **leasehold** or **lease**, making the occupant a **tenant**. Ownership thus needs to address the law of **landlord and tenant**, a landlord being the owner who leases occupancy to a tenant. Landlord/tenant law must address the *types* of leaseholds including how parties create and terminate them. Landlord/tenant law also must address tenant rights of *possession* versus landlord rights of *rent*. Landlords may *assign* their interest, while tenants may be able to *sublet*. The *termination* of tenancies is another subject as are issues of *habitability* and *suitability*, all addressed in the following sections.

Types of holdings: creation and termination

The law recognizes several different types of **tenancy**. The following sections address a *term of years*, which is a tenancy for a specific period whether measured in years or not, *tenancies at will*, terminable by either party, *holdovers* and other tenancies *at sufferance*, and *periodic tenancies*, typically measured by the period of the original lease. Landlords and tenants typically create the type of tenancy at least initially by entering into a lease. The conditions for terminating a lease depend on the type of tenancy that the lease or other circumstance has created.

Terms for years

A **term of years** is a common leasehold that conveys the right to occupy and use the land *for a specific period*. Although the law calls the leasehold a term of *years*, the landlord and tenant may provide for a period of days, weeks, months, years, or any other period, if the period is specific. The landlord and tenant need only know when the term will end. Thus, a lease that lasts *until the third full moon rises* is a term of years because the parties can calculate the date certain when the third full moon rises. A term of years may be **determinable**, meaning that although the lease provides for a specific period, the occurrence of a condition may shorten the period, terminating the lease. Thus, a lease *for one year, as long as tenant lives alone* is a determinable term of years. A term of years terminates automatically, meaning *without notice*, at the end of its term.

Tenancies at will

A **tenancy at will** is a leasehold that either party may terminate at any time, with or without reason. While the common law did not require notice to terminate, the modern rule and many state statutes require *reasonable notice*, particularly as to residential leases. Thus, a residential landlord may have to serve a thirty-day notice to quit. While a landlord may terminate a tenancy at will for any reason or no reason, a landlord must not terminate in violation of **anti-discrimination laws** protecting classes including race, color, national origin, sex, religion, age, disability, family status, meaning with or without children, and in some states marital status or other statuses, meaning with children.

Holdovers and other tenancies at sufferance

A **holdover** is a tenant who stays beyond the termination of the lease, whether the lease ends by term of years or at the end of a periodic tenancy. A holdover tenant has only a **tenancy at sufferance** during which the landlord may decide whether to evict the tenant or to hold the tenant to a renewed lease period equal to the original lease period. Thus, if the original lease was month-to-month, then the landlord could only hold the tenant over, meaning require the tenant to commit to and pay for, another month's lease. If, instead, the lease was year-to-year, many jurisdictions permit the landlord to hold the tenant to an additional year, although some states provide for only a month-to-month tenancy, particularly for *residential* leases. If the original lease was for more than one year, many jurisdictions would limit the landlord to holding the tenant over for a shorter period such as one month or one year. The landlord must make the decision within a reasonable time whether to hold over or to evict.

Periodic tenancies

A **periodic tenancy** is a tenancy that renews automatically for the initial lease period or other renewal period that the lease provides. Thus, for example, a *month-to-month* lease, providing that the tenant rents by the month, is a periodic tenancy that renews for one month as long as the landlord intends each month that the tenant stay and the tenant intends likewise. Landlord and tenant can also have longer periodic tenancy such as year-to-year or even providing for five-year renewal periods. The landlord or tenant may only terminate a periodic tenancy at the end of one of the periods. The lease may require notice a certain number of days before the end of a period.

Possession

A lease grants the tenant the right of **possession** and the landlord the right of **rent**. A lease fundamentally includes the landlord's *duty to deliver* to the tenant the *legal right of possession*. Most jurisdictions hold to the English rule that the landlord also has a duty to deliver *actual* possession, not just the legal right to possess. Thus, in those cases, a landlord who grants legal right of possession to a tenant but leaves the premises occupied by a holdover tenant would have breached duty to deliver actual possession. The tenant's remedies would then be to either withhold rent until the tenant can occupy the premises or void the lease and sue the landlord for any damages due to the lost possession. If the landlord delivers only partial possession, though, the tenant has a right only to reduce the rent for the lost portion. The tenant may alternatively sue to evict the holdover tenant. Jurisdictions following the minority American rule do not require the landlord to deliver actual possession, instead requiring the tenant to sue the holdover to evict and take possession.

Tenants must avoid **waste**, meaning that they must not destroy the property, allow its collapse into disrepair, or make other significant changes to the property. For example, if a tenant discovers a significant plumbing leak, the tenant must act or notify the landlord promptly to do so, rather than ignore the problem as it causes growing damage. Tenants must also not deliberately destroy walls, floors, appliances, and mechanical systems. Tenants do *not*, though, have a duty to renovate or remodel to address normal wear and tear. Tenants also have no duty to repair after catastrophic damages, for instance from hurricane or flood, although they must try to avoid such damage when reasonably able to do so. Tenants must also avoid **illegal uses** such as prostitution, drug sales, and the like. A landlord discovering such uses may terminate the lease or seek to enjoin such uses while enforcing the lease. Tenants must also not interfere with quiet use and enjoyment by *other tenants*.

Fluency Cards

Cover and uncover the response to each prompt until you fluently recall the exact response.

Tenancy types	**Term of years**
Term of years, determinable term of years, tenancy at will, tenancy at sufferance, periodic tenancy.	Conveys occupancy for specific period.

Determinable term	**Termination notice (no cause)**
Ends with occurrence of stated condition.	Required for periodic tenancy and often for at-will tenancy by statute.
Termination notice for cause (major breach)	**Tenancy at sufferance**
For leasing, amenities, & advertising. Protects race, religion, origin, handicap, & familial status.	Holdover overstaying end of term. Evict or hold to equal renewed term, within reasonable time.
Holdover renewal	**Periodic tenancy**
States may renew residential holdover for a month and limit multi-year holdover to 1 year.	Extends lease for same fixed period of time unless a party gives proper notice.
Possession	**Partial possession**
Landlord must deliver actual (English rule) or in a few states only legal (tenant must evict).	Tenant pays partial rent for landlord delivering only partial possession.

No possession

Tenant w/o possession withholds rent, voids lease and sues, or evicts holdover tenant.

Tenant duties

Don't waste, destroy, disrepair, alter significantly, interfere with other tenants, or conduct illegal activities.

Wear and tear

Tenants have no duty to renovate to fix normal wear and tear.

Rent

Tenant must pay lease rent or, if none, market value, when stated due or, if none, on term's last day.

Definitions Worksheet on Leasehold Estates

1.   Name and briefly define the types of tenancies.

_____

_____

_____

2.   What is a *determinable* term of years? Give an example. How does a term of years end?

_____

_____

_____

3.   What restrictions, if any, does law impose on terminating tenancies at will?

_____

_____

4.   How does the law treat holdover tenants? Give an example.

_____

_____

5.   What duties does a landlord have relating to possession?

_____

_____

6.   What duty and defenses do the tenant have as to rent?

_____

_____

7.   How does law limit to whom a landlord must lease, to protect certain classes?

_____

_____

_____

Answer Key for Definitions Worksheet on Leasehold Estates

1. ***Name and briefly define the types of tenancies.*** A *term of years* is a tenancy for a specific period whether measured in years or not, *tenancies at will* either party may terminate, holdovers create *tenancies at sufferance*, and *periodic tenancies* law typically measures by the period of the original lease.

2. ***What is a*** **determinable** ***term of years? Give an example. How does a term of years end?*** A *determinable* term of years means that although the lease provides for a specific period, the occurrence of *a condition may shorten the period*, terminating the lease. For example, a lease for one year "as long as tenant lives alone" is a determinable term ending if another person lives with the lessee tenant. A term of years terminates automatically, meaning without notice, at the end of its term.

3. ***What restrictions, if any, does law impose on terminating tenancies at will?*** While the common law permitted either party to terminate a tenancy at will at any time with or without reason, the modern rule and many state statutes require *reasonable notice*, especially as to residential leases. A residential landlord may have to serve a thirty-day notice to quit. Also, a landlord must not violate anti-discrimination laws protecting classes including race, color, national origin, sex, religion, age, disability, family status with or without children, and in some states marital status or other statuses.

4. ***How does the law treat holdover tenants? Give an example.*** A holdover, meaning a tenant who stays beyond the lease's end, has only a *tenancy at sufferance* during which the landlord decides whether to evict or hold the tenant to a renewed lease period equal to the original period. For example, if the original lease was for one year, then the landlord could hold the tenant over for another year's lease, although some states provide for only a month-to-month tenancy for *residential* leases, and if the original lease was for more than one year, many states limit the landlord to holding the tenant over for a shorter period such as one month or one year. The landlord must make the decision within a reasonable time whether to hold over or to evict.

5. ***What duties does a landlord have relating to possession?*** The landlord's lease delivers to the tenant the *legal right of possession*. Most states hold to the English rule that the landlord also has a duty to deliver *actual* possession, not just the legal right. If someone occupies against the tenant's right to possess, the tenant could then either withhold full or partial rent until full possession or void the lease and sue the landlord for any damages due to the lost possession. The tenant may alternatively sue to evict the holdover tenant. States following the minority American rule do not require the landlord to deliver actual possession, instead requiring the tenant to sue the holdover to evict and take possession.

6. ***What duty does the tenant have as to rent?*** The tenant owes the duty to pay rent, under modern rules dependent on habitability and suitability (studied in Week 3). If the lease fails to state the rent, then a court infers *fair market value*. If the lease fails to state when rent is due, then rent is due on the last day of the lease term. A landlord who complies with the lease may evict a non-paying tenant.

7. ***How does law limit to whom a landlord must lease, to protect certain classes?*** While a landlord may terminate a tenancy at will for any reason or no reason, a landlord must not refuse to lease or terminate a lease in violation of *anti-discrimination laws* protecting classes including race, color, national origin, sex, religion, age, disability, family status, meaning with or without children, and in some states marital status or other statuses.

8

Issue-Spotting Worksheet on Landlord and Tenant
State the law each scenario raises. No analysis. Just spot the issue and state the law.

1.   Your new client begins by telling you about her dispute with her landlord. Turns out, she is a recovering drug addict who signed a one-year lease in a residential rehabilitation program. With her now halfway through, the landlord has tried to kick her out, allegedly for doing drugs and sneaking in overnight roommates. She denies both allegations but admits that both are "against the rules." Although the program is difficult, she wants to stay in her apartment the rest of the year. You have some landlord-tenant law to share.

_____

_____

2.   Your client then pulls the lease out of her backpack for you to review. Turns out, the lease is not for a year but instead lets either landlord or tenant terminate at any time. You point that fact out to the client who, dumbfounded, asks if that means the landlord can kick her out today. You've got some advice.

_____

_____

3.   Your client is indignant, especially, she explains, because the landlord doesn't treat men who are in the program the same way as the landlord is treating her and has treated other women. She says angrily *that's illegal!* but then adds uncertainly, *isn't it?*

_____

_____

4.   Your client pauses to consider your last counsel before saying that she might just refuse to leave if the landlord tells her to do so, especially insofar as she says that the landlord promised her a year's lease. She doesn't look that confident, though. Sure enough, she asks you what could happen if she tried to stay, adding *I'd pay rent!*

_____

_____

5.   You look at your watch. Your client correctly takes it as your signal that she'd better wrap things up. Then it comes out: she's not paid rent for the past two months. She says she's not even sure what the rent really is or when it's due. She wants to know if you could tell her what she has to do about rent including if she has any "excuses" she could use not to pay.

_____

_____

Answer Key for Issue-Spotting Worksheet on Landlord and Tenant

1. ***This scenario implicates a determinable term of years.*** You might want to tell your new client about a *determinable* term of years, meaning a lease for a specific period but with *a condition that may shorten the period*, terminating the lease.

2. ***This scenario implicates termination of a tenancy at will.*** Consider telling your client that while the common law permitted either party to terminate a tenancy at will at any time without reason or notice, the modern rule and many state statutes require *reasonable notice*, especially as to residential leases. A residential landlord may have to serve a thirty-day notice to quit.

3. ***This scenario implicates anti-discrimination law.*** Consider telling your client that a landlord must not violate anti-discrimination laws protecting classes including race, color, national origin, sex, religion, age, disability, family status with or without children, and in some states marital status or other statuses. Those protections extend to lease termination.

4. ***This scenario implicates law on holdover tenants.*** Although this lease is only a tenancy at will, you might want to tell your client generally about holdover tenants who attempt to stay beyond the lease term. Holdovers have only a *tenancy at sufferance* during which the landlord decides whether to evict or hold the tenant to a renewed lease period equal to the original period. The landlord must make the decision within a reasonable time whether to hold over or to evict.

5. ***This scenario implicates the tenant's duty to pay rent.*** You'd better tell your client that a tenant owes the duty to pay rent, under modern rules dependent on habitability and suitability. If the lease fails to state the rent, then a court infers *fair market value*. If the lease fails to state when rent is due, then rent is due on the last day of the lease term. A landlord who complies with the lease may evict a non-paying tenant. Frustration of purpose or an illegal lease, such as failing to meeting housing codes, may be rent defenses.

Comprehensiveness Exercise for Leasehold Estates

Insert words at the ^ mark that would make for a more-accurate or more-detailed law statement.
Follow the italicized hints for help. Suggested answers are on the next page.

1.   ^ The forms of tenancy include a term of years ^ , tenancy at will ^ , and tenancy at sufferance ^ ^ . *[Care to include brief definitions after each form? And one form is left out.]*

2.   A ^ term of years terminates ^ at the end of its term but shortens that term if the identified condition occurs. *[What do you call this type of term of years that can end early on a condition? Does the term of years end automatically or require something at the end of its term?]*

3.   While either party may terminate a common law tenancy at will ^ , the modern rule and state statutes require ^ notice ^ . *[When and how may a party terminate? On what kind of notice? And especially for what kind of leases?]*

4.   A landlord must not violate anti-discrimination laws protecting classes including race ^ ^ and sex ^ ^ ^ ^ ^ . *[Can you think of several other protected statuses?]*

5.   A holdover tenant has only a tenancy at sufferance during which the landlord decides ^ whether to evict ^ . *[How quickly must the landlord decide? And does the landlord have another option other than to just evict?]*

6.   The lease gives the tenant the ^ right of possession, but who, whether the landlord or tenant, must deal with other occupiers of the premises depends on whether the state follows the English rule ^ or the American Rule ^ . *[What kind of right (qualify it)? Can you briefly define the English Rule? And the American Rule?]*

7.   A tenant owes the duty to pay the lease's stated rent ^ by the date the lease states ^ . *[What if the lease doesn't state rent? What if the lease doesn't state when to pay?]*

8.   A landlord ^ may evict a non-paying tenant, unless the tenant can show frustration of purpose ^ as rent defense. *[May the landlord always evict or only under a certain circumstance? Can you think of other rent defenses?]*

9.   A landlord must not refuse to lease ^ in violation of anti-discrimination laws protecting race, color, national origin, ^ ^ age, or disability ^ ^ . *[Just refuse to lease, or something else, too? Can you name several other protected classes?]*

Answer for Comprehensiveness Exercise on Leasehold Estates

1. The forms of tenancy include a term of years *for a specific period whether measured in years or not*, tenancy at will *that either party may terminate*, tenancy at sufferance *when a tenant holds over*, *and periodic tenancy that renews for the original lease period*.

2. A *determinable* term of years terminates *without notice* at the end of its term but shortens that term if the identified condition occurs.

3. While either party may terminate a common law tenancy at will *without reason or notice*, the modern rule and state statutes require *reasonable* notice, *especially as to residential leases*.

4.   A landlord must not violate anti-discrimination laws protecting classes including race, *color, national origin*, sex, *religion, age, disability, family status with or without children, and in some states marital status or other statuses*.

5.   A holdover tenant has only a tenancy at sufferance during which the landlord decides *within a reasonable time* whether to evict *or hold the tenant to a renewed lease period equal to the original period*.

6.   The lease gives the tenant the *legal* right of possession, but who must deal with other occupiers of the premises depends on whether the state follows the English rule *that the landlord also has a duty to deliver actual possession* or the American Rule *requiring the tenant to sue the holdover to evict and take possession*.

7.   A tenant owes the duty to pay the lease's stated rent *or fair market value if not stated* by the date the lease states *or the lease term's last day if not stated*.

8.   A landlord *who complies with the lease* may evict a non-paying tenant, unless the tenant can show frustration of purpose, *an illegal lease such as failing to meeting housing codes, or a similar circumstance* as rent defense.

9.   A landlord must not refuse to lease *or terminate a lease* in violation of anti-discrimination laws protecting race, color, national origin, *sex, religion*, age, disability, *family status, and in some states marital status or other statuses*.

Application Exercise on Types of Tenancies

Sort the fact patterns into *term of years* (Y), *tenancy at will* (W), *tenancy at sufferance* (S), or *periodic tenancy* (P). Answers are at the bottom of the page.

1. The uncle and his nephew agreed that the nephew could live in the carriage house as long as each agreed.

2. After haggling, the landlord and tenant finally signed a six-month lease with rent due the first of each month.

3. They'd had the arrangement so long, no one could remember how it started, the tenant just paying each month.

4. The four roommates were supposed to move out June 30th, but two remained through the summer and beyond.

5. When the year's lease ended, they talked and decided to just let it continue on as long as both agreed.

6. When the man overstayed the lease, the landlord sent a notice to quit, getting ready to evict for the new tenant.

7. The lawyer took out a five-year lease on the office with options for two five-year renewals.

8. The simple, one-page lease form provided for a one-year duration from the start of school.

9. The retail strip-mall owner let all his tenants renew annually on year-to-year leases with rent adjustment.

10. Neither party had signed or discussed anything. The drifter had just moved in and started paying rent.

11. The landlord had an eviction suit pending but was in no rush, hoping that the tenant might agree to renew.

12. The father let the son use the shed as a mechanic's shop, the son paying a little rent whenever he could.

13. The commercial landlord clearly could have evicted the shoe store but waited to see if it sold to a better owner.

14. The city had accepted two ten-year renewals already and looked to continue the practice with the vendor.

15. Odd, but the parties had signed a lease for 268 days, just long enough for the tenant to qualify as a resident.

16. The four-month lease enabled the college student to stay around all summer making some good money.

17. The bank liked having the lawyer renting an office upstairs month to month, for the free advice it got.

18. The landlord needed a new long-term tenant but hesitated to evict the holdover while waiting for one to sign.

19. With mall occupancy at a historic low, the landlord began accepting pop-up tenants without durational term.

20. The mechanic was handy fixing the marina's own equipment, so the marina owner let him use the shop.

21. The owner knew he should evict but told the nonpaying holdover tenant, a single mom, she could stay for now.

22. After much negotiation, they finally agreed to an eight-year lease with a two-year tenant renewal option.

23. They'd never discussed a durational term, but they had agreed that rent was due the first of every month.

24. The trailer-park owner liked the handy man's work and so let him stay in one of the empty units.

25. They finally agreed that the tenant would have the flat through the end of the growing season.

Answers: 1W 2Y 3P 4S 5W 6S 7Y 8Y 9P 10W 11S 12W 13W 14P 15Y 16Y 17P 18S 19W 20W 21S 22Y 23P 24W 25Y

Factors Exercise on Leasehold Estates

In cases in which the landlord and tenant dispute whether the landlord unlawfully discriminated, the factfinder may consider factors such as whether the landlord made ***derogatory comments*** about the tenant's protected class, the landlord's ***pattern*** of treating or mistreating the tenant's protected class, demographics of the ***applicant pool***, whether the landlord had **legitimate business reasons** for the landlord's action, how **compelling** those reasons may have been, and whether the asserted business reasons are **pretext** for discrimination. For each scenario, choose which factor would weigh heavily in favor of landlord or tenant and analyze that factor by filling in the blanks.

1.   **The landlord showed that the landlord's apartment complex had tenant demographics almost perfectly matching the demographics of the local area, especially as to the tenant's protected class.**

The [_choose a factor_] favors the [_choose a party_] when [_state relevant facts_] because [_explain your reasoning_].

2.   **The landlord testified that the landlord made an authorized credit check on the tenant, finding that the tenant had stiffed two prior landlords each of whom had to sue for back rent.**

The [_choose a factor_] favors the [_choose a party_] when [_state relevant facts_] because [_explain your reasoning_].

3.   **The tenant testified that the landlord had called the tenant an *old fogey* who wouldn't fit in with the hip demographic that the landlord sought.**

The [_choose a factor_] favors the [_choose a party_] when [_state relevant facts_] because [_explain your reasoning_].

4.   **While the landlord testified that the landlord terminated the tenant's at-will lease to renovate the apartment complex, the landlord admitted on cross-examination that no renovation subsequently occurred.**

The [_choose a factor_] favors the [_choose a party_] when [_state relevant facts_] because [_explain your reasoning_].

5.   **The Hispanic-Latino tenant showed from the landlord's records and independent witness testimony that the landlord had never rented to a Hispanic-Latino tenant despite that nearly one half of applicants were Hispanic-Latino.**

The [_choose a factor_] favors the [_choose a party_] when [_state relevant facts_] because [_explain your reasoning_].

6.   **The landlord testified that the landlord discovered that the tenant had a twenty-year-old misdemeanor conviction for domestic violence, as the reason why the landlord terminated the tenant's lease.**

The [_choose a factor_] favors the [_choose a party_] when [_state relevant facts_] because [_explain your reasoning_].

Discrimination Exercise on Leasehold Estates

Indicate whether each statement *overgeneralizes*, *undergeneralizes*, or *misconceives* the rule, explaining why. *Overgeneralizing* states the rule too broadly, *undergeneralizing* too narrowly, and *misconceiving* incorrectly.

1. A term of years, a type of tenancy, is for a specific period measured in years.
    ____OVER/____UNDER/____MIS/ Why? _____
    _____

2. A term of years shortens the lease term when the identified condition occurs.
    ____OVER/____UNDER/____MIS/ Why? _____
    _____

3. A tenancy at will is a tenancy that neither party may terminate.
    ____OVER/____UNDER/____MIS/ Why? _____
    _____

4. Either party may terminate a tenancy at will without reason or notice.
    ____OVER/____UNDER/____MIS/ Why? _____
    _____

5. A tenancy at sufferance is when the landlord holds the tenant over.
    ____OVER/____UNDER/____MIS/ Why? _____
    _____

6. The landlord decides whether to evict a holdover tenant or negotiate a new lease period.
    ____OVER/____UNDER/____MIS/ Why? _____
    _____

7. Landlords must not discriminate in their choice of tenants or in terminating a tenant's lease.
    ____OVER/____UNDER/____MIS/ Why? _____
    _____

8. The American rule is that the landlord has a duty to deliver actual possession, while the English rule requires the tenant to sue the holdover to evict and take possession.
    ____OVER/____UNDER/____MIS/ Why? _____
    _____

9. A lease that states no rent figure does not require the tenant to pay any rent.
    ____OVER/____UNDER/____MIS/ Why? _____
    _____

Answers for Discrimination Exercise on Leasehold Estates

1. The statement **UNDERgeneralizes** the rule. A term of years is for a specific period *whether or not* measured in years. The lease may measure the term in months, weeks, or some other period, not just years.

2. The statement **OVERgeneralizes** the rule. Only a *determinable* term of years shortens the lease term when the identified condition occurs. A term of years need not be a *determinable* term of years.

3. The statement **MISconceives** the rule. A tenancy at will is a tenancy that *either*, not *neither*, party may terminate.

4. The statement **OVERgeneralizes** the rule. While either party may terminate a *common law* tenancy at will without reason or notice, *the modern rule and state statutes require reasonable notice, especially as to residential leases*.

5. The statement **MISconceives** the rule. A tenancy at sufferance is when *a tenant holds over*, not when the landlord holds the tenant over. The tenant is the party to the lease who overstays the term.

6. The statement **UNDERgeneralizes** the rule. The landlord decides whether to evict a holdover tenant or *hold the tenant to a renewed lease period generally equal to the original period*. The landlord has a greater power than negotiation, which isn't a right but may be an option.

7. The statement **OVERgeneralizes** the rule. A landlord must not violate anti-discrimination laws *that protect specific classes including race, color, national origin, sex, religion, disability, family status, and in some states marital or other status*. Landlords may discriminate based on other criteria such as creditworthiness.

8. The statement **MISconceives** the rule. The English rule is that *the landlord has a duty to deliver actual possession*, while the American rule *requires the tenant to sue the holdover to evict and take possession*.

9. The statement **MISconceives** the rule. A tenant owes the duty to pay *fair market value rent by the lease term end if the lease omits the rent figure*.

Multiple-Choice Question with Answer Explanation

1. A senior-living complex owner agreed to allow a new tenant to occupy one of the complex's units only until the complex owner completed a new wing of units then under construction, when the tenant would have to move into the new wing. The owner completed construction of the new wing but allowed the tenant to remain in her current unit without any communication to her of the construction's completion or new terms. What interest has the tenant held?

A. A leasehold term of years followed now by a tenancy at will.
B. A leasehold periodic tenancy followed now by a tenancy at sufferance.
C. A defeasible fee terminable on the completion of construction.
D. A life estate also conditioned on completion of construction.

Answer explanation: Option A is correct because the owner and circumstances plainly enough indicated intent to retain ownership while offering only a leasehold interest. A leasehold or non-freehold estate, constituting a right to control property owned by another, comes in the form of a term of years, periodic tenancy, or tenancy at will including a tenancy at sufferance. A term of years lasts for a specific period, not necessarily years but any period that the parties can calculate with certainty, such as here the completion of current construction. A tenancy at will is one that either party may terminate at any time for any reason, as here the tenant may leave or the owner move the tenant to the new wing at any time. Option B is incorrect because while a periodic tenancy lasts from period to period without having any definite duration longer than one period, here the initial leasehold had no specific period and so was not a periodic tenancy. Moreover, while a tenancy at sufferance, which is a form of tenancy at will, involves the tenant wrongfully overstaying before the landlord decides whether to hold the tenant over for a new term or to evict, here the tenant has not wrongfully overstayed, not yet having any notice of completion or request to move. Options C and D are incorrect because both suggest ownership rather than leasehold interests, when the owner and circumstances clearly enough indicate only intent to lease.

Week 2
The Defaulting Tenant

QUESTIONS FOR THE ASSIGNED READING:

What are a tenant's primary responsibilities?

What is the difference between *abandonment* and *surrender*?

What is *self-help* by a landlord? Does law permit self-help? Why or why not?

Remember the concept of for-cause notice? How does that apply to this week's reading?

What does it mean to *mitigate damages*? Was mitigation originally a contract-law or property-law concept? When might a landlord not have to mitigate damages? When must a landlord mitigate damages? Who should carries the burden of proof on mitigation of damages?

What is the difference between assignment and sub-lease? How does one tell whether a transfer of rights is one or the other? Are privity of contract and privity of estate relevant? Why or why not?

What is the general rule whether a tenant can sublease or assign rights? What is the exception? How did California modify this doctrine? What is the majority rule today? How does the rule differ between residential and commercial leases?

Name something you did not understand from this week's reading.

SHORT OUTLINE:

Possession is the tenant's leasehold right while landlords have the right of **rent** and *duty to deliver possession*.
  Most states follow the English rule for the landlord to deliver *actual* possession, not just legal right.
    The tenant without actual possession could withhold rent for occupancy, void and sue for damages, or evict.
    If the landlord delivers only partial possession, the tenant could reduce rent for the lost portion or evict.
  Some states follow the American rule requiring landlords only to convey legal right, not actual possession.
    The tenant must then sue the holdover tenant to evict and take possession.
  Tenants must avoid **waste**, not destroying the property, allowing disrepair, or making significant changes.
    Tenants must also not deliberately destroy walls, floors, appliances, and mechanical systems.
  Tenants do *not* have a duty to renovate or remodel to address normal wear and tear.
  Tenants also have no duty to repair after catastrophic damage but must reasonably avoid such damage.
  Tenants must also avoid **illegal uses** such as prostitution, drug sales, and the like.
    A landlord discovering such uses may terminate the lease or seek to enjoin while enforcing the lease.
  Tenants must also not interfere with quiet use and enjoyment by *other tenants*.
Rent is the tenant's primary duty to the landlord, the lease stating the amount, absent infer *fair market value*.
  The lease also states when rent is *due*, absent rent is due on the last day of the term, monthly or otherwise.
  A landlord wishing to evict a non-paying tenant brings an action for **ejectment** also referred to as *eviction*.
  Frustration of purpose is a rent defense when the basis for forming the lease proves incorrect.
  Illegal leases, such as for residence that fails to meeting housing codes, void the obligation to pay rent.
    If law changes, making the use illegal, then the tenant may terminate if the tenant cannot use the premises.
Assignment and subletting involve transfer of the tenant's rights and obligations to a new tenant.
  The law allows assignment or sublet of a leasehold unless the lease prohibits, which many leases do.
  The rules for assignment and sublet implicate both *privity of contract* and *privity of estate*.

Assignment transfers the tenant's *entire* interest to a new tenant.

    Assignment ends privity of estate between landlord and tenant but not privity of contract.

    Assignment *creates* privity of estate between landlord and the tenant's assignee but *not* privity of contract.

    Assignee owes landlord rent and enforces landlord's obligations. Landlord collects from tenant or assignee.

Sublet transfers *part* of the leasehold to a subtenant, the tenant keeping the remainder interest.

    Sublease does *not* create privity of contract or estate between landlord and sublessee.

    Tenant retains privity of contract/estate with landlord, and creates privity of contract/estate with sublessee.

    Landlord collects rent from tenant, tenant from sublessee; tenant enforces lease, sublessee sublease.

Termination of a lease implicates other rights and obligations in addition to eviction and action for rent.

    A landlord may sue for contract damages in **anticipatory breach** if a tenant unconditionally refuses possession.

    A landlord may also pursue contract-breach damages if a tenant *abandons* a lease after having taken possession.

    Landlords must **mitigate damages** promptly and diligently seeking to relet the premises to another tenant.

    Tenants may help mitigate, sending prospective tenants, later proving landlord's failure to mitigate.

    A tenant may **surrender** a leasehold and landlord accept surrender with no rent, partial rent, or lease buyout.

    Rather than *self-help eviction*, landlords often get *court order* after notice, hearing, and even jury-trial rights.

    Landlords resorting to self-help may face civil liability and statutory or punitive damages.

    States requiring judicial proceedings for eviction typically offer streamlined procedures.

LONG OUTLINE:

Rent

    While the landlord owes the duty to provide the tenant with legal and likely also actual possession, the tenant owes the landlord the duty to pay **rent**. While the traditional rule made the tenant's duty to pay rent independent of the landlord's duties, the above section and a following section on habitability and suitability show the widespread abandonment of the traditional rule. The lease states the rent amount, in the absence of which a court will infer a *fair market value*. The lease also states when rent is due, in the absence of which rent is due on the last day of the month in a month-to-month lease or the last day of the term for a tenancy in term of years. A landlord who wishes to eject a non-paying tenant brings an action for **ejectment** also referred to as *eviction*. **Frustration of purpose** can be a rent defense when the basis on which the landlord and tenant agreed to the lease proves incorrect. **Illegal** leases, such as for a residence that fails to meeting housing codes, void the obligation to pay rent. If the law changes, making the use illegal, then the tenant may terminate if the tenant cannot use the property legally. A section well below treats the question of the landlord's right to **fixtures** on the tenant vacating.

Assignment and subletting

    A tenant may wish to **assign** the tenant's lease rights and obligations to a new tenant. An **assignment** transfers the tenant's *entire* interest to a new tenant. Tenants may also wish to **sublet** a part of the leasehold to a subtenant, keeping the remainder interest. A sublet refers to a conveyance of less than the tenant's full leasehold interest, such as to sublet for three months of a six-month lease. The law generally allows either assignment or sublet of a leasehold interest, unless the lease bars assignment or sublet, which many leases do. The rules for assignment and sublet implicate both *privity of contract*, referring to the agreement between landlord and tenant, and *privity of estate*, referring to the transfer of the leasehold estate from landlord to tenant.

    Assignment ends the privity of estate between landlord and tenant but not privity of contract. The tenant continues to owe whatever obligation the lease calls for in the event of assignment, which is typically full right to enforce the lease against the tenant notwithstanding assignment. Assignment *creates* privity of estate between landlord and the tenant's assignee but *not* privity of contract. By contrast, sublease does *not* create any privity, whether of contract or estate, between landlord and the tenant's sublessee. The tenant retains both privity of contract and of estate with the landlord, while creating privity of contract and estate only between tenant and sublessee. The rules, then, are that a landlord can collect rent from anyone with whom the landlord is in privity of contract *or* estate, but a tenant can enforce obligations only of a landlord with whom the tenant is in privity of *estate*. So, in assignments, the landlord can collect rent from *either* the tenant or assignee, while only the assignee can enforce the landlord's obligations. Yet in subleases, the landlord can collect rent *only* from the tenant and the tenant from sublessee, while the tenant can enforce the landlord's obligations, and the sublessee can enforce the tenant's obligations.

Termination (surrender, mitigation of damages, and anticipatory breach)

The above sections on the types of tenancies address how each type terminates. The above section on **rent** addresses a landlord's action for ejectment or eviction for nonpayment of rent. The law strongly discourages *self-help evictions*, particularly for residential leases. Landlords must usually instead get a *court order* following appropriate procedures including notice, hearing, and in some cases even jury-trial rights. Landlords who resort to self-help such as changing locks and putting personal property out at the curb may have civil liability or criminal responsibility for those actions. On the other hand, states that require judicial proceedings for eviction typically offer streamlined procedures. A tenant may **surrender** a leasehold. The landlord may accept the tenant's surrender without pursuing unpaid rent, accepting partial payment of past due rent, or accepting a lease buyout of future unpaid rent.

A landlord may sue for contract damages in **anticipatory breach** if a tenant makes a positive and unconditional refusal to take possession and fulfill the lease, or becomes unable to perform. Likewise, if a tenant *abandons* a lease after having taken possession for part of the lease term, and does so without the landlord's agreement as to surrender terms, then the landlord may pursue a contract-breach action on the lease for past unpaid rent, future unpaid rent, and other damages as contract law allows. However, in the case of anticipatory breach or breach in abandonment of the lease, landlords have the same contract-law obligation to **mitigate damages** that others enforcing contracts owe. In the case of a lease, the landlord's duty to mitigate means that the landlord must ordinarily promptly and diligently seek to re-lease the premises to another tenant. In practice, tenants may attempt to help the landlord do so by sending prospective tenants to the landlord, which may also help the tenant prove the landlord's failure or refusal to mitigate as a defense to a rent action.

Fluency Cards

Cover and uncover the response to each prompt until you fluently recall the exact response.

Ejectment	**Frustration of purpose**
Equitable action to evict a holdover tenant.	Rent defense when lease basis proves incorrect.
Illegal lease	**Lease assignment**
Voids rent obligation, giving tenant option to terminate.	Transfers interest to new tenant if lease permits, ending estate privity but not contract.

20

Assignment duties

Assignee pays and enforces obligations of landlord who may collect from tenant or assignee.

Sublet

Transfers only part, not whole, to subtenant. No estate or contract privity of subtenant to landlord.

Sublet duties

Landlord rent from tenant, tenant from subtenant. Tenant enforces lease, subtenant sublease.

Anticipatory lease breach

If tenant refuses to possess, landlord gets rent. Same with tenant abandonment.

Rent mitigation

Landlord must seek new tenant to mitigate rent loss.

Landlord self-help

Landlords must seek court order with notice and hearing. Self-help leads to statutory liability.

Federal Fair Housing Act

For leasing, amenities, advertising. Protects race, religion, origin, handicap, familial status.

Fair Housing Act exceptions

Owns just 3 single-family homes or owner-occupied with just 3 rental units. Don't apply to advertising.

14th Amendment

Guarantees equal protection for protected class. State action required.

Civil Rights Act, 42 USC 1982

Housing rights for African American citizens equal to rights of Whites. No state action required.

Definitions Worksheet on Defaulting Tenants

1.   What is an *assignment*? In assignment, which parties have *privity of contract* and which *privity of estate*?

_____

_____

_____

2.   In assignment, what rights and obligations do the landlord, tenant, and assignee have?

_____

_____

3.   What is a *sublease*? In a sublease, which parties have *privity of contract* and which *privity of estate*?

_____

_____

_____

4.   In sublease, what rights and obligations do the landlord, tenant, and subtenant have?

_____

_____

5.   What action may a landlord take, and must the landlord avoid, when the tenant defaults in paying rent?

_____

_____

6.   What defenses does the tenant have as to rent?

_____

_____

7.   What rights does a landlord have when a tenant *abandons* or *surrenders* a lease?

_____

_____

_____

Answers for Definitions Worksheet on Defaulting Tenants

1.   ***What is an assignment? In assignment, which parties have privity of contract and which privity of estate?*** *Assignment* transfers the tenant's *entire* interest to a new tenant, subject to any restrictions against assignment in the lease. Assignment *ends* the privity of estate between landlord and tenant but not privity of contract. Assignment *creates* privity of estate between landlord and assignee but *not* privity of contract. Tenant and assignee have privity of contract.

2.   ***In assignment, what rights and obligations do the landlord, tenant, and assignee have?*** The tenant continues to owe whatever obligation the lease calls for in the event of assignment, which is typically full right to enforce the lease against the tenant notwithstanding assignment, unless the landlord offers a novation. In assignment, the landlord may also collect rent from the assignee. Only the assignee, not the tenant, can enforce the landlord's obligations.

3.   ***What is a sublease? In a sublease, which parties have privity of contract and which privity of estate?*** Sublease refers to a conveyance of *less than the tenant's full leasehold interest*, such as to sublet for three months of a six-month lease, subject to any restrictions against sublease in the lease. Sublease does not create any privity, whether of contract or estate, between landlord and the tenant's sublessee. The tenant retains both privity of contract and estate with the landlord, while creating privity of contract and estate only between tenant and sublessee.

4.   ***In sublease, what rights and obligations do the landlord, tenant, and subtenant have?*** In subleases, the landlord can collect rent *only* from the tenant and the tenant from sublessee, while the tenant can enforce the landlord's obligations, and the sublessee can enforce the tenant's obligations. Landlord and subtenant have no rights or obligations with respect to one another.

5.   ***What action may a landlord take, and must the landlord avoid, when the tenant defaults in paying rent?*** A landlord may bring an action for ejectment, also known as eviction. The law strongly discourages *self-help evictions*, particularly for residential leases. Landlords must usually instead get a *court order* following streamlined procedures that include notice, hearing, and in some cases even jury-trial rights. Landlords who resort to self-help such as changing locks or putting personal property out at the curb may have civil liability or criminal responsibility.

6.   ***What defenses does the tenant have as to rent?*** Under modern rules, the tenant's duty to pay rent depends on habitability (for residential leases) or suitability (for commercial leases). Frustration of purpose may also be a rent defense when the basis on which the parties agreed to the lease proves incorrect. Landlords also have the same contract-law obligation to *mitigate damages* that others enforcing contracts owe. In the case of a lease, the landlord's duty to mitigate means that the landlord must ordinarily promptly and diligently seek to re-lease the premises to another tenant.

7.   ***What rights does a landlord have when a tenant abandons or surrenders a lease?*** A landlord may sue for contract damages in *anticipatory breach* if a tenant makes a positive, unconditional refusal to take possession and fulfill the lease or becomes unable to perform. If a tenant *abandons* a lease after having taken possession for part of the lease term, then the landlord may pursue a contract-breach action on the lease for past unpaid rent, future unpaid rent, and other damages as contract law allows. A tenant *surrenders* a leasehold when the landlord accepts without pursuing unpaid rent, accepts partial payment of past due rent, or accepts a lease buyout of future unpaid rent.

Comprehensiveness Exercise on Defaulting Tenants

Insert words at the ^ mark that would make for a more-accurate or more-detailed law statement.
Follow the italicized hints for help. Suggested answers are on the next page.

1.   Rights and responsibilities on assignment or sublease depend on who has privity of contract ^ ^ ^ . *[Define privity of contract? And what other form of privity affects the rules? Can you define that other form?]*

2.   Assignment transfers the tenant's ^ interest to a new tenant ^ . Assignment ends privity of estate between landlord and tenant ^ . Assignment creates privity of estate between landlord and assignee ^ . *[Transfers how much of the interest? Any restrictions on assignment? What about the other form of privity? And again, what about the other form of privity?]*

3.   In assignment, the landlord may collect rent from the assignee ^ ^ . The assignee ^ may enforce the landlord's obligations. *[Collect only from the assignee, or someone else, too? And always collect, or only sometimes collect? And only the assignee may enforce?]*

4.   Sublease conveys ^ the tenant's leasehold interest ^ . Sublease does not create privity of contract ^ between landlord and sublessee. The tenant retains privity of contract ^ with landlord, while tenant and sublessee have privity of contract ^ . *[How much of the tenant's interest? And whenever the tenant wishes, or subject to restriction? Does sublease create the other kind of privity between landlord and sublessee? Does the tenant retain the other kind of privity with the landlord? Do tenant and sublessee have the other kind of privity?]*

5.   In sublease, the landlord may collect rent only from the tenant ^ , while the tenant can enforce the landlord's obligations ^ . *[May the tenant collect any rent? May anyone else enforce obligations?]*

6.   Law discourages ^ landlords from using self-help in evicting, like changing locks ^ , providing civil liability ^ . Landlords must usually instead get a court order ^ after notice ^ . *[All landlords, or primarily a certain kind of landlord? Anything else that landlords sometimes do? Only civil liability or something else, too? Full procedures or something less? Only notice or something more?]*

7.   A landlord seeking to sue a ^ tenant for unpaid rent must seek to re-lease the premises to another tenant ^ . *[Just any tenant, or a certain kind of tenant? What does the law call the duty to re-lease?]*

8.   A landlord may sue for anticipatory breach when the tenant refuses ^ to possess the premises and fulfill the lease ^ . The landlord may also sue for unpaid rent ^ when a tenant abandons a lease after having taken possession. *[Refuses how? Refuse or something else, too? And only sue for unpaid rent or for other things?]*

Answers for Comprehensiveness Exercise on Defaulting Tenants

1. The rules for assignment and subleasing depend on who has privity of contract, *referring to the agreement between landlord and tenant, and privity of estate, referring to transfer of leasehold estate from landlord to tenant*.

2. Assignment transfers the tenant's *entire* interest to a new tenant *if the lease permits*. Assignment ends privity of estate between landlord and tenant *but not privity of contract*. Assignment creates privity of estate between landlord and assignee *but not privity of contract*.

3. In assignment, the landlord may collect rent from the assignee *or the tenant unless having given the tenant a novation*. The assignee, *not the tenant,* may enforce the landlord's obligations.

4. Sublease conveys *less than* the tenant's leasehold interest *if the lease permits*. Sublease does not create privity of contract *or estate* between landlord and sublessee. The tenant retains privity of contract *and estate* with landlord, while tenant and sublessee have privity of contract *and estate*.

5. In sublease, the landlord may collect rent only from the tenant *and the tenant from sublessee*, while the tenant can enforce the landlord's obligations, *and the sublessee can enforce the tenant's obligations*.

6. Law discourages *residential* landlords from using self-help in evicting, like changing locks *or putting personal property at the curb*, providing civil liability *and criminal responsibility*. Landlords must usually instead get a court order *under streamlined procedures* after notice *and hearing*.

7. A landlord seek to sue a *vacating* tenant for unpaid rent must seek to re-lease the premises to another tenant *in mitigation of damages*.

8. The landlord may sue for anticipatory breach when the tenant refuses *positively unconditionally* to possess the premises and fulfill the lease *or becomes unable to perform*.

9. The landlord may also sue for unpaid rent, *future rent, and other damages,* when a tenant abandons a lease after having taken possession.

Examples/Non-Examples Exercise on Lease Breaches

Identify whether each fact pattern is an example (E) or non-example (NE) of the *highlighted concept*. Answers follow. In the blanks, generate an additional example and non-example.

1.   A landlord may sue for damages in *contract (lease) breach* if a tenant refuses or abandons possession during the lease term without the landlord accepting surrender, except the landlord must mitigate in re-lease.

___   The tenant's vacating the premises mid-lease surprised the accommodating landlord who, unable to relet, filed suit.
___   Right after signing the lease, the tenant found a better apartment and so never showed up, leaving the landlord stuck with it.
___   The landlord had agreed that he was fine with the tenant's flush roommate taking over the lease but then sued anyway.

E: _____

N: _____

2.   The law implies a *covenant of quiet enjoyment* for the tenant to use the property as the lease intended without interfering nuisances, in breach of which the tenant may withhold rent.

___   The tenant lost her job due to disability halfway through the lease term and was unable to make some of the rent payments.
___   Drug deals and parties all night in the next-door apartment made such noise and threats that the tenant paid only half rent.
___   The landlord's renovations cut off power and water, blocked hallway access, and made such noise the tenant withheld $500.

E: _____

N: _____

3.   Some states imply in residential leases a *warranty of habitability* that the premises are fit, safe, and sanitary to inhabit, in breach of which the tenant can void the lease, withhold rent, or deduct for repairs.

___   Rats and other vermin made so much noise in the walls and left such filth around the apartment that the tenant left.
___   The restaurateur was not happy with the landlord's old décor and so spent $5,000 decorating, withheld from the next rent.
___   Official report showed significant lead-paint risk to the tenant's children, and so the tenant paid for repairs and withheld rent.

E: _____

N: _____

4.   In commercial leases, the law implies a *warranty of suitability* that the premises suit the commercial tenant's anticipated commercial use, failing which the tenant may void the lease and sue for damages.

___   The landlord leased to the tenant for a paint facility, but the city ruled the use illegal for the district, causing the tenant to quit.
___   When the couple had their first child, they felt that the apartment was too close to a highway for safety and so left mid-lease.
___   When health officials ruled the makeup-air deficient, refusing occupancy, the chef closed his diner and sued the landlord.

E: _____

N: _____

5.   A tenant may assert *constructive eviction,* void the lease, and recover damages, where the landlord commits such wrongful acts or so neglects the premises as to substantially interfere with ordinary uses.

___   The police and fire station next door meant that sirens went off frequently throughout the night, causing the tenant to leave.
___   The furnace gave out December 1st, and as the weather got colder, the tenant after many unmet demands finally moved out.
___   The tenant hated that the landlord had made a brothel out of the building, customers at all hours of the night, and so left.

E: _____

N: _____

Answers: 1 EEN; 2 NEE; 3 ENE; 4 ENE; 5 NEE

Assignment/Sublease Exercise

For each problem, state whom the landlord can sue, based on what theory, whom if anyone the tenant can sue, based on what theory, and whether anyone else can sue and, if so, based on what theory.

1. Landlord leases to tenant 1 who assigns to tenant 2 who assigns to tenant 3.

2. Landlord leases to tenant 1 who subleases to tenant 2 who assigns to tenant 3.

3. Landlord leases to tenant 1 for a term of three years at a monthly rent of $1,000. One year later tenant 1 "subleases, transfers, and assigns" to tenant 2 for "a period of one year from date." Thereafter neither tenant 1 nor tenant 2 pays rent to landlord.

4. Same as the prior problem, but the instrument of transfer includes a covenant (promise) whereby tenant 2 "agreed to pay the rents" reserved in the head lease. What effect might this have on landlord's rights?

5. Landlord leases to tenant 1 for a term of three years at a monthly rent of $1,000; the lease provides that "tenant 1 hereby covenants to pay said rent in advance on the first of each month." The lease also provides that "tenant 1 shall not sublet or assign without the permission of landlord." Six months later tenant 1, with landlord's permission, transfers to tenant 2 for the balance of the term. Thereafter tenant 2 pays the rent directly to landlord for several months, then defaults. Landlord sues tenant 1 for the rent due. What result, and why?

6. Landlord and tenant signed a 2-year written lease for tenant to rent an entire 2-story commercial building. Landlord's home is on a parcel adjacent to the commercial building. Tenant agreed to pay $2,000 monthly rent and to collect landlord's mail and send it to landlord by U.S. postal service monthly. The lease has no clause stating whether Tenant may assign or sublease the premises. Tenant met all obligations for one year. At the end of the first year, tenant moved out of the premises and entered into a written agreement with a new tenant. The new tenant agreed to rent the entire building for the rest of the lease at the original amount. The new tenant also agreed "to assume all of the responsibilities of the original lease." Six months later, the new tenant entered into an arrangement with a friend. The friend agreed to rent the upstairs space for one month for $400. The friend had possession of the second story for one month, then vacated without paying any rent. The new tenant remained in the building until the end of the lease. The new tenant did not pay any rent for the last 6 months. After the new tenant took possession, nobody picked up the landlord's mail for a year. **If Landlord sues all three parties, from whom may he collect rent and why? If Landlord sues all three parties for damage he suffered because nobody sent him his mail (assume he can prove some reasonably certain damage caused by this failure), from whom can he collect damages and why?**

Answer to Problem 6: The landlord is in privity of contract with the tenant and so can sue for breach of contract, demanding past rent and damages related to not picking up the mail. The landlord is no longer in privity of estate with the tenant. The landlord is also in privity of contract with the new tenant because the new tenant assumed all lease responsibilities, of which the landlord was a third-party beneficiary. Yet the landlord also has privity of estate with the new tenant. Thus, the landlord can sue for back rent under both theories. The promise to pick up mail is a personal promise that does not run with the land. It does not affect the leased premise's use and enjoyment, nor the landlord's reversionary interest. Therefore, the landlord cannot sue the new tenant for that promise under privity of estate. However, because the landlord is a third-party beneficiary of the new tenant's agreement with the tenant, the landlord can probably sue for the mail promise under privity of contract. The landlord is not in privity of contract nor in privity of estate with the friend and so cannot sue the friend. The new tenant is in privity of contract and privity of estate (for one month) with the friend and so can sue the friend on both theories. The friend is only responsible to the new tenant for rent, not for picking up the mail.

Application Exercise for Defaulting Tenants

Sort the following fact patterns into an *assignment (A)* or *sublease (S)*. Answers are at page bottom.

1. The tenant, moving to Hawaii, leased the apartment to a friend for the balance of the term at half rent.

2. The tenant, needing some help with rent, leased a bedroom to a friend for $250 a month and some dog walking.

3. The tenant, sick of Minnesota winters, leased the cabin and lands to another hunter for the balance of the term.

4. The tenant, wanting to move in with her fiancé, gave up her month-to-month lease to a co-worker.

5. The tenant, on assignment in Australia for six months, leased the walk-up to a stranger until the tenant's return.

6. The tenant, needing only two of the cooling ponds, leased the other two ponds to a neighboring smelter.

7. An artist, short on cash, moved in as a co-tenant in an art collector's apartment in exchange for two paintings.

8. A butcher, having just opened a business, rented the top bunk in a supplier's bungalow for a freezer of meat.

9. A medical student moved into an apartment vacated by a fellow student whom the medical school dismissed.

10. A steel distributor rented a parts supplier's rented warehouse until the supplier needed it back next model year.

11. A franchisee rented a restaurant from a chef whose diner had failed and who needed to cover the diner's lease.

Sort the following fact patterns into whether the party has a right (R) to enforce or not (N). Answers are at page bottom.

12. A residential assignee seeks to enforce the landlord's covenant of quiet enjoyment.

13. A commercial subtenant seeks to enforce the landlord's warranty of suitability.

14. A residential landlord seeks to collect rent from a tenant.

15. A residential landlord seeks to collect rent from an assignee.

16. A residential landlord seeks to collect rent from a subtenant.

17. A commercial landlord seeks damages for a subtenant's alleged waste.

18. A commercial tenant seeks to collect rent from a subtenant.

19. A residential assignee seeks to enforce the tenant's warranty of habitability.

20. Under the American rule, an assignee seeks to make the landlord deliver possession, ousting an occupier.

21. Under the American rule, a tenant seeks to make the landlord deliver possession, ousting an occupier.

22. Under the English rule, a tenant seeks to make the landlord deliver possession, ousting an occupier.

23. Under the English rule, an assignee seeks to make the landlord deliver possession, ousting an occupier.

Answers: 1A 2S 3A 4A 5S 6S 7S 8A 9A 10S 11A 12R 13N 14R 15R 16N 17N 18R 19R 20N 21N 22R 23R

Housing-Discrimination Exercise

The Fair Housing Act prohibits discrimination in housing based on color, disability, family status, national origin, race, religion, and sex, while 42 USC Section 1982 grants all citizens the same right as white citizens to inherit, buy, lease, sell, hold, and convey real and personal property. State whether the action unlawfully discriminates (D) in violation of 42 USC Section 1982 or Section 3604 of the Fair Housing Act or not (N). *Note that state and city laws may add other protected classes.* Answers are below.

1. Resident-landlord advertises "furnished basement apartment in private white home."

2. Landlord refuses to rent to white tenant because of tenant's poor credit history.

3. Landlord tells African-American applicant apartment is taken, then a few days later rents it to a White applicant.

4. Landlord refuses to rent to white applicant because "this is a Mexican neighborhood.:"

5. Landlord advertises "furnished basement apartment for one tenant only."

6. Landlord refuses to rent a one-occupant room in a private home to two applicants intending both to occupy.

7. Landlord advertises "furnished basement apartment for up to two occupants. No children allowed."

8. Landlord advertises "furnished basement apartment. No cohabitation. Only married couples allowed."

9. Landlord advertises "furnished home for rent to employed or otherwise financially secure persons."

10. Landlord tells leasing agent not to lease to "Christians, Jews, Muslims, or other religious people."

11. Landlord tells leasing agent to lease only to "people who appear to be strong and healthy."

12. Homeowner refuses to sell to Mexican immigrant because the offer included a financing contingency.

13. Homeowner refuses to sell to African-American couple because they offered a substantially below-market price.

14. Homeowner refuses to sell to black couple, wanting to keep the neighborhood white.

15. Homeowner refuses to sell to Hispanic-Latino couple because buyers offended homeowner with jokes.

16. Mexican-heritage homeowner refuses to sell to Honduran-heritage buyer because "you can't trust a Honduran."

17. Female homeowner refuses to sell to a male buyer because "you can't trust a man."

18. Lesbian homeowner refuses to sell to straight woman buyer because woman is straight.

19. Gay homeowner refuses to sell to straight male buyer because buyer is male.

20. Straight male homeowner refuses to sell to gay buyer because buyer is gay.

21. Apartment leasing agent refuses to lease to wheelchair-bound applicant because apartments are all full.

22. Apartment leasing agent refuses to lease to limping man who walks with a cane because "we don't allow gimps."

23. Apartment leasing agent refuses to lease to blind applicant because "we don't want anyone to get hurt."

24. Apartment leasing agent refuses to lease to couple with two Great Dane dogs because "no pets allowed."

25. Apartment leasing agent refuses to lease to applicant with therapy horse because no apartments were available.

Answers: 1D 2N 3D 4D 5N 6N 7D 8N 9N 10D 11D 12N 13N 14D 15N 16D 17D 18N 19D 20N 21N 22D 23D 24N 25N

Factors Exercise on Defaulting Tenants

Landlords use many factors to decide and justify whether to pursue a defaulting or vacating tenant for unpaid rent or instead to accept no-rent or reduced-rent surrender. Although not strictly relevant to the landlord's legal rights, those factors may also influence witnesses, judges, juries, mediators, and case evaluators. Factors can include the tenant's *ability to pay, willingness to pay, collectability, reasons* for not paying, *effort* to pay, *need* for support, *deservedness* of support, *honesty*, and other *character*, and the landlord's *morality, reputation, ability* to forego rent, and *affinity* for the tenant or the tenant's *family* or *situation*. For each scenario, choose a factor that would weigh heavily in favor of landlord or tenant and analyze that factor by filling in the blanks.

1.   **The defaulting tenant, recently disabled in a motor-vehicle accident, struggled mightily to pay rent, making incremental partial payments whenever able to raise small amounts of cash.**

The [*choose a factor*] favors the [*choose a party*] when [*state relevant facts*] because [*explain your reasoning*] .

2.   **The defaulting tenant is a single parent of three preschool-age children, who works two jobs and depends on grandparents, aunts, and uncles for daycare.**

The [*choose a factor*] favors the [*choose a party*] when [*state relevant facts*] because [*explain your reasoning*] .

3.   **The landlord, a leading member of a faith community who is personally and openly committed to caring for the orphan, widow, and poor, has a defaulting destitute elderly tenant whose spouse recently died.**

The [*choose a factor*] favors the [*choose a party*] when [*state relevant facts*] because [*explain your reasoning*] .

4.   **The landlord is a hardworking parent of six minor children, sole support for those children and a homemaker spouse, and self-employed as a low-income owner and manager of critical marginal housing.**

The [*choose a factor*] favors the [*choose a party*] when [*state relevant facts*] because [*explain your reasoning*] .

5.   **The defaulting tenant is a wealthy investment advisor who has grown tired of the apartment's Central Park view and so has leased three other apartments in which the tenant prefers to stay.**

The [*choose a factor*] favors the [*choose a party*] when [*state relevant facts*] because [*explain your reasoning*] .

6.   **The defaulting tenant is a fellow of the landlord's Masonic Lodge, a former high-school classmate of the landlord, and the landlord's occasional fishing buddy who hasn't paid rent because of overspending on a boat.**

The [*choose a factor*] favors the [*choose a party*] when [*state relevant facts*] because [*explain your reasoning*] .

Discrimination Exercise on Defaulting Tenants

Indicate whether each statement *overgeneralizes*, *undergeneralizes*, or *misconceives* the rule, explaining why. *Overgeneralizing* states the rule too broadly, capturing circumstances to which it does not apply. *Undergeneralizing* states the rule too narrowly, omitting circumstances to which it applies. *Misconceiving* states the rule incorrectly.

1. Assignment transfers part of the tenant's interest to an assignee, so that both the tenant remains responsible and in control, while the assignee must look only to the tenant.
_____OVER/_____UNDER/_____MISS/ Why? _____
_____
_____

2. Sublease transfers all the tenant's interest to the sublessee so that the sublessee owes the landlord rent and can enforce landlord obligations.
_____OVER/_____UNDER/_____MISS/ Why? _____
_____
_____

3. The law strongly discourages self-help evictions for residential leases, so that landlords must usually get a court order after notice to the tenant.
_____OVER/_____UNDER/_____MISS/ Why? _____
_____
_____

4. Frustration of purpose is a rent defense when the tenant's expectation that led the tenant to enter into the lease proves incorrect.
_____OVER/_____UNDER/_____MISS/ Why? _____
_____
_____

5. States that require judicial proceedings for eviction typically offer streamlined procedures under which tenants have the option of surrendering the leasehold.
_____OVER/_____UNDER/_____MISS/ Why? _____
_____
_____

6. A landlord discovering a tenant's illegal use has as remedy that the landlord may terminate the lease.
_____OVER/_____UNDER/_____MISS/ Why? _____
_____
_____

Answers for Discrimination Exercise on Defaulting Tenants

1. The statement **MISconceives** the rule. Assignment transfers the tenant's *entire* interest to the assignee, *ending* privity of estate with the landlord, continuing contract (lease) obligations, and creating privity of estate between landlord and assignee who may enforce leasehold rights.

2. The statement **MISconceives** the rule. Sublease transfers *only part* of the tenant's interest, thus *not* creating any privity, whether of contract or estate, between landlord and sublessee, meaning the landlord can collect rent *only* from the tenant and the tenant from sublessee, while the tenant can enforce the landlord's obligations, and the sublessee can enforce the tenant's obligations.

3. The statement **UNDERgeneralizes** the rule. The law strongly discourages *self-help evictions* for residential leases, so that landlords must usually get a court order after not only notice but also hearing and in some cases jury-trial rights, *and may have civil liability and criminal responsibility for changing locks and putting personal property out at the curb.*

4. The statement **OVERgeneralizes** the rule. Frustration of purpose is a rent defense when the basis on which *both the landlord and tenant agreed* to the lease proves incorrect.

5. The statement **OVERgeneralizes** the rule. States that require judicial proceedings for eviction may offer streamlined procedures facilitating the tenant's surrender, but the landlord may accept *or reject* surrender, either pursuing or not pursuing unpaid rent, or accepting a lease buyout of future unpaid rent.

6. The statement **UNDERgeneralizes** the rule. A landlord discovering a tenant's illegal use may either terminate the lease *or seek to enjoin such uses while enforcing the lease.*

Problem-Solving Exercise on Landlord and Tenant

Think-aloud problem solving (TAPS) is a proven method of using vocalization to become a more creative and better problem solver. Professionals are effective problem solvers when they speak aloud to another, speaking aloud to themselves, or let their mental operations taking the silent form of words, concepts, principles, and strategies to reach partial solutions and then chain partial solutions toward final novel solution. Read the following example (EX) and non-example (NE) of an unknown new rule (RU), one that the judges writing their opinions and orders have not expressly stated but that you must instead discern and record as your problem solution. Vocalize each mental operation taken toward a partial solution, until you reach and record the final novel rule. Check your answer against the model answer at the bottom of the next page when the professor says to do so.

EX   OPINION AND ORDER: In this landlord/tenant case, the plaintiff landlord seeks unpaid rent from the defendant tenant for the period after the tenant vacated during the lease term. The landlord possesses the premises so that ejectment is not in issue. The court so orders that defendant retains no leasehold claim. The defendant tenant presented evidence that the tenant sent three persons to the landlord, each of whom were willing to assume the lease for the balance of defendant's leasehold term but that the landlord refused. The unrepresented defendant has moved to dismiss on that uncontested evidence. The Court grants defendant's motion, dismissing plaintiff's case with prejudice.

NE   OPINION AND ORDER: In this landlord/tenant case, the plaintiff landlord seeks unpaid rent from the defendant tenant for the period after the tenant vacated during the lease term. The landlord possesses the premises so that ejectment is not in issue. The court so orders that defendant retains no leasehold claim. The defendant tenant presented evidence that most apartments in the area are rented because of high demand, despite the landlord's contradicting evidence that advertising failed to lease the premises. The defendant tenant has moved to dismiss. The Court denies defendant's motion, setting plaintiff's rent claim for bench trial.

RU   _____

_____

_____

_____

_____

_____

_____

Answer to problem: Tenants may help the landlord mitigate damages by sending prospective tenants to the landlord, evidence of which the tenant may use to prove the landlord's failure or refusal to mitigate, as a defense to a rent action.

Multiple-Choice Questions with Answer Explanations

2.   Ralph, a third-generation American of Italian and Greek descent saw an ad for an apartment online. Ralph has dark, olive-colored skin. He e-mailed the landlord and asked to see the apartment. When he arrived, the landlord appeared taken aback and said to him, "What are you, a Muslim?" Ralph murmured "Why does it matter?" The landlord said, "I'm sorry, but something has come up and I am no longer able to rent the unit." Ralph went home. The next week, he discovered that a friend of his, Jenny Jones, a very light-skinned Muslim-American woman, had rented the unit. When he expressed surprise, Jenny said, "That landlord is kind of weird. The first thing he said to me was, "At least you're not a Muslim. I really liked the place so I didn't let him know he was wrong." Which is Ralph's strongest claim?

A.   A claim under the 14th Amendment to the U.S. Constitution.
B.   A claim under 42 U.S.C. § 1982.
C.   Ralph has no valid claim because he was a White person and not a Muslim.
D.   A claim under the Fair Housing Act.

Answer explanation: Option D. The Fair Housing Act prohibits discrimination in rental based on color, ethnicity, and religion, including based on perceived rather than actual characteristics. Even if the landlord was incorrect about Ralph's religion or ethnicity, basing his decision on that perception is discrimination. Also, Ralph's dark skin may have made the landlord think he was Muslim. Option A is incorrect because the 14th Amendment protects only against state action (government actors), and this matter involves a private landlord. Option B is not the best answer because although the federal statute provides that all citizens have the same right to enjoy property as White citizens, it is unclear whether an Italian-Greek American would be considered non-white, even though Ralph's dark skin was likely a contributing factor to the denial of housing. The Fair Housing Act's inclusion of ethnicity, race, color, and religion make it a stronger claim. Option C is incorrect because the landlord's perception that the applicant is of a certain protected class is enough.

3.   Linda rented a commercial building to Terry for a term of years, ten years in length. After two years, Terry's business was suffering, and so he reached an agreement with Dennis where Dennis agreed to take over all of Terry's interests in the building for the duration of the lease. In that agreement, Dennis promised to assume all obligations under Terry's lease with Linda. After two more years passed, Dennis needed to take a medical leave of absence from his business and so entered an agreement with Joyce where Joyce would rent the entire premises for one year; at the end of the year, Dennis would resume possession. What best describes the relationship between Linda and each of the other parties?

A.   Privity of contract and privity of estate with both Terry and Dennis but not with Joyce.
B.   Privity of contract and privity of estate with Dennis but not with Terry or Joyce.
C.   Privity of contract with Terry and privity of contract and estate with Dennis but not with Joyce.
D.   Privity of contract with Terry and privity of estate with Dennis but not with Joyce.

Answer explanation: Option A. A lease of the full premises conveys privity of contract and estate. When Linda entered into the lease with Terry, she had privity of estate and privity of contract with Terry. A tenant's assignment of the full premises benefitting the landlord conveys privity of contract and estate. Terry's arrangement with Dennis was an assignment (Terry retained no current possessory interest nor any reversionary interest) benefitting Linda (when Dennis agreed to assume all lease obligations), so Terry remained in privity with Linda, but Dennis was now in privity of contract and estate with Linda. A conveyance of less than the full lease term is a sublease, not an assignment, creating neither privity of contract nor estate with the landlord. The agreement between Dennis and Joyce did not convey the full term and so is a sub-lease. Thus, Linda is neither in privity of contract or privity of estate with Joyce. Option B is incorrect because Linda retains privity with Terry. Option C is incorrect because Linda retains privity of estate with Terry. Option D is incorrect because Linda retains privity of estate with Terry and privity of contract with Dennis.

4.   A property owner leased an artist's studio to a sculptor for three years at $1,000 per month rent. The lease permitted sublease or assignment. After one year of paying the property owner rent, the sculptor subleased the studio to a painter for one year at the same rent. However, the painter moved out after six months without having paid any rent. When the sublease expired, the sculptor moved back in for the final year of the three-year lease but paid no rent. Who owes the property owner how much in rent?

A.   The sculptor owes $12,000 and the painter owes $12,000.
B.   The sculptor owes $18,000 and the painter owes $6,000.
C.   The sculptor owes the property owner $24,000 in rent.
D.   The sculptor owes the property owner $12,000 in rent.

Answer explanation: Option C is correct because a sublease is the lease of less than all of the property or for less than the full term, while an assignment is a lease of the entire property for the entire term. A sublease of less than the entire tenancy leaves only the tenant and not the subtenant liable to the property owner, while an assignment would make both tenant and subtenant liable unless the owner discharges the tenant. Here, the tenant remained liable for the last two unpaid years of rent. The subtenant would be liable only to the sculptor and only for the one unpaid year of rent. Option A is incorrect because the sculptor would owe both years of unpaid rent, not just the last year, and the subtenant would owe only the tenant, not the property owner. Option B is incorrect because the sculptor owes for all of the two unpaid years, and the painter owes only the tenant and would owe $12,000, not $6,000. Option D is incorrect because the sculptor also owes for the unpaid sublet year, although the sculptor would have an action against the subtenant for that year.

5.   A company sent a painting crew to paint a bridge, giving crew members housing stipends to find their own accommodations over the six- to nine-month expected duration of the project. One painter negotiated with a local homeowner to rent a carriage house above a detached garage. The painter and homeowner agreed in a signed writing that the painter was on a month-to-month lease with rent due in advance on the first day of the month. The painter paid timely on or before the first day of each month for the first seven months until the project looked near completion. The painter did not pay on the first day of the eighth month. The homeowner could tell that the bridge was nearly painted and suspected that the painter was going to stiff the homeowner for the last month's rent. What interest does the painter hold, giving the homeowner what if any recourse?

A.   Periodic month-to-month tenancy, giving the homeowner only the right of suing for the month-eight rent but not to evict.
B.   Tenancy at sufferance, giving the homeowner the option of holding the painter to another month's rent or evicting the painter.
C.   Term of years for a total of nine months, giving the homeowner the right to sue for rent through the eighth and ninth months.
D.   No interest, giving the homeowner the right to change the locks or otherwise take self-help to prevent the painter's trespass.

Answer explanation: Option B is correct because a tenancy at sufferance, which is a form of tenancy at will, involves the tenant wrongfully overstaying beyond the lease term, before the landlord decides whether to hold the tenant over for a new term equal to the original lease term (but no longer than one year and possibly shorter by statute) or to evict, which are the landlord's options. By failing to pay rent, the painter has breached the lease and is wrongfully overstaying, giving the landlord the right to evict or hold the painter to the full month even if the painter leaves before the month's end. Option A is incorrect because the periodic tenancy ended when the painter failed to pay rent and wrongfully overstayed, creating a tenancy at sufferance. Option C is incorrect because while the parties may have discussed that the painter would want to stay for as long as nine months (the expected longest duration of the project), they contracted instead for a month-to-month lease. If the homeowner wants to treat the painter as a holdover, then the holdover period would be another month (the periodic tenancy), not nine months. Option D is incorrect because landlord-tenant law discourages self-help and instead treats the wrongful holdover as a tenant at sufferance whom the owner can hold to another periodic term or file suit to evict.

6.   A strip-mall owner leased storefront space to a discount shoe store for a four-year term. After two years, the discount shoe store, which wasn't making enough income to support the lease, subleased to a used sporting-goods reseller for the remaining two-year duration of the original lease. The sporting-goods reseller then made the shoe store's lease payments to the mall owner. After one year of subleasing, the sporting-goods reseller complained to the mall owner that the mall's sidewalks littered were and trash cans full, in insubstantial breach of the shoe store's original lease for clean premises. When the mall owner did nothing, the sporting-goods reseller quit the premises, leaving the storefront vacant for the last year of the four-year lease and two-year sublease. Who owes what obligations?

A.   The owner owes neither the shoe store nor the sporting-goods store clean premises, while neither store owes the owner rent.
B.   The owner owes both the shoe store and sporting-goods store clean premises, while both stores owe the owner rent.
C.   The owner owes only the shoe store clean premises, while only the shoe store owes the owner the last year's rent.
D.   The owner owes only the sporting-goods store clean premises, while only the sporting-goods store owes the owner the last year's rent.

Answer explanation: Option C is correct because a sublease is the lease of less than all of the property or for less than the full term, while an assignment is a lease of the entire property for the entire term. A sublease of less than the entire tenancy leaves only the tenant and not the subtenant liable to the owner, while an assignment would make both tenant and subtenant liable unless the owner discharges the tenant. While a tenant can enforce the owner's obligations, a subtenant on a sublease cannot. Option A is incorrect because the owner would owe the shoe store the lease obligation of clean premises, while the shoe store would owe the lease rent. Option B is incorrect because the owner owes the sporting-goods store no performance because not in privity of contract or estate, while only the shoe store owes the owner rent because the sporting-goods store has no contract with the owner. Option D is incorrect because the sporting-goods store only has a sublease with the shoe store, owing only the shoe store rent. Only the shoe store has a lease with the owner on which the shoe store owes rent. The reverse is also true that the owner owes the sporting-goods store nothing because the owner has no privity of contract or privity of estate with the sporting-goods store.

7.   A landlord agreed in writing to lease an apartment to a tenant for one year beginning on an upcoming date. When the date arrived, though, the tenant found a prior tenant still in the apartment and refusing to leave. The tenant notified the landlord who confirmed that the prior tenant's lease had expired just before the new tenant's occupancy date. What legal action would properly provide the new tenant with actual possession?

A. Only an eviction action by the landlord to remove the prior tenant.
B. An eviction action by either the landlord or new tenant to remove the prior tenant.
C. Only an eviction action by the new tenant to remove the prior tenant.
D. Nothing other than the new tenant's self-help because the prior tenant is a holdover.

Answer explanation: Option B is correct because any party with the lease right to possession may enforce that right. The landlord retains the right to terminate the prior lease while the new tenant has the right to actual possession that the new tenant may enforce under the new lease. Option A is incorrect because the new tenant also has a right under the new lease to actual possession. Option C is incorrect because the landlord retains a right to enforce the prior lease. Option D is incorrect because no circumstances suggest any right of the prior tenant to remain as a holdover.

8. A landlord and tenant entered into a written, signed, and otherwise enforceable lease for an apartment unit near the university at which the tenant was a student. The lease term was for one year. The tenant stayed throughout the year, paying rent on time at the beginning of each month. The tenant had one year remaining at the university and so remained in the apartment at the end of the lease term. The tenant paid the landlord the next month's rent at the beginning of each of the next two months after the lease ended, consistent with the tenant's prior obligation and practice. At first, the landlord accepted the tenant's rent payments while tendering the next year's lease for the tenant's signature. The tenant did not sign, hoping that the landlord would accept rent each month instead so that the tenant could leave without obligation when school ended after nine months. But the landlord instead served a notice to quit. The tenant paid another months' rent, which the landlord accepted despite the notice. If during that month for which the tenant paid rent the landlord sues to evict, then what is the tenant's status?

A. Tenant at will with a month-to-month lease because the landlord accepted rent.
B. Tenant at sufferance with no possessory rights because of the landlord's notice to quit.
C. Tenant on a periodic tenancy from year to year because of the prior one-year term.
D. Trespasser subject to both contract damages under the lease and tort damages.

Answer explanation: Option B is correct because although a tenant is at will month to month when the landlord accepts monthly rent after the lease term expires, the tenant is at sufferance with no possessory rights once the landlord protests the tenant's continued occupancy, such as by serving a notice to quit. Option A is incorrect because although the tenant was initially at will month to month when the landlord accepted rent and offered a lease, the tenant became at sufferance when the landlord served the notice to quit. Option C is incorrect because a periodic tenancy, one that adopts the prior lease's term, follows the rental payments (monthly, not yearly, here) rather than the full prior lease's term unless the lease specifies the same term for a tenant holding over after the original term. The lease term would be month to month, not year to year, but for the notice to quit making the tenancy at sufferance. Option D is incorrect because the tenant had consent for possession and the landlord has accepted rent although having served a notice to quit and filed suit to evict. The tenant would remain liable for lease damages but likely not damages in tort.

9. The owner of a small-town sandwich-shop business and the building housing the shop decided to rent the shop along with the apartment upstairs. The owner entered into a five-year written lease calling for the tenant, a youthful entrepreneur, to take possession in three months. Two months before the tenant took occupancy, the sandwich shop had a small fire the modest damage from which the owner took pains to clean up. At about the same time, the entrepreneur's inspection revealed some mold in the apartment upstairs. Thus, one

month before the tenant was to take occupancy, the entrepreneur notified the owner that the entrepreneur was refusing to take occupancy but that he had a buddy who was interested in taking over the lease. The owner simultaneously discovered that the entrepreneur had joined the military and already left for training. If the owner sues the entrepreneur accelerating damages for the entire lease term, then what legal arguments should each side raise?

A.   The entrepreneur the servicemembers' civil relief act, and the owner breach of the duty of occupancy and specific performance.
B.   The entrepreneur the protection of the recording statute, and the owner breach of the warranty of habitability.
C.   The owner breach of the duty of good faith and fair dealing, and the entrepreneur impossibility and impracticality, and the absence of any damage.
D.   The owner anticipatory breach, and the entrepreneur breach of the warranties of habitability and suitability, and the obligation to mitigate damages.

Answer explanation: Option D is correct because a landlord may sue for anticipatory breach whenever a tenant refuses to perform a lease before the lease term begins or it reasonably appears that the tenant has made it impossible to perform the lease. On the other hand, a landlord owes a residential tenant a warranty that the apartment is habitable, a commercial tenant a warranty that the premises is suitable for the anticipated business, and owes a tenant a duty to mitigate damages. The facts implicate each of these legal theories. Option A is incorrect because although the servicemembers' civil relief act ordinarily holds immune from civil suit a servicemember whom authorities call up for active duty, here the entrepreneur apparently just voluntarily joined rather than received a call up. Even if the relief act applies, the law doesn't recognize a duty of occupancy or give the landlord a right of specific performance to force the tenant to occupy. Option B is incorrect because the recording act does not in any way apply, and the landlord doesn't have a claim against a tenant for breach of the warranty of habitability. It would be the other way around that the landlord owes the residential tenant that duty. Option C is incorrect because the landlord would sue for anticipatory breach, not breach of the duty of good faith and fair dealing. The entrepreneur would not defend on impossibility (the premises could with appropriate repair or cleaning still be occupied) or impracticality (the facts give no indication of occupancy being impractical other than the need to complete any clean up after the fire and remediate any dangerous mold). And the landlord hasn't found another tenant yet, even if the entrepreneur had an interested friend, so the landlord may well suffer damage.

Week 3
Leasehold Covenants and Warranties

QUESTIONS FOR THE ASSIGNED READING:

What are a landlord's primary obligations?

What are the elements of constructive eviction? How can a tenant benefit from claiming constructive eviction? What are constructive eviction's limits? How does society benefit from recognizing constructive eviction?

What are the elements of the implied warranty of habitability? May a tenant waive the warranty? How does one prove the warranty's breach? How does law limit the warranty? Is the warranty a claim or defense?

How is retaliation for claiming housing discrimination the same or different from retaliation for claiming breach of the implied warranty of habitability?

Name something you do not understand about this week's material.

SHORT OUTLINE:

Habitability and suitability warranties may grant tenants greater rights to use the premises as intended.
    The common law imposes no landlord duty to maintain and repair, the tenant instead owing that duty.
        Yet many states today require a *residential* landlord to maintain and repair the premises.
        States also prohibit landlords from evicting tenants for reporting housing-code violations.
    Some states also imply a *residential* landlords' **warranty of habitability** for safe and sanitary premises.
        Where the warranty exists, a tenant has the option of deducting cost of necessary repairs from the rent.
    Leases imply a **covenant of quiet enjoyment** for leasehold use, free of interfering actions and nuisances.
        Nuisances that so badly disturb as to frustrate uses gives a tenant a right of **constructive eviction**.
            Non-functioning heating, cooling, plumbing, and electricity are common constructive-eviction grounds.
            Constructive eviction, a damages action and rent defense, requires the tenant to *leave the premises*.
            The landlord must act so wrongfully or so neglect as to *substantially interfere* with tenant use.
            The tenant must also *give notice* of interference, and landlord must fail to remedy.
        States split whether landlords must prevent interfering but hold landlords responsible for common areas.
        Landlords also breach by wrongfully locking out or allowing others to do so, from all or any part.
        Common law also allows tenants to withhold rent for a landlord's breach of quiet enjoyment.
    Commercial leases imply a landlord's warranty of **suitability** for the anticipated commercial use.

LONG OUTLINE:

Habitability and suitability

    The law implies in every lease a **covenant of quiet enjoyment**, not referring solely to peaceful premises but rather to use the property for the purpose that the lease intended including to be free of nuisances that interfere with that use. The common law, followed in most jurisdictions, allows the tenant to withhold rent if the landlord violates the covenant. Landlords can violate the covenant by either wrongfully locking out or evicting the tenant, or allowing another to do so, from all or any part of the premises. The landlord's doing so relieves the tenant of *all* liability to pay rent, unlike the forgoing rule for partial evictions in which the tenant must continue to pay partial rent.

    In some jurisdictions, the law also implies in every *residential* lease a **warranty of habitability** that assures the tenant that the premises are fit for the tenant to inhabit the premises safely and sanitarily, even though the common law does not imply the warranty. Where the warranty exists, a tenant can add to the above remedies the option of deducting repairs from the rent. The common law, though, generally imposes no duty on the landlord's part to maintain and repair the premises, which instead becomes the tenant's responsibility on taking possession unless the lease provides otherwise. Many jurisdictions today require a residential landlord to maintain and repair the premises, creating an obligation much like that of the warranty of habitability. Jurisdictions do prohibit landlords from evicting tenants for reporting housing-code violations. In commercial leases, the law implies a warranty of **suitability**, which is roughly equivalent to the residential warranty of habitability. Unless the lease provides otherwise, the commercial premises must be suitable for the anticipated commercial use.

A tenant, whose possession nuisances so badly disturb as to frustrate or destroy those uses, has a right of **constructive eviction**. The landlord must have committed such wrongful actions or so neglected the premises as to *substantially interfere* with its uses. The tenant must also have *given notice* of the interference, and the landlord must have failed to remedy the interference. Constructive eviction also requires the tenant to *leave the premises*. Constructive eviction is both an action that the tenant may maintain for damages due to the interference *and* a defense to the landlord's rent action. Non-functioning mechanical systems for heating, cooling, plumbing, electricity, and access, often constitute grounds for constructive eviction. Jurisdictions split on whether landlords must prevent others from interfering if able to do so but do routinely hold landlords responsible for common areas.

Fluency Cards

Cover and uncover the response to each prompt until you fluently recall the exact response.

Habitability

Many states require landlords to maintain and repair residential units and protect reporting tenants.

Tenant repairs

Landlord must reimburse residential tenant for necessary repairs.

Suitability

Commercial leases imply warranty that premises suit anticipated use.

Quiet enjoyment

Implied covenant against actions interfering with use. Lack of heat and plumbing are examples.

Quiet-enjoyment remedies

Tenant claims constructive eviction, first notifying for cure. Withhold and abate rent.

Definitions Worksheet on Leasehold Covenants and Warranties

1. What is the *covenant of quiet enjoyment*?

_____

_____

_____

2. What *remedy* does a tenant have for breach of the covenant of quiet enjoyment?

_____

_____

3. How might a *landlord* violate the covenant of quiet enjoyment? What remedy would a tenant have?

_____

_____

4. What is the *warranty of habitability*? Where does it apply?

_____

_____

_____

5. Who, landlord or tenant, has the obligation to *maintain and repair* the premises?

_____

_____

6. What is the *warranty of suitability*? Where does it apply?

_____

_____

_____

7. What is *constructive eviction*? Give an example.

_____

_____

_____

8. What must a tenant do to claim constructive eviction?

_____

_____

Answers for Definitions on Leasehold Covenants and Warranties

1.   ***What is the covenant of quiet enjoyment?*** The law implies in every lease a *covenant of quiet enjoyment*, not referring solely to peaceful premises but rather for the tenant to use the property for the purpose that the lease intended including to be free of nuisances that interfere with that use.

2.   ***What remedy does a tenant have for breach of the covenant of quiet enjoyment?*** Common law allows the tenant to *withhold that portion of the rent representing the interference*.

3.   ***How might a landlord violate the covenant of quiet enjoyment? What remedy would a tenant have?*** Landlords violate the covenant by either wrongfully locking out or evicting the tenant, or allowing another to do so. The landlord's doing so relieves the tenant of *all* liability to pay rent.

4.   ***What is the warranty of habitability? Where does it apply?*** In some jurisdictions, beyond the common-law covenant of quiet enjoyment, law implies in every *residential* lease a *warranty of habitability* that assures the tenant that the premises are fit for the tenant to inhabit the premises safely and sanitarily.

5.   ***Who, landlord or tenant, has the obligation to maintain and repair the premises?*** Unless the lease provides otherwise, common law makes maintenance and repair the tenant's duty, but many states require a residential landlord to maintain and repair the premises, creating an obligation like that of the warranty of habitability. States prohibit landlords from evicting tenants for reporting housing-code violations.

6.   ***What is the warranty of suitability? Where does it apply?*** In commercial leases, the law implies a *warranty of suitability*, somewhat like the residential warranty of habitability. Unless the lease provides otherwise, the commercial premises must be suitable for the anticipated commercial use.

7.   ***What is constructive eviction? Give an example.*** A tenant whose possession nuisances so badly disturb as to frustrate or destroy those uses has a claim of *constructive eviction* against the landlord. The landlord must have committed such wrongful actions or so neglected the premises as to *substantially interfere* with its uses. Non-functioning mechanical systems for heating, cooling, plumbing, and electricity are common grounds for constructive eviction.

8.   ***What must a tenant do to claim constructive eviction?*** The tenant must *give notice* of the interference, *allow the landlord to remedy* the interference, and then on failure of remedy *leave the premises*. Constructive eviction is both an action that the tenant may maintain for damages due to the interference *and* a defense to the landlord's rent action.

Comprehensiveness Exercise for Leasehold Covenants

Insert words at the ^ mark that would make for a more-accurate or more-detailed law statement.
Follow the italicized hints for help. Suggested answers are on the next page.

1.   The law implies in a lease a covenant of quiet enjoyment referring to ^ a peaceful premises ^ ^ . *[Whose right to peace, landlord or tenant? Do you have a more-robust definition? Can you include an example category?]*

2.   In breach of the covenant of quiet enjoyment, common law allows the tenant to withhold ^ rent ^ . *[How much rent, all or some? And how do you measure how much to withhold?]*

3.   In some jurisdictions, beyond the common-law covenant of quiet enjoyment, law implies in a ^ lease a warranty ^ that assures ^ that the premises are fit ^ . *[In all leases or only one kind of lease? What kind of warranty? Assures whom? Can you give a brief definition of fitness?]*

4.   Common law makes maintenance and repair the tenant's duty ^ ^ . *[Except on two big exceptions.]*

5.   In commercial leases, the law implies a warranty ^ in which the premises must fit ^ commercial use ^ . *[What's the name of the warranty? What (whose) commercial use? Any exceptions?]*

6.   A landlord who commits such wrongful actions ^ as to ^ interfere with the tenant's use ^ evicts the tenant. *[What about omitting to act? Any little interference? What kind of eviction?]*

7.   Non-functioning heating ^ ^ and electricity are common grounds for constructive eviction. *[Can you add a couple of other common examples?]*

8.   A tenant claiming constructive eviction must first ^ ^ leave the premises. *[Just up leave, or do two other things first?]*

Answer for Comprehensiveness Exercise on Leasehold Covenants

1. The law implies in a lease a covenant of quiet enjoyment referring to *the tenant's right to* a peaceful premises *and to use the property for the purpose that the lease intended including to be free of nuisances*.

2. In breach of the covenant of quiet enjoyment, common law allows the tenant to withhold *that portion of the* rent *representing the interference*.

3. In some jurisdictions, beyond the common-law covenant of quiet enjoyment, law implies in a *residential* lease a warranty *of habitability* that assures *the tenant* that the premises are fit, *generally meaning safe and sanitary*.

4. Common law makes maintenance and repair the tenant's duty, *unless the lease provides otherwise or, as is common, the state requires a residential landlord to maintain and repair*.

5. In commercial leases, the law implies a warranty *of suitability* in which the premises must fit *the anticipated* commercial use, *unless the lease provides otherwise*.

6. A landlord who commits such wrongful actions *or allows such wrongful conditions* as to *substantially* interfere with the tenant's use *constructively* evicts the tenant.

7. Non-functioning heating, *cooling, plumbing,* and electricity are common grounds for constructive eviction.

8. A tenant claiming constructive eviction must first *give notice of the interference, allow the landlord to remedy the interference, and then on failure of remedy* leave the premises.

Application Exercise on Leasehold Covenants and Warranties

Sort the fact patterns into breach of the covenant of quiet enjoyment (QE), warranty of habitability (H), or warranty of suitability (S). Answers are at the bottom of the page.

1. The elderly tenant was unable to sleep or hear the telephone or television due to raucous parties upstairs.

2. The heat in the college-student tenant's upstate New York apartment didn't work in January.

3. Though leased specifically for restaurant use, the premises didn't have the code-required makeup-air system.

4. The toilets would not flush in the five-member family's apartment due to tree roots growing into sewer lines.

5. The accounting firm's office suite had frequent power failures, shaking, and loud noise from nearby construction.

6. The single mother couldn't get her toddler children safely out to see doctors because of hallway drug deals.

7. The disabled couple could not navigate the lobby and hallways because of derelicts passed out on drugs.

8. The medical-clinic tenant could not get state approval to occupy because of asbestos in the walls and floors.

9. The elevator did not work to the wheelchair-bound tenant's tenth-floor apartment.

10. The church tenant could not conduct Sunday services because of land-use restrictions against use and parking.

11. Rats in the apartment walls kept the tenants up all night and left feces on kitchen and bathroom counters.

12. The landlord's rebel son used the apartment building's basement as a firing range and weapons facility.

13. The federal government restricted river waters, leaving the marina tenant high and dry.

Sort the fact patterns into constructive eviction (CE) or not (N). Answers are at the bottom of the page.

14. The landlord locked out the tenant because the landlord decided he didn't like retired punk rockers.

15. The tenant vacated the apartment because his girlfriend moved out and he needed a smaller place.

16. The tenant vacated the apartment because the tenant tired of the green shag carpet.

17. The tenant gave notice and, when the landlord failed to repair, left the apartment that had lost electricity.

18. The tenant gave notice and, when the landlord failed to repair, left the apartment that had no plumbing.

19. The tenant left the apartment that had no plumbing and refused to pay rent after the landlord repaired.

20. The landlord put the tenant's personal property out at the curb and changed the locks to sell the premises.

21. The tenant vacated after losing a job and moving in with her parents, and the landlord sued for rent.

22. The landlord called the police when the tenant dealt drugs out of the apartment, resulting in the tenant's arrest.

23. The tenant moved out after the landlord refused to repair heavy smoke damage from a hallway fire.

Answers: 1QE 2H 3S 4H 5S 6QE 7QE 8S 9H 10S 11H 12QE 13S 14CE 15N 16N 17CE 18CE 19N 20CE 21N 22N 23CE

Factors Exercise on Leasehold Covenants and Warranties

Tenants must avoid **waste**, defined under any one or combination of the following factors: the property's **destruction**, allowing collapse into **disrepair**, making significant **changes** to the property, affecting the property's intended **use**, causing the property to fall into **noncompliance**, bringing the property into value-reducing **disrepute**, or deliberately destroying or altering **mechanical systems** or **structures**. For each scenario, choose which factor that would weigh heavily in favor of landlord or tenant and analyze that factor by filling in the blanks.

1.   The commercial tenant, though paying rent, went to Florida for the winter, leaving the premises unoccupied, allowing pipes to freeze and break, and resulting flood to destroy walls, floors, and ceilings.
The [_choose a factor_] favors the [_choose a party_] when [_state relevant facts_] because [_explain your reasoning_].

2.   The commercial tenant, a frustrated architect and builder, had made so many dramatic changes to the suite's previously traditional layout that the landlord knew he'd never lease it again without major renovations.
The [_choose a factor_] favors the [_choose a party_] when [_state relevant facts_] because [_explain your reasoning_].

3.   The property had been a premier retail/office location until the investment advisor, now imprisoned, had utterly ruined the location's ambience, goodwill, and character, to the point that the landlord couldn't find a renter.
The [_choose a factor_] favors the [_choose a party_] when [_state relevant facts_] because [_explain your reasoning_].

4.   The premises looked about like it had when the massage-parlor tenant had first occupied it, but the city shut it down for lice, bed bugs, and other health-code violations, quarantined while awaiting fumigation.
The [_choose a factor_] favors the [_choose a party_] when [_state relevant facts_] because [_explain your reasoning_].

5.   The programmer tenant had monkeyed with the office's every electronic system including wifi, server units, remote HVAC controls, and remote security, to the point that they were effectively inoperable.
The [_choose a factor_] favors the [_choose a party_] when [_state relevant facts_] because [_explain your reasoning_].

6.   As a parting shot following their bitter rent dispute, the tenant left graffiti all over the many natural tile, stone, and other masonry surfaces.
The [_choose a factor_] favors the [_choose a party_] when [_state relevant facts_] because [_explain your reasoning_].

Discrimination Exercise on Leasehold Covenants and Warranties

Indicate whether each statement **_overgeneralizes_**, **_undergeneralizes_**, or **_misconceives_** the rule, explaining why. *Overgeneralizing* states the rule too broadly, *undergeneralizing* too narrowly, and *misconceiving* incorrectly.

1. The law implies in a lease a covenant of quiet enjoyment referring to the tenant's right to a peaceful premises.
____OVER/____UNDER/____MIS/ Why? _____
_____

2. In breach of the covenant of quiet enjoyment, common law allows the tenant to withhold rent.
____OVER/____UNDER/____MIS/ Why? _____
_____

3. Law implies in a lease a warranty of habitability.
____OVER/____UNDER/____MIS/ Why? _____
_____

4. The warranty of habitability assures the tenant that the premises are fit, meaning safe.
____OVER/____UNDER/____MIS/ Why? _____
_____

5. Common law makes maintenance and repair the landlord's duty unless the lease provides otherwise or, as is common, the state requires a residential tenant to maintain and repair.
____OVER/____UNDER/____MIS/ Why? _____
_____

6. In commercial leases, the law implies a warranty of suitability in which the premises must fit the anticipated commercial use.
____OVER/____UNDER/____MIS/ Why? _____
_____

7. A landlord who commits such wrongful actions or allows such wrongful conditions as to interfere with the tenant's use constructively evicts the tenant.
____OVER/____UNDER/____MIS/ Why? _____
_____

8. A tenant may claim constructive eviction, leave the premises, and refuse to pay rent.
____OVER/____UNDER/____MIS/ Why? _____
_____

Answers for Discrimination Exercise on Leasehold Covenants

1. The statement **UNDERgeneralizes** the rule. The law implies in a lease a covenant of quiet enjoyment *not referring solely to peaceful premises but also for the tenant to use the property for the purpose that the lease intended including to be free of nuisances that interfere with that use*.

2. The statement **OVERgeneralizes** the rule. In breach of the covenant of quiet enjoyment, common law allows the tenant to withhold *only that portion of the rent representing the interference*.

3. The statement **OVERgeneralizes** the rule. *Some states* imply in a *residential* lease a warranty of habitability. The common law does not imply the habitability warranty, and the habitability warranty does not apply to commercial leases.

4. The statement **UNDERgeneralizes** the rule. The warranty of habitability assures the tenant that the premises are fit, *meaning both safe and sanitary, and otherwise habitable (and so including things like heating and cooling)*.

5. The statement **MISconceives** the rule. Common law makes maintenance and repair the *tenant's* duty, unless the lease provides otherwise or, as is common, the state requires a residential *landlord* to maintain and repair.

6. The statement **OVERgeneralizes** the rule. In commercial leases, the law implies a warranty of suitability in which the premises must fit the anticipated commercial use, *unless the lease provides otherwise*. Commercial landlords and tenants are free to negotiate a lease in which the tenant takes the premises as is.

7. The statement **OVERgeneralizes** the rule. A landlord who commits such wrongful actions or allows such wrongful conditions as to *substantially* interfere with the tenant's use constructively evicts the tenant. The interference must frustrate or destroy the use.

8. The statement **MISconceives** the rule. A tenant claiming constructive eviction *must first give notice of the interference, allow the landlord to remedy the interference, and then on failure of remedy* and only then may leave the premises.

Multiple-Choice Question with Answer Explanation

10.   The owner of a mechanic's facility decided to retire but to keep the facility in case he needed or wanted to resume work. He leased the mechanic's shop to a young man who had just graduated from a vocational program. He separately leased a bungalow on the back of the property to a young woman who had just quit college to find herself. A city inspector tagged and closed the shop because it lacked the fire-suppression equipment mandated for commercial rentals. The inspector simultaneously tagged the bungalow as uninhabitable for not having a second means of egress in the event of fire. If the leases did not address such events, then what if any would be the owner's obligations to the young man running the shop and young woman living in the bungalow, and the tenants' remedies?

A.   Warranty of suitability owed the young man and warranty of habitability owed the young woman, requiring renovation and repair, or reduction in rent or lease termination.
B.   Duty of commercial care owed the young man and duty of ordinary care owed the young woman, requiring compensation for damages caused by unreasonable conditions.
C.   Obligation to hold harmless both the young man and young woman in the event of injury, property damage, or other loss, to the tenants and visiting third parties.
D.   No duties owed to either tenant because the leases did not address these eventualities, and the tenants have possession, leaving the tenants with no remedies.

Answer explanation: Option A is correct because a landlord owes a residential tenant a warranty that the apartment is habitable and owes a commercial tenant a warranty that the property is suitable for the anticipated business. If the breach is substantial, then a tenant may leave without lease liability, repair the breach and withhold rent in the cost of repairs, withhold rent representing the breach's reduction in the leasehold value, or sue for damages. Option B is incorrect because while tort law imposes duty of care, real-property law imposes warranties of suitability and habitability. Option C is incorrect because hold-harmless clauses might be appropriate if the tenants became liable to a non-party to the lease because of the owner's breach, but the concern as to the tenants is not their future loss but their present inability to use their premises. Option D is incorrect because the law imposes warranties of suitability for commercial use and habitability for residential use. Commercial leases may shift those obligations, but residential leases by law cannot.

Essay Question with Model Answer

A Tenant rented a one-bedroom apartment in a small city for $900 per month. The lease was for one year beginning the first of January until the end of December. When the Tenant first saw the apartment, he told the Landlord he had a severe breathing problem as well as severe allergies, making a point to ask if the apartment had central air conditioning. The Landlord indicated that the apartment did have central air, which the lease also specified. The Landlord was responsible for general repairs under the lease.

Because the Tenant started renting in January, he did not need to turn the air conditioner on until May. May was an unusually hot month, and when Tenant turned on the air conditioner, it did not work. The Tenant notified the Landlord that he needed the air conditioning repaired, but the Landlord did not send anyone to repair. The apartment windows were not designed to open, although some of them did. The Tenant spent $200 on fans and didn't say anything for a week, thinking it would get better.

When the temperature suddenly rose in a June heat wave, it became unbearable. Normally, in this city the highs were around 75 degrees but this June the highs were between 98 and 100 degrees, with lows of 78 degrees at night. The Tenant was retired and home all day. During this time, the Tenant suffered from the heat, which caused his breathing to become labored and his allergies to flare up. He opened the few windows he could manage to pry open just to breathe, but then the allergies became much worse. He had to buy extra inhalers because his condition worsened. After two weeks (mid-June to end of June), the Tenant decided to withhold July rent; instead of a payment, he sent the Landlord a letter stating that he would pay rent when the air conditioning was fixed.

After five additional weeks (with no August rent payment sent either), the Tenant filed a complaint with the local human-rights office, alleging discrimination based on disability. A few days later, the Tenant received an apparently valid notice to quit alleging non-payment of rent, stating the Tenant had to leave in seven days. Eight days later, the Landlord filed a lawsuit seeking possession, back rent, and future rent for the remainder of the lease. The air conditioning has not yet been fixed.

The Tenant comes to your law firm for legal advice. Your supervising attorney has asked you to send her a short memo answering these client questions and providing the legal grounds for your responses:

1. Can the Landlord evict me? My lease extends until the end of December. Do I have any defense?
2. Do I owe for the months I didn't pay?
3. Can I find another place and leave without owing future rent?

Model Answer:

1. A landlord cannot generally terminate a tenancy in the middle of a term-of-years lease. This lease is a term-of-years lease because it has start and end dates. The lease ends on the last day of the term (December 31), requiring no notice. Landlord may send a notice to quit for failure to pay rent. If Landlord did serve a valid notice to quit for nonpayment of rent, then the Landlord could properly proceed with ejectment.

However, the tenant may have valid defenses to eviction for nonpayment of rent. First, he can allege a breach of the implied warranty of habitability. The described conditions of no air conditioning in extreme heat, in a building that is not designed to allow for air flow, is likely to violate local housing codes and create an unlivable condition. This argument is bolstered by the inclusion of working air conditioning in the lease terms. If the conditions are found to be a breach of the implied warranty of habitability, then the court determines how much rent to abate. If the Court finds no rent is due until the landlord repairs the condition, then Tenant won't owe any past due rent and cannot be evicted for non-payment of rent. Tenant notified the Landlord of the situation and Landlord failed to repair, and Tenant did not begin deducting rent until after giving Landlord a reasonable opportunity to repair.

Tenant can also allege a breach of the Fair Housing Act based on not providing housing in such a way as to accommodate the Tenant's disability. The Tenant notified Landlord that his medical condition required air conditioning, so Landlord was aware of the disability. The only potential problem with this claim is whether the medical conditions are seen to interfere with daily living or merely a temporary medical problem; the breathing problems create a stronger claim in this regard than the allergies. This claim could be a successful defense to eviction.

Finally, Tenant can allege retaliatory eviction under the Fair Housing Act. The timing of the notice to quit shortly after Tenant made a claim with the Fair Housing Commission suggests one caused the other. While Landlord can defend by stating that the eviction is based on non-payment of rent, courts will look at the timing of a fair housing complaint compared to an eviction action. This claim is a strong.

2. As indicated above, Tenant may not have to pay the back rent or any rent until the air conditioning is fixed. However, the court might find the lack of air conditioning to only equal a portion of the rent, in which case Tenant will be given an opportunity to pay any rent deemed owed, to prevent eviction.

3. Tenant is normally liable for future rent in a term-of-years lease breached mid-term. However, such a claim might be defended against by alleging constructive eviction; Tenant can claim that conditions were so bad he had to leave because the unit was unlivable. This claim is weakened by the fact that Tenant stayed in the unit with no air conditioning for a couple of months already and left only when Landlord filed for eviction. But Tenant's notice bolsters the claim. Landlord is responsible for maintaining the air conditioning per the lease, and Tenant's medical condition continued to worsen. A court might or might not find that the unit was

completely unlivable on these facts. In either case, Landlord must try to mitigate damages by putting the unit up for re-letting.

Week 4
Nuisance

QUESTIONS FOR THE ASSIGNED READING:

What are the elements of nuisance? Which elements are both sides most likely to dispute on the facts? Why?

If someone has created a nuisance that either affects private land use or affects the public, why shouldn't a court automatically issue an injunction? What are the policy reasons for weighing factors on both sides? Can money be enough of a remedy?

What is the difference between an intentional nuisance and unintentional nuisance?

What is the difference between a public nuisance and private nuisance?

Name something you do not understand about this week's material.

SHORT OUTLINE:

Nuisance claims protect those who own and use real property. Define nuisance as:
> *intentional, unreasonable, substantial, non-trespassory invasion of another's interest in using lands.*
Private nuisance claims protect the individual interest of one who owns or controls private lands.
> Only those who own or control the private land have *standing to sue*.
Public nuisance claims protect the general interest of all who may use public lands.
> Only public officials, private affected-class reps, and private persons with special injury may sue.
Weigh these factors to determine whether nuisance exists:
> utility or value of the activity, how common the activity is, suitability to the locale,
> impracticality of avoiding invasion, and gravity of the harm that it produces.
Nuisances are usually intentional but may include negligent or reckless conduct, in some states.
> Nuisance may also include conditions giving rise to strict liability as an abnormally dangerous activity.
> Other tort claims or law violations of law increases the likelihood of the conduct being a nuisance.
The jury determines *nuisance in fact* based on the above factors.
> Some authority exists for a judge to determine a *nuisance in law* for conduct violating statute.
Remedies include not only damages to those who prove harm but also a preliminary injunction.
> To enjoin, must show irreparable harm, substantial likelihood of success on the merits, and
> balance of hardships weighing in plaintiff's favor.

LONG OUTLINE:

Nuisance

   Nuisance is a tort claim protecting those who own and use real property. A nuisance is an *intentional, unreasonable, substantial non-trespassory invasion of another's interest in using lands*. A **private nuisance** claim protects the individual interest of one who owns or controls private lands, while a **public nuisance** claim protects the general interest of all who may use public lands. In the case of private nuisance, only those who own or control the private land have *standing to sue*. In the case of public nuisance, public officials or private representatives of the affected class, and private individuals who show special injury, have standing to sue.

   Determining whether a nuisance exists depends on weighing factors. In general, one compares the utility or value of the activity, including how common the activity is, its suitability to the locale, and the impracticality of avoiding invasion, with the gravity of the harm that it produces. Nuisances do not always involve intentional conduct. Liability may exist for unintentional conduct that is negligent or reckless, or for conditions giving rise to strict liability as an abnormally dangerous activity. The existence of other tort claims or violations of law, rule, or regulation increases the likelihood of the conduct being a nuisance. As to who determines whether a nuisance exists, a jury determines *nuisance in fact* based on the factors mentioned above, while some authority exists for a judge to determine a *nuisance in law* when the conduct violates statutes and regulations. The remedies for a nuisance may include not only damages to those who prove harm but also a preliminary injunction on a showing of irreparable harm, substantial likelihood of success on the merits, and a balance of hardships weighing in plaintiff's favor.

Fluency Cards

Cover and uncover the response to each prompt until you fluently recall the exact response.

Nuisance	**Public nuisance**
intentional, unreasonable, substantial non-trespassory invasion of another's interest in using lands.	Protects the general interest of all using public lands. Standing with public official or private person with special injury.

Private nuisance
Protects the interest of one owning or controlling private lands, having standing to sue.

55

Definitions Worksheet on Nuisance

1. What interest does a *nuisance* claim protect?

    _____

    _____

2. What are the elements of a nuisance claim?

    _____

    _____

    _____

3. What is the difference between private and public nuisance claims?

    _____

    _____

4. How does nuisance law determine an activity's unreasonableness?

    _____

    _____

5. Can unintentional conduct constitute a nuisance?

    _____

    _____

    _____

6. Who (judge or jury) decides a nuisance?

    _____

    _____

7. Who may sue for nuisance?

    _____

    _____

    _____

8. What remedies does law offer for nuisance claims?

    _____

    _____

Answers for Definitions Worksheet on Nuisance

1.   ***What interest does a nuisance claim protect?*** Nuisance is a tort claim protecting those who own and use real property.

2.   ***What are the elements of a nuisance claim?*** A nuisance claim is an intentional, unreasonable, substantial non-trespassory invasion of another's interest in using lands.

3.   ***What is the difference between private and public nuisance claims?*** A private nuisance claim protects the individual interest of one who owns or controls private lands, while a public nuisance claim protects the general interest of all who may use public lands.

4.   ***How does nuisance law determine an activity's unreasonableness?*** Compare the utility or value of the activity, including its suitability to the locale and impracticality of avoiding invasion, with the gravity of the harm that it produces.

5.   ***Can unintentional conduct constitute a nuisance?*** Under the Restatement, yes, if liability would exist for negligent or reckless conduct, or strict liability as an abnormally dangerous activity, so better to just apply those other theories when so, while keeping nuisance an intentional tort.

6.   ***Who (judge or jury) decides a nuisance?*** A jury determines nuisance in fact based on the factors mentioned above, although authority exists for a judge to determine a nuisance in law (a nuisance under all circumstances).

7.   ***Who may sue for nuisance?*** In the case of private nuisance, only those who own or control the private land have standing to sue. In the case of public nuisance, public officials or private representatives of the affected class, and private individuals who show special injury, have standing to sue.

8.   ***What remedies does law offer for nuisance claims?*** Damages to those who prove harm and an injunction on a showing of irreparable harm, success on the merits, and a balance of hardships weighing in plaintiff's favor.

Differentiation Exercise on Nuisance

For each of the following scenarios, indicate whether the nuisance is public or private, and intentional or unintentional, and who has standing to sue. Answers are on the next page.

1. The factory created an odor that the adjacent property owner smelled night and day.

2. The center's bells rang every Sunday morning so that people who regularly brunched downtown couldn't hear each other for at least 15 minutes each week.

3. The plant deposited chemicals in the river that flowed downstream. The plant's CEO indicated she had no idea the chemicals were unsafe. The president of the wildlife-protection club lived in a nearby town that was upstream.

4. The factory created an odor that everyone in the neighborhood could smell during the day.

5. The privately owned museum imperfectly covered a hole left over from completion of an outdoor exhibit, which created a cave-in potential if someone stepped on it.

6. The apartment dweller kept his television turned up very high, with the result that the next-door neighbor couldn't concentrate on homework.

7. The homeowner had parties every Saturday night, blasting music until midnight.

8. The kids lit firecrackers in their yard every July 4th until at least 10 p.m.

9. The college student liked to study to loud music, often playing it throughout the week until about 3 a.m.

10. The Farmer's Market offered large bags of fresh manure that the storm unfortunately ripped apart, stinking up the public building where the Market was located.

11. Although the plant had tested the noise levels to ensure they would not be bothersome to people, the noises were heard by dogs that barked all night, every night, because of the noise.

12. The neglected area of woods on the land had carved a dangerous gully that washed out the neighbor's path every time there was a storm, of which the woods' owner was unaware.

Answers to Differentiation Exercise on Nuisance

1. The factory created an odor that the adjacent property owner smelled night and day. ***Private; intentional; adjacent owner.***

2. The center's bells rang every Sunday morning so that people who regularly brunched downtown couldn't hear each other for at least 15 minutes each week. ***Public; intentional; people who brunched.***

3. The plant deposited chemicals in the river that flowed downstream. The plant's CEO indicated she had no idea the chemicals were unsafe. The president of the wildlife-protection club lived in a nearby town that was upstream. ***Public or private depending on who sues; intentional; people who live downstream or who use the water.***

4. The factory created an odor that everyone in the neighborhood could smell during the day. ***Public or private; intentional; owners in neighborhood or people who regularly frequent it.***

5. The privately owned museum imperfectly covered a hole left over from completion of an outdoor exhibit, which created a cave-in potential if someone stepped on it. ***Public; unintentional; people who walk across the property.***

6. The apartment dweller kept his television turned up very high, with the result that the next-door neighbor couldn't concentrate on homework. ***Private; intentional; neighbor.***

7. The homeowner had parties every Saturday night, blasting music until midnight. ***Private; intentional; neighbors.***

8. The kids lit firecrackers in their yard every July 4th until at least 10 p.m. ***Private; intentional; neighbors.***

9. The college student liked to study to loud music, often playing it throughout the week until about 3 a.m. ***Private; intentional; nearby affected persons.***

10. The Farmer's Market offered large bags of fresh manure that the storm unfortunately ripped apart, stinking up the public building where the Market was located. ***Public or private; unintentional; people who regularly frequent the area around the market or live nearby.***

11. Although the plant had tested the noise levels to ensure they would not be bothersome to people, the noises were heard by dogs that barked all night, every night, because of the noise. ***Private; probably intentional; neighbors.***

12. The neglected area of woods on the land had carved a dangerous gully that washed out the neighbor's path every time there was a storm, of which the woods' owner was unaware. ***Private; unintentional; neighbor.***

Comprehensiveness Exercise on Nuisance

Insert words at the ^ mark that would make for a more-accurate or more-detailed law statement.
Follow the italicized hints for help. Suggested answers are on the next page.

1. A nuisance claim protecting those who own ^ real property is an intentional ^ ^ ^ invasion of another's interest in using lands. *[Only those who own, or someone else, too? Missing three other invasion qualifiers, too.]*

2. A private nuisance claim protects the individual interest of one who owns ^ private lands. *[Only owners, or someone else, too?]*

3. A public nuisance claim protects the general interest of all who may use ^ lands. *[What lands (limit the lands to a certain type)?]*

4. To determine unreasonableness, nuisance law compares the activity's utility or value ^ ^ with the gravity of the harm that it produces. *[Name two specific factors determining utility.]*

5. Law addresses unintentional conduct affecting use and enjoyment of lands under negligent ^ conduct liability ^ . *[Name another kind of conduct worse than negligence but not as bad as intentional conduct. And name another kind of liability addressing activities on land.]*

6. A jury determines nuisance ^ ^ . *[Which kind of nuisance does a jury determine? What role does a judge have?]*

7. ^ Only those who own or control the land have standing to sue ^ . *[Which kind of nuisance claim do owners or controllers pursue? And isn't there another kind?]*

8. Nuisance remedies include damages for those who prove harm and an injunction ^ ^ ^ . *[When can a plaintiff win an injunction (three requisites)?]*

Answer for Comprehensiveness Exercise on Nuisance

1.   A nuisance claim protecting those who own *or use* real property is an intentional, *unreasonable, substantial non-trespassory* invasion of another's interest in using lands.

2.   A private nuisance claim protects the individual interest of one who owns *or controls* private lands.

3.   A public nuisance claim protects the general interest of all who may use *public* lands.

4.   To determine unreasonableness, nuisance law compares the activity's utility or value, *including its suitability to the locale and impracticality of avoiding invasion,* with the gravity of the harm that it produces.

5.   Law addresses unintentional conduct affecting use and enjoyment of lands under negligent *or reckless* conduct liability, *or strict liability as an abnormally dangerous activity.*

6.   A jury determines nuisance *in fact, while a judge determines a nuisance in law (a nuisance under all circumstances).*

7.   *In the case of private nuisance,* only those who own or control the land have standing to sue. *In the case of public nuisance, public officials or private representatives of the affected class have standing, as do private individuals who show special injury.*

8.   Nuisance remedies include damages for those who prove harm and an injunction *on a showing of irreparable harm, success on the merits, and a balance of hardships weighing in plaintiff's favor.*

Application Exercise on Nuisance

Sort the fact patterns into public nuisance (PU), private nuisance (PV), or no nuisance (NN). Answers are at page bottom.

1. Three homeowners in the subdivision sued an adjacent homeowner for operating an illicit brothel.

2. A township sued a farmer for letting a huge pile of old tires smolder for weeks, creating thick black smoke.

3. A landowner sued a hunter for cutting branches, spreading feed corn, and building a hunting blind on the land.

4. An environmental group representing bike-path users sued a farmer for repeatedly spreading manure on the path.

5. A New York advocacy group sued an oil driller legally burning off methane in a huge West Texas oil field.

6. An apartment owner sued a new big-box retailer for building a light tower that brightly lit bedrooms all night.

7. A homeowner with toddler children sued a neighbor for continous raucous outdoor pot parties all night.

8. A village sued a tree service for frequent burning of timber piles creating thick smoke across a busy roadway.

9. A new gun range sued a neighboring blasting-and-mining operation for noise abatement.

10. An association of homeowners sued an adjacent new granite-countertop cutting operation for noise abatement.

11. Elderly couple buying and moving into a home sued neighbor for playful children screams from pool patio.

12. Office-building tenants sued an adjacent new electrical-transformer business for destroying wifi capability.

13. Public-safety officials sued smelting plant to abate weekend noxious-gas emissions onto public soccer fields.

14. Old Buddhist meditation temple sued new neighboring puppy mill to abate constant loud barking at all hours.

15. Airport authority sued neighboring landowner for hosting frequent large amateur drone-club events.

16. Homeowners association sued nearby Wiccan lodge to abate weekly indoor secretive occult seances.

17. Parent-teacher association sued outdoor theater to abate XXX film showings during nearby school hours.

18. VFW Post sued nearby American Legion post for starting Friday fish fries that undercut similar VFW events.

19. Homeowners along new railroad track sue railroad for chemical dust and rock debris from passing open rail cars.

20. Neighborhood group sued nearby vacant-lot owner for hosting drug-dealers, gamblers, pimps, and prostitutes.

21. Daycare center sued neighboring orchard for pesticide dust constantly drifting into daycare play yard.

22. Homeowner sued nearby hospital to abate occasional late-night ambulance sirens.

23. Cattlemen's association sued uranium-storage facility for excessive radiation on nearby open-range lands.

24. Cosmetology salon sued new adjacent smoke shop for smoke and smells permeating salon during salon hours.

Answers: 1PV 2PU 3NN 4PU 5NN 6PV 7PV 8PU 9NN 10PV 11NN 12PV 13PU 14PV 15PU 16NN 17PU 18NN 19PV 20PU 21PV 22NN 23PU 24PV

Factors Exercise on Nuisance

To determine the reasonableness or unreasonableness of an activity, nuisance law considers factors including the activity's **utility** or **social value,** suitability to its **locale,** **impracticality** of avoiding invasion, **gravity** of harm that it produces, **nature** of the harm or injury, **frequency** of the harm or injury, and injury or harm **cost**. For each scenario, choose a factor weighing heavily in favor of either claimant or respondent, analyzing that factor by filling in the blanks.

1. **The oil-sands refiner emitted a constant tar-like smoke across the adjacent residences, businesses, and farm fields.**

    The [*choose a factor*] favors the [*choose a party*] when [*state relevant facts*] because [*explain your reasoning*] .

2. **The hospital's ambulances emitted occasional loud sirens through the adjacent neighborhood on the rare occasion that the ambulances encountered neighborhood traffic on an emergency run.**

    The [*choose a factor*] favors the [*choose a party*] when [*state relevant facts*] because [*explain your reasoning*] .

3. **The ballpark's late-night fireworks after every home game awoke and scared young children in neighboring homes and severely disturbed the mentally disabled residents of an adjacent adult foster home.**

    The [*choose a factor*] favors the [*choose a party*] when [*state relevant facts*] because [*explain your reasoning*] .

4. **The twice-a-year Saturday-night rock concerts on the private parking lot annoyed nearby condominium residents who preferred other music forms.**

    The [*choose a factor*] favors the [*choose a party*] when [*state relevant facts*] because [*explain your reasoning*] .

5. **Cattle-manure stench from the rancher's feedlot wafted across the neighboring hog farms and large commercial poultry operations.**

    The [*choose a factor*] favors the [*choose a party*] when [*state relevant facts*] because [*explain your reasoning*] .

6. **Light from the softball-field towers kept the neighborhood lit until the fields closed at 10 p.m. during summer and 8 p.m. on school nights.**

    The [*choose a factor*] favors the [*choose a party*] when [*state relevant facts*] because [*explain your reasoning*] .

Discrimination Exercise on Nuisance

Indicate whether each statement *overgeneralizes*, *undergeneralizes*, or *misconceives* the rule, explaining why. *Overgeneralizing* states the rule too broadly, *undergeneralizing* too narrowly, and *misconceiving* incorrectly.

1. A nuisance claim protecting those who own or use real property is an intentional, non-trespassory invasion of another's interest in using lands.

____OVER/____UNDER/____MIS/ Why? _____

_____

2. A private nuisance claim protects the personal, private interest of those individuals who own private lands.

____OVER/____UNDER/____MIS/ Why? _____

_____

3. A public nuisance claim protects the individual interest of all who may use private lands.

____OVER/____UNDER/____MIS/ Why? _____

_____

4. To determine reasonableness or unreasonableness, nuisance law compares the activity's utility, including suitability to locale and impracticality of avoiding invasion, with its social value.

____OVER/____UNDER/____MIS/ Why? _____

_____

5. Law addresses unintentional conduct affecting use and enjoyment of lands under negligent or reckless conduct liability.

____OVER/____UNDER/____MIS/ Why? _____

_____

6. Only those who own or control the land have standing to sue in nuisance.

____OVER/____UNDER/____MIS/ Why? _____

_____

7. Nuisance remedies are damages for those who prove the loss or harm and an injunction abating the nuisance.

____OVER/____UNDER/____MIS/ Why? _____

_____

Answers for Discrimination Exercise on Nuisance

1. The statement **OVERgeneralizes** the rule. A nuisance claim protecting those who own or use real property is an intentional, ***unreasonable, substantial*** non-trespassory invasion of another's interest in using lands.

2. The statement **UNDERgeneralizes** the rule. A private nuisance claim protects the personal, private interest of those individuals who ***either*** own ***or control*** private lands. A lessee of lands, for instance, could maintain a private nuisance claim.

3. The statement **MISconceives** the rule. A public nuisance claim protects the ***general, not individual***, interest of all who may use ***public, not private***, lands.

4. The statement **MISconceives** the rule. To determine reasonableness or unreasonableness, nuisance law compares the activity's utility, including suitability to locale and impracticality of avoiding invasion, with ***the gravity of the harm that it produces***, not its social value, which is like utility.

5. The statement **UNDERgeneralizes** the rule. Law addresses unintentional conduct affecting use and enjoyment of lands under negligent or reckless conduct liability, ***and strict liability as an abnormally dangerous activity***.

6. The statement **UNDERgeneralizes** the rule. Only those who own or control the land have standing to sue in ***private*** nuisance, but as to ***public nuisance, public officials or private representatives of the affected class have standing, as do private individuals who show special injury***.

7. The statement **OVERgeneralizes** the rule. Nuisance remedies are damages for those who prove the loss or harm and an injunction abating the nuisance ***only on a showing of irreparable harm, success on the merits, and a balance of hardships weighing in plaintiff's favor***.

Multiple-Choice Questions with Answer Explanations

11.   A resident lived in a posh development with the houses crowded closely together. A neighbor with teenage children moved in next door. The neighbor's teenagers frequently played amplified guitars, drums, and other rock-band instruments late into the night in the neighbor's garage. The resident called the police over the noise, who confirmed that the noise probably violated local ordinance but who also indicated that nothing would be done about it. The resident was fed up calling the police over the neighboring garage band's noise-ordinance violations. Wondering whether there was anything else he could do to put a stop to the sleep-shattering racket, the resident consulted an attorney. What would be proper legal advice?

A.   The resident may be able to pursue a nuisance action to stop the ordinance violations.
B.   The resident may be able to pursue a trespass action to stop the ordinance violations.
C.   The resident may be able to pursue invasion of privacy claims to stop the teenagers.
D.   The resident has no tort remedy and can only hope the city enforces the ordinance.

Answer explanation: Option A is correct because intangible entries (noise, smell, light, etc.), while not a trespass, may be addressed through the tort of nuisance, which involves unreasonable interference with use and enjoyment rather than, as in trespass, interference with exclusive possession. The violation of law may provide a stronger basis on which to maintain that the noise was unreasonable. Option B is incorrect because there was no interference with exclusive possession (no entry). Option C is incorrect because there was no invasion of privacy (no exploitation, intrusion, false light, or public disclosure). Option D is incorrect because there may be a nuisance remedy.

12.   A farmer periodically watered his truck garden by opening and closing sluice gates to briefly flood the garden fields. Often, the sluicing of the fields would result in a pond forming across a public bike path and road running alongside the truck garden. The pond that formed across the bike path and road when the farmer sluiced his truck garden received more and more complaints from passersby using the bike path and road. The board of a nearby homeowner's association asked its legal counsel for an opinion on what could be done to correct the pond problem so that it no longer interfered with homeowner use of the bike path and road. What tort rights should counsel address in the opinion?

A.   The pond problem is just something to live with because the truck garden is productive.
B.   The pond problem may constitute a trespass to land to abate by damages action.
C.   The pond problem may constitute a private nuisance to discourage by damages action.
D.   The pond problem may constitute a public nuisance that could be abated by injunction.

Answer explanation: Option D is correct because a public nuisance is one that interferes with public enjoyment, while a private nuisance is one that substantially affects the use and enjoyment of private lands. Here, the pond may have interfered substantially enough with the use of the road and bike path so as to warrant a court action to abate the problem by injunction. Option A is incorrect because there may be a public-nuisance remedy. Option B is incorrect because no private land has been identified onto which the pond encroached as an entry. Option C is incorrect because there was no private nuisance, and no single individual would be likely to be able to prove sufficient damages to discourage the problem.

Week 5
Easements and Licenses

QUESTIONS FOR THE ASSIGNED READING:

What is an easement? What are the elements of an easement?

What is the difference between an easement appurtenant and easement in gross? Which do you think law should favor and why? Which does the law currently favor and why?

Should law permit a landowner to tie up land use through easements? Don't easements go against free alienability of land, one of property law's key tenets? Why does law favor easements?

List the elements of each of these different ways of creating easements: express; prescriptive; by estoppel; implied by prior existing use; and implied by necessity.

Name something you do not understand about this week's material.

SHORT OUTLINE:

Easements involve ownership rights in land limited to use or restriction.
Nature and type of easements include **affirmative easements** entitling use and **negative easements** restricting use.
  Easements appurtenant are rights of a dominant-parcel owner over the servient parcel, running with the land.
    Run with land means easement restrictions benefit and burden successors to dominant and servient parcels.
  Easements in gross are rights over the servient parcel *not* attached to any dominant parcel, not running.
    Beneficiaries in gross may *not* transfer rights unless parties agree or rights are for *commercial purpose*.
    The servient land remains subject to an easement in gross on the servient land's conveyance.
  Licenses in land involve right to use another's land for a *limited and temporary purpose*, not ownership.
    Courts construe a license when parties are unclear what they intend but intend something temporary.
    Licensors giving permission for limited use may generally revoke it at any time.
      Estoppel prevents revocation if the grant so states *or* if the holder *substantially and detrimentally relies*.
      Easement that fail the statute of frauds or otherwise may give rise to an **irrevocable license**.
        Not all states recognize estoppel, and construed licenses last only as justice requires.
Methods of creating easements are numerous.
  Express easements arise by **grant** of the servient land's owner in favor of the easement's grantee.
    Easements also arise by **reservation** of an owner who transfers the servient land to another, reserving rights.
    Law presumes easement by grant intends the easement to be permanent, unless expressly stated otherwise.
    If the grant or reservation does not mention duration, then the court will construe as a permanent easement.
  Implied easements arise from the circumstances of the conveyance, indicating easement intent.
    Quasi-use easements involve an owner dividing land into dominant and servient parcels reflecting prior use.
      The owner or a purchaser of the dominant parcel get to continue the use after division.
      A single owner must have owned dominant and servient lands, use must be reasonably necessary,
      use must be continuous rather than sporadic, parties must intend the burden, and use must be apparent.
    Necessity easements arise when an owner divides land, leaving one parcel needing an easement.
      Easements of necessity arise when not satisfying requirements for easement by implication/ prescription.
      The land division must deprive a parcel of a right that is *necessary* for the property's use.
      Easements of necessity require *strict necessity*, not just convenience or other general benefit.
    Plat easements arise by implication from a recorded **plat**, a map of the owner's newly divided land.
      Owners reference plat restrictions when granting deeds to lot buyers, including for express easements.

Law may imply plat easements omitted from deed, from the plat map and apparent uses of other parcels.
This rule of *beneficial enjoyment* depends on plat and use indicating the owner's intent.
Prescription: easements also arise by **prescription**, referring to *adverse possession* like for freehold estates.
The easement use must be open, notorious, continuous, hostile, and under claim of right, for the period.
The exclusive-use requirement of adverse possession is absent for a prescriptive easement.
An easement by prescription grants the holder only the earned adverse right, not greater rights.

LONG OUTLINE:

Rights in land

Real-property law addresses and provides for other **rights in land** beyond the ownership estates that the above sections address. Those other rights in land include *covenants at law and in equity*, restricting and controlling the use of land, and *easements*, *profits*, and *licenses*, creating rights in others than the owners of the land to use the land, even if inconsistent with the owner's wishes. Covenants differ from easements in that covenants involve *contract* obligations while easements create *ownership* interests in the land. Keep that distinction in mind as you review the law of covenants and easements. Real-property issues also arise around *fixtures* permanently affixed to the land and *zoning* restrictions. The following sections address these other rights in land beyond the ownership issues addressed above.

Easements, profits, and licenses

An **easement** involves an ownership right in land limited to its use or restriction, in contrast to the freehold estates described in sections above that reflect ownership interests in the full bundle of ownership rights. Easements function like *covenants at law or in equity*, addressed above, except again that an easement is an ownership interest rather than, as in the case of a covenant at law or in equity, only a contract interest. Consider the *nature* and *types* of easements in the following section, followed by sections on their *creation*, *scope*, and *termination*.

Nature and type

The law first distinguishes between **affirmative easements**, entitling the holder to use of the servient land, and **negative easements**, *restricting* the *owner* from some use. For example, an easement that permits one neighbor to use the driveway of another neighbor has an *affirmative* easement, while an easement that prohibits one neighbor from building a structure on a portion of that neighbor's *own* land, for the benefit of the other neighbor, is a *negative* easement. The law also distinguishes between **easements appurtenant**, referring to rights that owners of a dominant parcel have relative to the servient parcel, and **easement in gross**, referring to rights that owners hold relative to the servient parcel but *not* attached to any dominant parcel. For example, both above examples involve easements *appurtenant* because they both benefit a specific neighboring parcel of land. By contrast, an easement *in gross* would entail a person's right to enter another's land to, for example, put one's boat in the water, without that person's right benefitting any specific land. The law also labels types of easement by their manner of creation, as the next section addresses.

Easements appurtenant *run with the land*, while easements in gross do *not* run with the land. As indicated above in the sections on covenants at law and in equity, to run with the land means that the easement's restriction benefits the successors in interest to the dominant parcel while burdening successors in interest to the servient parcel. For example, the right to put one's boat in the water in the above example, being merely in gross, would *not* run with the land, while the other rights to driveway use or prevent building of structures, being appurtenant, *would* run with the land. Beneficiaries of easements in gross may *not* generally transfer their rights unless the parties so agree or the rights are for a *commercial purpose*, such as when a company buys the right to maintain a billboard on an owner's servient land. However, the servient land remains subject to an easement in gross on the servient land's conveyance.

The law also recognizes **licenses** in land. A license involves the right to use another's land for a *limited purpose*, such as if a landowner permits a friend to temporarily park the friend's motor home on the landowner's land. Unlike an easement, a license is *not* an interest in land. When the parties are not clear whether they intend a license or an easement in gross, the courts tend to construe a *license* unless the parties clearly intend the restriction to be more than temporary. The grantor of a license who gives oral or written permission to the limited use may generally revoke it at any time. However, under the **doctrine of estoppel**, the grantor must *not* revoke if the grant specifically stated that it would be irrevocable *or* if the license's holder has *substantially and detrimentally relied* on the license, although some jurisdictions refuse to recognize estoppel. Thus, in the above example, if the friend *had* to park the motor home on the owner's land overnight or for another short period to avoid a fine or fee that the friend would incur for having relied on the owner's license, then estoppel could prevent the landowner from objecting. Indeed, an easement that fails due to the statute of frauds or other reason may give rise to an **irrevocable license** of this type. However, an irrevocable license, while like a permanent easement in gross, lasts only until it no longer prevents an injustice.

Methods of creation

Parties create easements in several ways, each addressed in the following sections. Easements arise most easily and obviously by express **grant** of the owner of the servient land. Yet easements also arise by **reservation** of the owner who transfers the then-servient land to another. Easements also arise by **implication** from the circumstances of the conveyance, indicating transferor and transferee intent to recognize an easement. Easements also arise of **necessity** when an owner divides land and leaves one parcel needing an easement across the other to make use of the land. Finally, easements also arise by **prescription**, referring to *adverse possession*, in the manner that freehold estates arise by adverse possession.

Express

Parties create easements by **grant**, in which the servient land's owner transfers the right to the easement's grantee, and by **reservation**, in which the owner transfers land to another while reserving the easement right to the transferring owner. The law presumes that an easement by grant intends the easement to be permanent, unless the grant expressly states otherwise. For example, if a landowner agrees in exchange for a neighbor's consideration that the neighbor and successors to the neighbor's land may cross the landowner's property to reach a nearby beach, the landowner may grant the neighbor an easement that the neighbor can record to document the right. Alternatively, if the landowner decided to sell half of the land but reserve a path across the sold portion for the landowner and successors to reach the beach, the landowner could *reserve* the easement in the deed conveying the sold half. If the grant or reservation does not mention duration, then the court will construe the path as a permanent easement.

Implied

The law recognizes three types of **implied easement**, each treated in the following sections. Implied easements arise from the circumstances rather than by express grant. The first type of implied easement is a *quasi-use* easement that begins with an owner using the land in an apparent way that, when the owner later divides the land into dominant and servient parcels reflecting the prior use, allows the owner or a purchaser of the dominant parcel to continue the use. A second type of implied easement is an easement *of necessity* that the law implies to ensure that the dominant parcel would not otherwise be without use. A third type of implied covenant arises from the owner recording a *plat* on the land's division, burdening the platted lots with the initial restrictions.

Quasi-use

Parties can create an implied easement of **quasi-use** when a landowner begins with a single parcel on which the landowner conducts an apparent use, such as maintaining a driveway or providing for utilities. The owner's uses at that time are not easements, only *quasi* easements, because the owner holds the whole of the land. When the landowner then divides the land into two or more parcels at least one of which requires an easement to *continue the apparent use*, then an easement can arise by implication as necessary to continue the use. For example, if an owner maintains a driveway that the owner's land division subsequently interrupts, and the driveway is necessary to the owner's continued use of the parcel that the owner retains, then an easement by prescription will burden the parcel that the owner sells. Easements by implication, though, require that a single owner have owned the dominant and servient lands, that the use is reasonably necessary to the dominant land, that the use was continuous rather than sporadic before division, that the owner and successor have intended the burden of the continued use, and that the use was apparent to the successor when taking.

Necessity

Easements **of necessity** can arise even when the circumstances do not satisfy all requirements for an easement by implication or prescription. An easement of necessity requires that the land division have deprived a parcel of a right that is *necessary* for the property's use, such as access to a public roadway. Thus, for example, if a landowner divides a property front to back rather than side to side, leaving the back parcel landlocked without public-road access, the law will recognize an easement of necessity even if prior use had not established the access, access use was not apparent, or the parties had not intended access, as a quasi-use easement would have required. Because easements of necessity do not satisfy the conditions for a quasi-use easement or easement by prescription, easements of necessity require *strict necessity*, not just convenience or other general benefit to the dominant land.

Plat

Easements can also arise by implication from a recorded **plat**. A plat is a map of the owner's land divided into new parcels. The plat map may include descriptions of and restrictions on the land's use when divided, such as for single-family housing only. A master deed, master agreement, plat map, or other document recorded or referenced in recordings may include other restrictions, such as subjecting the parcels to control of an association, payment of association fees, and the like, and other benefits, such as use of the land's private streets, parks, and beach or other access. Prudent owners reference plat restrictions when granting deeds to individual lot buyers, including for express easements. However, when an owner neglects to include express easements in a deed, the law may imply those easements from the plat map and apparent uses of other parcels complying with the platted restrictions, under a rule of *beneficial enjoyment*. The plat and circumstances, though, must indicate the owner's intent to create the easement. Just because an easement would benefit all owners does not authorize the court to imply it.

Prescription

An easement by **prescription** can arise when a person adversely possesses the easement right. The use must be open and notorious, continuous, hostile to the owner's use, and under a claim of right, for longer than the state's statutory period for **adverse possession**. Notice that only the exclusive-use requirement of adverse possession is absent among the requirements for a prescriptive easement. When not creating a freehold estate because of the limited nature of the use or the absence of *exclusive* use, the use can give rise instead to an easement by prescription. Thus, for example, if neighbors cross an owner's land to reach a beach satisfying each of the above conditions and do so for the statutory period, then the neighbors acquire an easement by prescription to continue beach access. An easement by prescription grants the holder only the earned adverse right, not greater rights. Thus, the neighbors acquiring the access right would have no right to burden the easement further by, for instance, widening and improving their path, and building a deck for a beach overlook.

Fluency Cards

Cover and uncover the response to each prompt until you fluently recall the exact response.

Easement

Ownership right of use or restriction.

Easement appurtenant

Dominant over servient parcel, running with the land (benefiting and burdening successors).

Easement in gross

Unattached right over servient parcel. Does not run with land but binds servient successors.

Creating easement

Owner reserves easement on transfer of servient land.

License

Limited, temporary right to use land. Licensor revokes anytime unless reliance or grant says not.

Easement by necessity

Dominant parcel continues use if continuous, apparent, intended, and strictly necessary.

Plat easement

Recorded plat referenced in deed implies apparent restrictions.

Prescriptive easement

When open, notorious, continuous, hostile, and claim of right for period. No need for exclusivity.

Definitions Worksheet on Easements

1.   What is an *easement*?

_____

_____

2.   Name three ways to create an easement.

_____

_____

3.   What does law call an easement that grants one landowner use of other land?

_____

4.   What does law call an easement that allows one to restrict the land of another?

_____

5.   When do express easements run with the land?

_____

_____

_____

6.   How do implied easements arise?

_____

_____

_____

7.   What is a license?

_____

_____

8.   May the landowner revoke a license? If so, when does law limit revocation?

_____

_____

9.   How does a prescriptive easement arise?

_____

_____

Answers for Definitions Worksheet on Easements

1.   ***What is an easement?*** An easement is a nonpossessory right to enter, use, or restrict another's land.

2.   ***Name three ways to create an easement.*** Easements arise by express grant, including reservation, and by implication or prescription.

3.   ***What does law call an easement that grants one landowner use of other land?*** An easement granting one landowner use of another's land is an easement *appurtenant*. The benefited land is the *dominant* estate and the restricted land is the *servient* estate.

4.   ***What does law call an easement that allows one to restrict the land of another?*** An easement granting an individual the right to use or restrict the land of another is an easement *in gross*, having only a servient estate because the right is personal rather than benefiting land.

5.   ***When do express easements run with the land?*** An easement runs with the land when the signed grant describing the right intends to benefit and burden future owners, the right touches and concerns the land, and the parties record the easement to protect against bona-fide purchasers.

6.   ***How do implied easements arise?*** An implied quasi easement arises when an owner divides land one part of which openly benefits the other part and the owners expect that benefit to continue. The easement is one of strict necessity if the benefit is access. Merger of the parcels extinguishes the easement.

7.   ***What is a license?*** A license is a landowner's permission for another to enter the land to do something that would otherwise be a trespass.

8.   ***May the landowner revoke a license?*** A landowner may revoke a license unless tied to the licensee's ownership in personal property on the land or, by estoppel, if the licensee relied on the owner's representation such that revocation would be inequitable.

9.   ***How does a prescriptive easement arise?*** A prescriptive easement arises on another's open, continuous, adverse, claim-of-right use of the land for more than the prescriptive period.

Issue-Spotting Exercise on Servitudes

For each scenario below, indicate whether the statement describes an easement, negative easement, real covenant, equitable servitude, or license. Answers are on the next page. Use these definitions:

<u>Easement</u>: nonpossessory right to use or enter onto another's property, or the legal right to use another's land for a specific purpose. The holder of an easement has an interest in land owned by someone else but not a possessory interest.

<u>Negative easement</u>: nonpossessory right to prevent someone else from using his or her land in a way that blocks artificial water-flow, light, view through window, or support of a building (maybe also scenic view and conservation to preserve land in natural state).

<u>Real covenant</u>: promise by one landowner made to another landowner that the landowner would do or not do something on his or her own land, intended to bind future owners of the land who are in privity of estate and that relates in some way to the use of the land itself (runs with the land). Remedy is money damages.

<u>Equitable servitude</u>: promise by one landowner made to another landowner that the landowner would do or not do something on his or her own land, intended to bind future owners of the land whether they are in privity of estate or not, with notice. Remedy is injunctive relief.

<u>License</u>: grant of permission to enter another's land for a specific purpose, not intended to be irrevocable or bind successors to the land.

<u>Appurtenant easement</u>: use given to whoever owns the land that the easement benefits.

<u>In gross easement</u>: gives the right to someone without regard to ownership of land (only a servient estate, not a dominant estate). A dominant estate is the land the servitude benefits. A servient estate is the land that the servitude burdens.

1.   Homeowner bought her property from Sarah. The deed noted that Homeowner has the right to use Neighbor's driveway to get to Homeowner's property.

2.   Jerry bought part of his property from Donna. Jerry's sewer line is under Donna's yard, which is between his place and the street.

3.   Alice has a document (not the deed) between her mother, from whom she inherited her land, and Stewart, stating that her mother and her mother's heirs, successors, and assigns, have the right to use a path across Stewart's land to get to a beachside park.

4.   In a conversation, Stewart gave Alice permission to use a path across Stewart's land to get to a beachside park.

5.   Sylvester has the right to park his car in a lot owned by Miriam.

6.   Muhammed and his neighbor each promised the other, in writing, that each of them and their heirs, successors, and assigns, would build only a single-family residence on their respective properties. Muhammed sold his land to Florence.

7.   When Shirley sold half of her land to Alex, Alex promised in writing that he and his heirs, successors, and assigns would keep his house always Colonial blue paint color. Alex sold his land to Madiha.

8.   Smith bought a townhouse from Jones. At the time of purchase, Smith promised Jones in writing she would not block Jones' view from his window, in his adjacent townhouse. Smith then sold her townhouse to Brown.

9.   Sharese bought a house in a lake association. Her deed gave her the right to use a common lake for recreational purposes.

10.   Lori parks on Janice's property, which is next to the stadium, for the duration of a football game. The lot is nowhere near Lori's home.

11.   Lori purchases a right for herself and her heirs, successors, and assigns, to park on Janice's property, which is next to the stadium, for the duration of the football season. The lot is nowhere near Lori's home.

12.   In her deed, Lori is given permission to park on her subdivision property, which is next to the stadium, on game nights during each football season. The lot is in the same subdivision as Lori's home.

Answers to Issue-Spotting Exercise on Servitudes

1.   Homeowner bought her property from Sarah. The deed noted that Homeowner has the right to use Neighbor's driveway to get to Homeowner's property. ***Easement.***

2.   Jerry bought part of his property from Donna. Jerry's sewer line is under Donna's yard, which is between his place and the street. ***Easement.***

3.   Alice has a document (not the deed) between her mother, from whom she inherited her land, and Stewart, stating that her mother and her mother's heirs, successors, and assigns, have the right to use a path across Stewart's land to get to a beachside park. ***Easement.***

4.   In a conversation, Stewart gave Alice permission to use a path across Stewart's land to get to a beachside park. ***License.***

5.   Sylvester has the right to park his car in a lot owned by Miriam. ***Might be easement or license.***

6.   Muhammed and his neighbor each promised the other, in writing, that each of them and their heirs, successors, and assigns, would build only a single-family residence on their respective properties. Muhammed sold his land to Florence. ***Covenant or equitable servitude, depending on more information.***

7.   When Shirley sold half of her land to Alex, Alex promised in writing that he and his heirs, successors, and assigns would keep his house always Colonial blue paint color. Alex sold his land to Madiha. ***Negative easement.***

8.   Smith bought a townhouse from Jones. At the time of purchase, Smith promised Jones in writing she would not block Jones' view from his window, in his adjacent townhouse. Smith then sold her townhouse to Brown. ***Easement.***

9.   Sharese bought a house in a lake association. Her deed gave her the right to use a common lake for recreational purposes. ***License.***

10.   Lori parks on Janice's property, which is next to the stadium, for the duration of a football game. The lot is nowhere near Lori's home. ***License.***

11.   Lori purchases a right for herself and her heirs, successors, and assigns, to park on Janice's property, which is next to the stadium, for the duration of the football season. The lot is nowhere near Lori's home. ***Easement.***

12.   In her deed, Lori is given permission to park on her subdivision property, which is next to the stadium, on game nights during each football season. The lot is in the same subdivision as Lori's home. ***Easement.***

Issue-Spotting Exercise on Creating Easements

For each scenario, state how the parties created the easement, whether expressly, impliedly by prior existing use, impliedly by necessity, prescriptively, or by estoppel. Answers are below.

1. Larry lived on a large parcel, using a driveway from the southern edge of his land to his house on the northern edge. He sold the southern half to Jane. At the time of sale, that he used the driveway to get to his home was obvious, although Larry and Jane did not discuss Larry's use of the driveway.

2. Jorge bought a land-locked parcel from Ned. Jorge's new neighbor, adjacent-land-owner Sue, told Jorge he could build a road from the highway across her land to get to Jorge's land. Jorge spent six months and $8,000 to put in a state-of-the-art paved driveway. Sue then became angry with Jorge and told him he could no longer cross her land.

3. Mary sold to Jennifer the right for Jennifer to walk through her woods to get from Jennifer's land to a park. They both signed a document that gave this right to Jennifer, her heirs, successors, and assigns.

4. Katerina owned a large parcel of land. Her home was on the land's eastern edge. She sold the land's western half to Mark. The only road was on the eastern half. As a result, Mark's parcel was landlocked. All borders, other than Katerina's land, consisted of state parkland on which Mark could not drive or build.

5. Jerome bought a parcel adjacent to a parcel his neighbor Lester owned and occupied. The easiest way for Jerome to get to his land was by traversing Lester's land. Jerome could build another way out on the other side of his parcel at great expense. Jerome started using an old road across Lester's property. He did so with no permission. In fact, from time to time Lester would tell Jerome that he didn't want him using the road, even erecting large "No Trespass" signs all along the road. Jerome used the road to access his land for 25 years. Then, Lester put up a gate with a lock to block Jerome's access.

Answers: 1 implied prior existing use 2. By estoppel 3. Express 4. Implied by necessity 5. prescriptive

Comprehensiveness Exercise on Easements

Insert words at the ^ mark that would make for a more-accurate or more-detailed law statement.
Follow the italicized hints for help. Suggested answers are on the next page.

1.   An easement is a nonpossessory right to enter ^ another's land. *[Only entry, or two other forms of right?]*

2.   Easements arise by express grant, including reservation ^ ^ . *[Can you think of two other ways easements arise?]*

3.   An easement granting one landowner use of another's land is an easement *appurtenant*. The benefited land is the *dominant* estate ^ . *[What does law call the other land?]*

4.   An easement granting an individual the right to use or restrict the land of another is an easement *in gross*, having only a servient estate ^ . *[Can you briefly say why no dominant estate?]*

5.   An easement runs with the land when the signed grant describing the right intends to benefit and burden future owners ^ ^ . *[Can you name two other conditions?]*

6.   An implied quasi easement arises when an owner divides land one part of which ^ benefits the other part ^ . *[Is any benefit enough, or only certain benefits? And doesn't law impose another condition?]*

7.   A landowner may revoke a license ^ ^ . *[Can you name two exceptions?]*

8.   A prescriptive easement arises on another's open ^ ^ ^ use of the land for more than the prescriptive period. *[Can you name the three other conditions?]*

Answers for Comprehensiveness Exercise on Easements

1.　An easement is a nonpossessory right to enter, ***use, or restrict*** another's land. *Some easements do not require entry, just use or restriction.*

2.　Easements arise by express grant, including reservation, ***and by implication or prescription***.

3.　An easement granting one landowner use of another's land is an easement *appurtenant*. The benefited land is the *dominant* estate ***and the restricted land is the servient estate***.

4.　An easement granting an individual the right to use or restrict the land of another is an easement *in gross*, having only a servient estate ***because the right is personal rather than benefiting land***.

5.　An easement runs with the land when the signed grant describing the right intends to benefit and burden future owners, ***the right touches and concerns the land, and the parties record the easement to protect against bona-fide purchasers***.

6.　An implied quasi easement arises when an owner divides land one part of which ***openly*** benefits the other part ***and the owners expect that benefit to continue***. The easement is one of strict necessity if the benefit is access. Merger of the parcels extinguishes the easement.

7.　A landowner may revoke a license ***unless tied to the licensee's ownership in personal property on the land or, by estoppel, if the licensee relied on the owner's representation such that revocation would be inequitable***.

8.　A prescriptive easement arises on another's open, ***continuous, adverse, claim-of-right*** use of the land for more than the prescriptive period.

Application Exercise on Easements

Sort the fact patterns into express easement (E), implied easement (I), prescriptive easement (P), or license (L). Answers are at page bottom.

1. A farmer carved a back parcel out of farmlands for a daughter to buy and build a home, granting a driveway.

2. A landowner divided the land, selling a landlocked parcel that required road access across the retained land.

3. Back-lot owners beat a clear path across a lakefront lot owner's land for twenty years to use the lake and beach.

4. An industrial manufacturer permitted paintballers to hide, play, and shoot on the manufacturer's scrap yard.

5. A neighbor used a landowner's driveway for thirty years to build and access the neighbor's work shed.

6. A landowner divided the land, selling a residence the utilities for which were across the retained land.

7. An urban commercial lot owner divided the lot to deed half to another business, reserving a utility easement.

8. A suburban homeowner with children permitted a neighbor to erect their trampoline on the homeowner's lot.

9. A building owner divided the building, selling a half stairway access for which was across the retained half.

10. A lakefront-lot owner permitted other owners to pull their boats up onto the lakefront-lot owner's beach.

11. A homeowner sold the carriage house behind the home, driveway access to which was across the retained land.

12. A subdivision developer granted in the subdivision plat lot-owner use easements for a clubhouse and pool.

13. A neighbor put in a gravel driveway partway on a landowner's land, using the drive for fifteen years.

14. A lakefront owner selling a back lot deeded a lake-access easement to the back-lot buyer.

15. An office-building owner sold office suites, retaining common areas through which the suites needed access.

16. A farmer permitted mushroom hunters to harvest morels from woodlands on the farm's back forty.

17. Lot owners built a fire pit and placed stumps and chairs on a landowner's wide side lot, using it twenty years.

18. A trailer park sold lots, retaining the back driveway that lot owners must use to bring trailers onto their lots.

19. A woodlands homeowner deeded the land along the highway for a buyer to build, reserving driveway access.

20. A gas station sold its car-repair facility, retaining the parking area repair-facility customers must use.

21. Lot owners built an overlook deck and stairs to the beach on a lakefront lot owner's bluff, using it thirty years.

22. A woodlot owner permitted a friend to spread feed corn and hunt deer on the back of the woodlot.

23. A homeowner sold a side yard to a neighbor, reserving in the deed of conveyance an access easement.

24. An apartment-building owner sold third-floor apartments accessed by a retained elevator and stairway.

25. A homeowner permitted a neighbor to park a recreational vehicle on the homeowner's back lot.

Answers: 1E 2I 3P 4L 5P 6I 7E 8L 9I 10L 11I 12E 13P 14E 15I 16L 17P 18I 19E 20I 21P 22L 23E 24I 25L

Factors Exercise on Easements

To determine whether an implied easement has arisen, law considers factors including the **conveyance terms, consideration, necessity, reciprocal benefit, prior use, knowledge,** and how **apparent** the use was. For each scenario, choose a factor that would weigh heavily in favor of either the landowner or one claiming the implied easement, and analyze that factor by filling in the blanks.

1.   **An executive paid a lakefront-lot price for a divided back lot that accessed and viewed the lake only across the seller's retained parcel.**

The [_choose a factor_] favors the [_choose a party_] when [_____ _state relevant facts_____] because [_____ _explain your reasoning_ _____] .

2.   **A woodlands owner divided and sold a back parcel that accessed the main highway only across the owner's retained woodlands.**

The [_choose a factor_] favors the [_choose a party_] when [_____ _state relevant facts_____] because [_____ _explain your reasoning_ _____] .

3.   **The divided lot owner knew before dividing and selling the parcel that the parcel's water, gas, and sewer utilities were underground across the retained lot.**

The [_choose a factor_] favors the [_choose a party_] when [_____ _state relevant facts_____] because [_____ _explain your reasoning_ _____] .

4.   **Anyone, including seller and buyer, could plainly see that electric, cable-television, and internet utilities reached the divided and sold lot across the seller's retained parcel.**

The [_choose a factor_] favors the [_choose a party_] when [_____ _state relevant facts_____] because [_____ _explain your reasoning_ _____] .

5.   **Before dividing and selling, the seller herself had used the retained parcel for driveway access to the residence on the divided and sold lot.**

The [_choose a factor_] favors the [_choose a party_] when [_____ _state relevant facts_____] because [_____ _explain your reasoning_ _____] .

6.   **Though not expressly reserving an easement, the conveyance documents for the divided and sold lot clearly anticipated that the buyer would build and reside in a home on the divided and sold lot, accessed across the retained lot.**

The [_choose a factor_] favors the [_choose a party_] when [_____ _state relevant facts_____] because [_____ _explain your reasoning_ _____] .

Discrimination Exercise on Easements

Indicate whether each statement *overgeneralizes*, *undergeneralizes*, or *misconceives* the rule, explaining why. *Overgeneralizing* states the rule too broadly, *undergeneralizing* too narrowly, and *misconceiving* incorrectly.

1. An easement is a nonpossessory right to enter or use another's land.

____OVER/____UNDER/____MIS/ Why? _____

_____

2. Easements can arise by express grant or by implication.

____OVER/____UNDER/____MIS/ Why? _____

_____

3. An appurtenant easement grants an individual the right to use or restrict the land of another, while an easement in gross grants one benefited landowner use of another's servient land.

____OVER/____UNDER/____MIS/ Why? _____

_____

4. An easement runs with the land when the right touches and concerns the land.

____OVER/____UNDER/____MIS/ Why? _____

_____

5. An implied quasi easement arises when one land openly benefits another land and the owners expect that benefit to continue.

____OVER/____UNDER/____MIS/ Why? _____

_____

6. A license arises only when tied to the licensee's ownership of personal property on the land.

____OVER/____UNDER/____MIS/ Why? _____

_____

7. A prescriptive easement arises on another's open, continuous, adverse, claim-of-right use of the land.

____OVER/____UNDER/____MIS/ Why? _____

_____

Answers for Discrimination Exercise on Easements

1. The statement **UNDERgeneralizes** the rule. An easement is a nonpossessory right to enter or use *or restrict* another's land. *Many easements restrict use rather than grant entry.*

2. The statement **UNDERgeneralizes** the rule. Easements can arise *not only* by express grant or implication *but also by prescription*.

3. The statement **MISconceives** the rule. *An appurtenant easement grants one benefited landowner use of another's servient land, while an easement in gross grants an individual the right to use or restrict another's land.*

4. The statement **OVERgeneralizes** the rule. An easement runs with the land *not just* when the right touches and concerns the land *but when a signed grant describing the right intends to benefit and burden future owners and the parties record the easement to protect against bona-fide purchasers*.

5. The statement **OVERgeneralizes** the rule. An implied quasi easement arises when *an owner divides land* one part of which openly benefits the other part and the owners expect that benefit to continue. *One land benefiting another land is not alone enough.*

6. The statement **UNDERgeneralizes** the rule. While a license arises when tied to the licensee's ownership of personal property on the land, *a license may arise for any other reason not involving personal property, when the owner grants permission*.

7. The statement **OVERgeneralizes** the rule. A prescriptive easement arises on another's open, continuous, adverse, claim-of-right use of the land *for more than the prescriptive period*.

Multiple-Choice Questions with Answer Explanations

13. A season-ticket holder to an outdoor summer commercial concert series brought intoxicating drinks and marijuana into the venue for the first several events. Each time, when other patrons called the season-ticket holder's rowdy behavior to security's attention, the event producer confiscated the drinks and marijuana, and warned the season-ticket holder not to do so again because it violated well-publicized event rules. If the conduct occurred yet again, may the producer revoke the holder's season tickets?

A. Yes, because the producer has an obligation to comply with law.
B. Yes, because the season-ticket holder had only a license.
C. No, because the season-ticket holder had a contract right to attend.
D. No, because the season-ticket holder would still have a right to comply.

Answer explanation: Option B is correct because tickets to a commercial event are a license revocable at the will of the licensor. Here, the producer may revoke the license for any reason or likely no reason but especially for violation of well-publicized rules. Option A is incorrect because the facts give no clear indication that either the producer or even the rowdy patron was violating the law, which would in any case not necessarily justify terminating the season tickets. Option C is incorrect because the law construes attending a commercial event as a revocable license notwithstanding the ticket purchase. The producer would have to pay damages if the revocation breached the purchase terms, but revocation would remain the producer's right. Option D is incorrect because the holder had several warnings, and even without warning the producer would have had a right to revoke the license.

14. A landowner granted a valid written driveway easement to a neighbor who in exchange agreed to pay for paving both adjacent parcels' driveways. The neighbor neglected to record the easement but did complete and regularly use the paved driveway on the landowner's land, sometimes even parking vehicles on the landowner's land. The landowner then granted a bank a deed of trust for a construction loan to build a house on the land. The bank promptly recorded the deed of trust. When the landowner failed to complete the house, the bank foreclosed on the trust deed and sought to sell the land free and clear of the neighbor's driveway easement. What right does the neighbor have, assuming that the jurisdiction has a conveyance statute that requires either recording or constructive notice?

A. The neighbor retains the easement right because the bank received its trust deed later.
B. The neighbor retains the easement right because of the bank's constructive notice.
C. The neighbor loses the easement right for having failed to record the writing.
D. The neighbor loses the easement right because trust deeds precede easements.

Answer explanation: Option B is correct because although trust deeds (a mortgage substitute used in some states in which the landowner grants a deed in the lender's favor for a trustee to hold and auction if the landowner defaults) are usually enforceable much like a mortgage, one taking an interest in land takes subject to easements over which one has constructive notice in a jurisdiction having a statute requiring recording or constructive notice. Here, the bank either would or should have seen the neighbor's paved driveway and driveway use, and known of the neighbor's easement interest, when loaning in exchange for a trust deed. The neighbor's completed easement thus has priority due to constructive notice. Option A is incorrect because the order of easement before trust deed is alone not enough without considering recording or constructive notice. Option C is incorrect because the neighbor does not lose the easement right over failure to record if as here the

83

bank had constructive notice. The neighbor would have lost the right if the neighbor never built the driveway and the bank did not otherwise have notice. Option D is incorrect because no general rule places trust deeds ahead of easements. And by the way, the neighbor would likely not have the right to park vehicles on the landowner's land because the easement was for a driveway, driveways are generally for ingress and egress, and parking vehicles may be beyond the easement's scope.

15. In exchange for a few calves, a farmer executed a writing sufficient to convey an undescribed easement for a driveway for ingress and egress by a neighboring dairy herder and successors and assigns. The drive that the herder began using substantially improved the herder's access to the herder's own barns and lands even though not strictly necessary for access. The herder thereafter used the drive more and more consistently, even making small improvements such as lightly grading and filling the drive. In time, much longer than the jurisdiction's period for adverse possession, both the farmer and the herder conveyed their lands to adult children between whom a dispute arose as to the continued use of the undescribed drive. What are their respective rights?

A.   The farmer's children have the right to exclude the herder's children from any drive.
B.   The farmer's children must allow some drive but may designate a different drive.
C.   The herder's children still have the right to use the same drive.
D.   The herder's children have only the right to compensation for the lost drive.

Answer explanation: Option C is correct because a grantee may enforce an express written grant for value of an undescribed easement later defined by use and acquiescence. The farmer granted the easement, which the herder then defined and as to which the farmer acquiesced. Note that although the herder used the easement for much longer than the period for adverse possession, a prescriptive easement would not have arisen because the use was by the farmer's consent rather than hostile. Option A is incorrect because the farmer's children had no right to exclude the heirs who succeeded to the enforceable easement. Option B is incorrect because the farmer's children may not relocate an easement that the parties to the grant had defined by use and acquiescence. The easement then is as good as if described. Option D is incorrect because the herder's children may keep the easement and would not have a theory for compensation in relinquishing it.

16. The owner of a home on a city lot discovered that his lot was large enough to divide front and back. The lot was between two city streets, one running along the lot's front and one running along the lot's back. The new back lot would have a new drive to the street in back, while the old front lot with the house would retain its drive to the street in front. The owner then sold the back lot to a buyer who constructed a house on the new back lot. When the buyer completed the new house and moved in, the buyer objected to the seller walking across the new back lot to a bus stop that the seller had used for twenty years to go to work. The deed to the new back lot said nothing about the bus stop and seller's use, but the buyer had known of and orally agreed to the use before buying. Does the seller have the right to continue to walk across the back lot to the bus stop?

A.   Yes because an easement by implication arose from prior use.
B.   Yes because the seller has a real covenant with the buyer to enforce.
C.   No because the seller failed to include the easement in the deed.
D.   No because by doing so, the seller would interfere with the buyer's privacy.

Answer explanation: Option A is correct because an easement is an interest in land allowing the holder to make or prevent use of another's property. Easements arise by grant expressly transferring the easement to another, reservation when transferring land to another, implication from circumstances showing that the parties must have intended the easement, and prescription through adverse possession. Easements by implication arise from either prior use or of necessity, when an owner divides and conveys parcels of land in ways that frustrate prior or necessary uses. Prior uses must be necessary, continuous, intended to continue, and apparent to the burdened purchaser. Option B is incorrect because the buyer made no promise to preserve the use, and so no real covenant arose to enforce. Option C is incorrect because easements by implication from prior use or necessity can arise without the easement in the deed or even in any other writing. Option D is incorrect because the facts do not indicate privacy interference, and moreover, even if the use affected some privacy, then the buyer would have known when taking the property subject to the use.

17. A bay-side landowner enjoyed visiting his land to watch seabirds bathe, swim, fish, and dig for food in the land's ponds and tidal pools. While the landowner wanted the land unspoiled, the annual taxes burdened the landowner just enough to contract in a signed writing with a local for the local to remove frogs, crabs, and clams from the land's ponds and pools in exchange for an annual payment approximating the taxes. One day, the local built a campfire on the land and invited some buddies to join him for a few beers and steamed clams. The local shooed the landowner's visiting grandchildren away when they came over to the campfire to see what was going on. What right, if any, does the landowner have to discourage or prevent the local's activity?

A. No right because the activity is reasonably incident to the easement in gross's purpose.
B. Limited right not to renew the license for another year after the end of the current year.
C. Full right to enforce the profit's limited scope and prevent other activity such as here.
D. Absolute right to terminate the servitude at any time without reason or advance notice.

Answer explanation: Option C is correct because a profit a prendre is a right to take from the land, including the right to enter the land to do so, but is not an interest in the land itself. A profit arises by express agreement or by prescription and can be either appurtenant to adjacent land or in gross, and transferable or nontransferable according to its terms. Profits terminate by voluntary release, merger of the benefitted lands, waste, or terms of the agreement. Here, the profit was to remove frogs, crabs, and clams, not to build fires, drink beer, and cook. Option A is incorrect because the interest here was only a profit, not an easement, and the profit had a much more-limited scope. Option B is incorrect because the interest is a profit, not a license, and because the landowner may at any time restrict the use to the profit's limited scope. Option D is incorrect because the interest is a profit, not a servitude, and termination would not be possible during a year for which the local had paid the profit's cost, the right being contractual.

18. A retailer owned land along a public highway. The owner of a salvage yard behind the retailer's land negotiated with the retailer for a right of way for ingress and egress across the retailer's land. The salvage yard had other access from a side street, but the right of way across the retailer's land was significantly more convenient. The salvage-yard owner duly recorded the retailer's deed that expressly granted the right of way to the salvage-yard owner "and successors, heirs, and assigns." The deed did not include a description of the right of way's specific location across the retailer's land. The retailer and salvage-yard owner agreed on a route that the salvage-yard owner then used for five years. The salvage-yard owner then sold the business and land to a new owner. The retailer also sold to an investor who demanded that the new salvage-yard owner move the right-of-way route to a different but reasonable alternative location on the investor's land. What result if the new salvage-yard owner refuses and the investor sues to either terminate or move the right of way?

A. Investor loses because the deed granted the right of way, and use defined it.
B. Investor loses because successive use fixed the right of way's location by prescription.
C. Investor wins but only on moving the right of way to the proposed reasonable location.

D.   Investor wins and the right of way is extinguished for lack of its location description.

Answer explanation: Option A is correct because use can establish the location of a deeded but undescribed right-of-way easement, and once use establishes the location, the restriction at that location persists. Option B is incorrect because the facts suggest only five years of use, which would not meet the typical statute on prescriptive use for ten years or more, and here the use was not adverse and prescriptive but instead by grant, so that prescriptive-use rights would not arise. Option C is incorrect because once the grantor and grantee fix the granted and deeded easement's location, the easement remains fixed. The grantee need not move it whenever the grantor shows an alternative reasonable location. Option D is incorrect because a grantor and grantee may establish an easement's location in addition to by express description.

19.   A husband and wife constructed a small home on one half of their own home's lot in which the wife's elderly mother then lived. When the mother passed away, the couple divided their lot and sold the small home to a college student. The couple later sold their own home to a surveyor. The surveyor promptly confirmed that the student's driveway to the small home was on the surveyor's main lot. The student pointed out that the surveyor's utility pole and line to the surveyor's house was on the student's lot. What rights if any do the surveyor and student have to continue their current uses on one another's lots?

A.   Neither gets to continue use of the other's lot unless the lot owner grants an easement.
B.   Neither gets to continue use of the other's lot unless able to prove necessity.
C.   Each gets to continue use of the other's lot under quasi easement implied by use.
D.   Each gets to continue use of the other's lot under implied reciprocal servitude.

Answer explanation: Option C is correct because apparent uses that existed when a landowner divides the land and that benefit the divided lots may exist as quasi easements implied by use even when not confirmed in the landowner's deed or other signed writing. Option A is incorrect because the law will imply a quasi easement by the evident use that existed at the time the owner divided the lots. Option B is incorrect because necessity is not a condition for an implied quasi easement by use to arise. Easements by necessity typically apply to landlocked lands. Here, the surveyor may be able to run utility lines or the student build a driveway on their own lots, but the evident use when the owner divided the lots is sufficient to establish the quasi easement. Option D is incorrect because the utility line and driveway are different uses rather than reciprocal (same, mutual) uses. Reciprocal servitudes typically arise by common plan, whereas here the two lots have different servitudes requiring different easements.

20.   Adjacent landowners hunted and fished on one another's wild lands at first by courtesy and later by express written agreement. Seeking to maximize the value of each land by this mutually beneficial agreement, the owners made their written agreement not only for the benefit of one another but for successors, heirs, and assigns. After years of mutual use, each landowner sold to other owners. One of those owners began to sell licenses to friends to come and hunt and fish on the both lands. The other owner protested and attempted to prohibit not only the other owner's friends but also the other owner from making any further use of the land. What result if the two owners seek a court declaration of their rights?

A.   Each owner may hunt and fish on the other's land by profit but not extend that right to others.
B.   Each owner must not hunt or fish on the other's land because any such right ceased on land transfer.
C.   The owner who sold licenses to friends to use the other's land has lost all right, and so has the other owner.

86

D.   The owner who sold licenses to friends must disgorge to the other owner half of the profits to retain the right.

Answer explanation: Option A is correct because a profit is a right to take from the land, including the right to enter the land to do so, but is not an interest in the land itself. A profit arises by express agreement or by prescription, and can be either appurtenant to adjacent land or in gross and transferable. Profits terminate by voluntary release, merger of the benefitted lands, waste, or terms of the agreement. Here, the profits appear to be appurtenant and thus not transferable in gross but only on conveyance of the land. Option B is incorrect because the original profits by their terms were also for the benefit of successors, heirs, and assigns. The rights appurtenant to each land may run with the land where, as here, so provided. Option C is incorrect because although one could make an argument that the sale of licenses was a sufficient waste of the profit as to terminate it, depending on the damage to the fish and wildlife, the rest of the answer is incorrect because the other owner committed no waste and should have a continued right. Option D is incorrect because the profits were for the benefits of the landowners and their successors, heirs, and assigns, not the benefit of friends or for commercial licensing to friends. So disgorging half of the profits would not perfect such a right.

Week 6
Easements Assignability, Scope, and Termination, and Negative Easements

QUESTIONS FOR THE ASSIGNED READING:

Review leasehold estates. Of what are you unsure about leasehold estates?

Review nuisance. What is still unclear about nuisance?

SHORT OUTLINE:

Scope of an easement, meaning the use it affords, depends on how the easement arose.
   Easements *by express grant or reservation* depend on the **terms of the express grant**.
      The easement's holder must not use beyond the express grant, nor the servient owner restrict to less.
      Right of use changes only when the parties creating the easement intended that it change.
      Easements may limit use by quantity, such as for only a single person or residents of a single parcel.
   Easements *by implication* look to the use from which the law implied the easement.
      Quasi-use easements from prior use have the scope of the prior use.
   Easements *by prescription* have the scope of the prescriptive use.
Termination of easements, typically *permanent* without ending date, can nonetheless occur in several ways.
   Express easements, by grant or reservation, terminate per the *expressed* terms.
   Easements appurtenant terminate by **merger** when the dominant land's owner acquires the servient land.
   Easements in gross terminate by **merger** when the holder acquires the servient land.
   Easements also terminate when the holder **releases** the servient land from the burden.
      A release is effective only when satisfying the *statute of frauds*.
   Easements terminate when the holder acts in ways that clearly express the holder's intent to **abandon**.
      A holder simply not using an easement is *not* abandonment.
   Easements terminate with **cessation of purpose**, but only if the easement was one *of necessity*.
   Easements for facility use terminate when the facility suffers **destruction**, if *not* by the servient land's owner.
   A servient land's owner may **adversely possess** and thereby terminate an easement.
      The owner's possession must be open, notorious, continuous, hostile, and a claim of right, for the period.

LONG OUTLINE:

Scope

An easement's **scope**, meaning what rights it affords and burdens it imposes, depends on how the easement arose. If the easement arose by *express grant or reservation*, then the easement's scope depends on the **terms of the express grant**. The easement's holder must not expand the scope of the grant, such as by widening an area of use, improving the easement beyond the grant, or making a different use than the grant expressed. Likewise, the owner of the servient land must not restrict the grant to less than the rights that it expresses, such as by denying vehicular ingress and egress as the grant expressed while permitting only foot traffic. An easement's right of use should change only when the parties creating the easement intended that it change, such as for vehicular travel rather than horse-and-buggy travel on the advent of the automobile. Easements may also limit or grant use by quantity, such as for only a single person or residents of a single parcel to pass or for residents of multiple parcels or even the public to pass.

If, by contrast, the easement arose *by implication*, then the court must look to the use from which the law implied the easement. *Quasi-use* easements, arising from prior use, would have the scope of the prior use. Thus, if an owner divided the land in a way that one parcel depended on an apparent utilities easement across the other parcel, the dominant parcel would have the right to continue the utilities use but *not* to construct a driveway or otherwise expand the use. The same rule holds for easements *by prescription* that the prescriptive use determines the easement's scope. Thus, if the prescriptive use was beach access, then the users creating the prescriptive easement would have that right but not the right to widen and improve the access, or increase the use to include building decks or other structures, or partying on the servient land.

Termination

Although easements are typically *permanent*, without ending date, easements can nonetheless **terminate** in several ways. An express easement, whether by grant or reservation, may terminate per the *expressed* terms. Thus, if the grant creates an easement across servient land for as long as the dominant land is within a certain family, or used as a vacation home but for no other use, then the easement would terminate on a change in either expressed condition. Easements can also terminate by **merger**, when the easement in gross's holder acquires the servient land or when the owner of the dominant land acquires title also to the servient land, even if the owner later re-divides the land. Easements can also terminate when the easement's holder **releases** the servient land from the burden, often after negotiation and for consideration. A release is effective, though, only when satisfying the *statute of frauds* insofar as the release reflects a transaction in an interest in land.

Easements can also terminate when the holder acts in a way that clearly expresses the holder's intent to **abandon** the easement, such as by building a fence across that part of the path on the holder's dominant land. A holder simply not using an easement is *not* abandonment. Easements can also terminate with **cessation of purpose**, but only if the easement was one *of necessity*. Thus, a landlocked parcel that had an easement of necessity across another parcel would lose the easement if a new public road provided the formerly landlocked parcel with access. Easements for use of a facility may also terminate when the facility suffers **destruction**, if the destruction was *not* at the hands of the servient land's owner. Finally, a servient land's owner may **adversely possess** and thereby terminate an easement, if the owner's possession meets the open, notorious, continuous, hostile, and claim-of-right conditions for the statutory period.

Fluency Cards

Cover and uncover the response to each prompt until you fluently recall the exact response.

Scope of easement	**Terminating easement**
As express grant states, or of necessity or by prescription (prior use). May limit to certain persons.	Merger of dominant and servient land, holder release or abandonment, or end of necessity.

Assigning easement appurtenant

If grantor intended and servient estate is on notice.

Assigning easement in gross

If grantor intended but not if personal, recreational, or overburdens servient land.

Definitions Worksheet on Easements

1.   When may a holder assign an easement appurtenant?

_____

_____

_____

2.   When may a holder assign an easement in gross?

_____

_____

3.   How does the grant determine an easement's scope?

_____

_____

_____

4.   May an easement's holder expand the easement's use?

_____

_____

_____

5.   What is the landowner's remedy when an easement holder exceeds the easement's scope?

_____

_____

6.   How can easements terminate?

_____

_____

_____

7.   How do easements differ from covenants?

_____

_____

_____

Answers for Definitions Worksheet on Easements

1.   ***When may a holder assign an easement appurtenant?*** The holder of an easement appurtenant may assign if the grantor intended assignment and the servient estate is on notice.

2.   ***When may a holder assign an easement in gross?*** The holder of an easement in gross may assign when the grantor intended assignment but may not assign a personal, recreational right or assign when doing so would overburden the servient estate.

3.   ***How does the grant determine an easement's scope?*** The grant defines the dominant parcel, the easement's treatment on the dominant parcel's division, and the nature and extent of use rights. Limit the scope of a prescriptive easement to the adverse use.

4.   ***May an easement's holder expand the easement's use?*** The grant determines limits to an easement's expansion, but if silent, then law allows normal development that does not overburden the servient parcel.

5.   ***What is the landowner's remedy when an easement holder exceeds the easement's scope?*** A landowner has a trespass action for damages and injunction when an easement holder exceeds the easement's scope.

6.   ***How can easements terminate?*** Easements can terminate by written release of the holder, expiration of the grant, end of the necessity, estoppel by servient owner's reliance on dominant holder's representation, abandonment, landowner's prescription, merger of dominant and servient parcels, and eminent domain.

7.   ***How do easements differ from covenants?*** An easement is a holder's right to use the servient parcel, while a covenant is a right to compel the servient owner to do something as to the servient parcel. Both an easement and a covenant can restrict the servient parcel's use.

Issue-Spotting Exercise on Scope and Termination of Easements

For each example, indicate whether Homeowner is likely to face a challenge
from Neighbor and, if so, whether is Homeowner likely to succeed.

Homeowner bought her property from Seller. The deed noted that Homeowner and her heirs, successors, and assigns have the right to use Neighbor's driveway to get to Homeowner's property. Consider these additional facts for each scenario:

1.   Homeowner's property abuts a lake, and she has a canoe that she stores in a shed a few miles from her home. When she wants to use the canoe, she loads it in her truck to drive across Neighbor's driveway.

2.   Homeowner's property abuts a lake. She runs a business where she drops people in canoes on the lake opposite from where she lives and then drives and picks them up on her property's side of the lake. She drives the canoes and paying guests across Neighbor's driveway several times a day every day during the summer. After a week, Neighbor notifies Homeowner he wants her to stop using the driveway for commercial purposes.

3.   Before Homeowner started the business, she asked Neighbor if she could use the driveway for this purpose. He said "yes" but never put it in writing. After Neighbor sold his property to Buyer, Buyer told Homeowner she had to stop using the easement for business purposes.

4.   Homeowner built a second driveway to access her home. She stopped using Neighbor's driveway. After Homeowner died, her daughter inherited the place and started using Neighbor's driveway for personal use. Neighbor told her to stop because Homeowner abandoned the easement.

5.   After Homeowner built the second driveway, Homeowner gave Friend permission to fish in her lake, assigning her use of Neighbor's driveway to Friend. Friend used it to drive onto Homeowner's property to fish. He used it mostly on weekends.

Comprehensiveness Exercise on Easements

Insert words at the ^ mark that would make for a more-accurate or more-detailed law statement.
Follow the italicized hints for help. Suggested answers are on the next page.

1.   The holder of an easement appurtenant may assign when the grantor intended assignment ^ . *[Can you name a second condition?]*

2.   The holder of an easement in gross may assign when the grantor intended assignment but may not assign a personal, recreational easement in gross ^ . *[Can you name a second limitation?]*

3.   An easement's grant defines ^ ^ the nature and extent of use rights. *[Can you name two other significant aspects that the grant defines?]*

4.   The grant determines limits to an easement's expansion, but if silent, then law allows normal development ^ . *[Can you name a limitation on development?]*

5.   A landowner has a trespass action for damages ^ when an easement holder exceeds the easement's scope. *[Can you name a second remedy?]*

6.   Easements can terminate by written release of the holder, expiration of the grant, or end of the necessity ^ ^ ^ ^ ^ . *[Can you name five other ways an easement can terminate?]*

7.   An easement is a holder's right to use the servient parcel, while a covenant is a right to compel the servient owner to do something ^ . *[Just do something, or do something specific?]*

Answers for Comprehensiveness Exercise on Easements

1. The holder of an easement appurtenant may assign when the grantor intended assignment *and the servient estate is on notice.*

2. The holder of an easement in gross may assign when the grantor intended assignment but may not assign a personal, recreational easement in gross *or assign when doing so would overburden the servient estate.*

3. An easement's grant defines *the dominant parcel, the easement's treatment on the dominant parcel's division, and* the nature and extent of use rights.

4. The grant determines limits to an easement's expansion, but if silent, then law allows normal development *that does not overburden the servient parcel.*

5. A landowner has a trespass action for damages *and injunction* when an easement holder exceeds the easement's scope.

6. Easements can terminate by written release of the holder, expiration of the grant, or end of the necessity, *estoppel by servient owner's reliance on dominant holder's representation, abandonment, landowner's prescription, merger of dominant and servient parcels, and eminent domain.*

7. An easement is a holder's right to use the servient parcel, while a covenant is a right to compel the servient owner to do something *related to the servient parcel.*

Application Exercise on Easements

Sort the fact patterns into whether the easement holder may assign (A) or not (N). Answers are below.

1. A back-lot owner with a recorded lake-access easement desires to assign to a buyer of the back lot.

2. A boat owner with a right to put the boat in the river on a riverfront-lot owner's land desires to convey the right.

3. An amateur photographer with permission to take photographs from an oceanfront lot wishes to convey the right.

4. A company paying to display a billboard on the owner's freeway-adjacent land wishes to convey the billboard.

5. A manufacturer paying to draw treatment water from a landowner's pond wishes to convey the right.

6. A camper owner with permission to park the camper on a farmer's field wishes to convey the right.

7. A landowner wishes to convey the land with unrecorded, personal lake-access rights across a lakefront lot.

8. A subdivision-lot owner with a platted utility easement across other lots wishes to convey the lot with utilities.

9. A landlocked parcel owner with a recorded driveway easement over an adjacent lot desires to convey the parcel.

10. A concert season-ticket holder with unassignable ticket rights desires to sell the rights to the highest bidder.

11. A carpenter who enjoys hunting desires to assign personal hunting-blind rights on a former customer's land.

Answers: 1A 2N 3N 4A 5A 6N 7N 8A 9A 10N 11N

Sort the following fact patterns into whether the easement terminates (T) or not (N). Answers are below.

1. The lot-owner holder of a lake-access easement across an adjacent lot releases the easement for $5,000.

2. Five years passes after the grant of a five-year easement to set off riverfront fireworks on Independence Day.

3. The county builds a road to a formerly landlocked parcel served by easement of necessity across another's land.

4. An owner sells a residence the utilities for which use a recorded easement across an adjacent lot.

5. A lot owner builds a fence at the lot's boundary after a neighboring easement holder says she no longer needs it.

6. A trailer owner removes the trailer from its easement site on a farmer's land, letting the site go to brush.

7. A landowner plants trees and bushes, for ten years blocking a driveway formerly used by a neighbor.

8. A lot owner with a neighbor's driveway easement across it sells to a buyer who doesn't want the easement on it.

9. A builder buys back unbuilt subdivision sites with recorded easements across one another, to build a mansion.

10. The county condemns several parcels with access and utility easements on them, to extend a highway.

11. An elderly couple for twenty years stop using their recorded back-lot lake-access easement because of illness.

Answers: 1T 2T 3T 4N 5T 6T 7T 8N 9T 10T 11N

96

Factors Exercise on Easements

Whether the expansion of an easement's use overburdens the servient parcel, thus limiting the use, can depend on several factors including **grantor intent, grantor knowledge at grant, nature of the use, parties' expectation of expansion at grant, degree of expansion, nature of the burden, cost of the burden, benefit to the easement users,** and **benefit if any to the landowner**. For each scenario, choose a factor that would weigh heavily in favor of either the landowner or easement holder, and analyze that factor by filling in the blanks.

1.   The lakefront-lot grantor of a back-lot lake-access easement had no idea at the time of the grant that a back-lot owner would someday build a hotel on the back lot, bringing dozens of hotel guests across the easement at all hours of day and night.

The [_choose a factor_] favors the [_choose a party_] when [_____ state relevant facts_____] because [_____ _explain your reasoning _____].

2.   The holders of a recreational-use-path easement across ranchland gradually graduated from walking use to bicycle use to motorbike use, until constant loud and fast motorbikes were causing injury and even death to the ranch's cows and calves.

The [_choose a factor_] favors the [_choose a party_] when [_____ state relevant facts_____] because [_____ _explain your reasoning _____].

3.   The developer of a platted subdivision with reciprocal easements for access to and use of the subdivision's grounds, pool, and fitness club unexpectedly built a casino on unsold lots, the patrons of which swarmed the grounds, pool, and fitness club.

The [_choose a factor_] favors the [_choose a party_] when [_____ state relevant facts_____] because [_____ _explain your reasoning _____].

4.   Greater use of a utility easement across the back of a business owner's lot first brought cable service, then higher-speed internet service to the business owner, and finally less-expensive, higher-quality service.

The [_choose a factor_] favors the [_choose a party_] when [_____ state relevant facts_____] because [_____ _explain your reasoning _____].

5.   The farmland grantor of a billboard easement along a freeway expected billboards advertising goods and services, not billboards promoting political candidates and positions with which the grantor disagreed.

The [_choose a factor_] favors the [_choose a party_] when [_____ state relevant facts_____] because [_____ _explain your reasoning _____].

6.   Heavier use of a beach-access easement across the lakefront owner's land eroded a bluff into a large dune blowout that would soon, with continued heavy easement use, require constructing elaborate retaining walls.

The [_choose a factor_] favors the [_choose a party_] when [_____ state relevant facts_____] because [_____ _explain your reasoning _____].

Discrimination Exercise on Easements

Indicate whether each statement *overgeneralizes*, *undergeneralizes*, or *misconceives* the rule, explaining why. *Overgeneralizing* states the rule too broadly, *undergeneralizing* too narrowly, and *misconceiving* incorrectly.

1. The holder of an easement appurtenant may assign the easement.
_____OVER/_____UNDER/_____MIS/ Why? _____

_____

2. The holder of an easement in gross may assign a personal, recreational easement in gross even when doing so would overburden the servient estate.

_____OVER/_____UNDER/_____MIS/ Why? _____

_____

3. An easement's grant defines the dominant parcel and the easement's treatment on the dominant parcel's division.

_____OVER/_____UNDER/_____MIS/ Why? _____

_____

4. The grant determines limits to an easement's expansion, but if silent, then law allows normal development.

_____OVER/_____UNDER/_____MIS/ Why? _____

_____

5. A landowner has a trespass action for an injunction when an easement holder exceeds the easement's scope.

_____OVER/_____UNDER/_____MIS/ Why? _____

_____

6. Easements do not terminate by written release of the holder, end of the necessity, abandonment, landowner's prescription, merger of dominant and servient parcels, or eminent domain.

_____OVER/_____UNDER/_____MIS/ Why? _____

_____

Answers for Discrimination Exercise on Easements

1. The statement **OVERgeneralizes** the rule. The holder of an easement appurtenant may assign *when the grantor intended assignment and the servient estate is on notice*.

2. The statement **MISconceives** the rule. The holder of an easement in gross may *not* assign a personal, recreational easement in gross or when doing so would overburden the servient estate.

3. The statement **UNDERgeneralizes** the rule. An easement's grant defines not only the dominant parcel, the easement's treatment on the dominant parcel's division *but also the nature and extent of use rights*.

4. The statement **OVERgeneralizes** the rule. The grant determines limits to an easement's expansion, but if silent, then law allows normal development, *but development must not overburden the servient parcel*.

5. The statement **UNDERgeneralizes** the rule. A landowner has a trespass action for *damages and* injunction when an easement holder exceeds the easement's scope.

6. The statement **MISconceives** the rule. Easements *may, rather than do not*, terminate by written release of the holder, end of the necessity, abandonment, landowner's prescription, merger of dominant and servient parcels, and eminent domain.

Multiple-Choice Questions with Answer Explanations

21. A homeowner had long lived next to a vacant lot owned by a gardener who would visit her vacant lot to garden. The homeowner often allowed the gardener to use the home's restroom. The homeowner one day agreed to let the gardener's guests use the home's restroom at an upcoming garden party that the gardener planned. The homeowner helped the gardener erect a tent on the vacant land and with the invitations for the garden party, which included food and drink. Yet on the day of the garden party, the homeowner refused any guest the use of the restroom, frustrating and discomforting the guests, spoiling the event, and embarrassing the gardener. Did the homeowner violate a right of the gardener?

A. Yes because the gardener acquired an irrevocable easement in gross for the usage.
B. Yes because the gardener acquired a license that the homeowner is estopped to revoke.
C. No because a grantor may revoke a license at any time and without reason or cause.
D. No unless the gardener gave the homeowner valuable consideration for the usage.

Answer explanation: Option B is correct because the grantor of a license to use the grantor's property for a limited purpose may generally revoke the license at will except where the grantor expresses intent to make the license irrevocable for the license period or, in the case of estoppel, the license holder substantially and detrimentally relied and revocation would be unfair for a limited period. Here, revocation at the event was unfair, although the homeowner probably could have revoked the day before or a few days before giving the gardener time to rent a portable toilet. Option A is incorrect because the gardener's interest was a license, not an easement in gross. A license differs from an easement in gross in that the easement is an interest in the land rather than a contract promise and is of indefinite duration rather than limited in time. Option C is incorrect because, as explained above, circumstances may bar a grantor from revoking a license, particularly when the grantee substantially and detrimentally relies. Option D is incorrect because a license may arise without consideration, as here.

22. A cabin owner had access to his land and cabin from a dirt road but wanted access instead to a paved road nearby, both for ease of use and to increase the cabin's value. The cabin owner negotiated with the neighbor for a driveway easement across the neighbor's land and out to the paved road. For valuable consideration, the neighbor signed and delivered to the cabin owner a written driveway easement, one that the cabin owner did not record. The cabin owner promptly completed the driveway. The neighbor then mortgaged his property to borrow money from a bank to construct his own cabin. The bank promptly recorded the neighbor's mortgage. Learning of the neighbor's plans, the cabin owner recorded the driveway easement. The neighbor decided not to build a cabin and instead defaulted on the loan and absconded with the loan money. The bank filed suit to foreclose on the mortgage to recover the defaulted loan from the sale of the neighbor's land, in doing so seeking to extinguish the cabin owner's easement. What would be the strongest grounds on which the court would preserve the easement?

A. The bank had notice or constructive notice of the cabin owner's driveway use.
B. The driveway easement was appurtenant and attached to the neighbor's land.
C. The driveway easement was necessary for access to a paved public road.
D. The cabin owner's recording before the foreclosure action protects the easement right.

Answer explanation: Option A is correct because a recording act ordinarily protects only bona fide purchasers who take and record without notice of superior rights. Purchasers who are or should be aware of the superior right, in this case the driveway easement, take subject to that right. Here, the cabin owner had a written easement but just hadn't recorded it. The bank knew or should have known of the easement because of the driveway's construction. Option B is incorrect because although an appurtenant easement, one pertaining to a particular benefitted parcel, ordinarily passes with the property, the question here is not whether the easement continues but which interest, mortgage or easement, is superior under the recording act. Because the bank took the mortgage with notice or constructive notice of the driveway, the bank does not get the protection of the recording act. Option C is incorrect because access to a paved road doesn't matter when the cabin owner already had access to a dirt road. Easements by necessity do not arise simply to improve access but rather to create access that doesn't exist. Option D is incorrect because recording before foreclosure would not matter. Recording before the bank recorded would matter, except that the bank had notice in any case.

Week 7
Real Covenants and Equitable Servitudes

QUESTIONS FOR THE ASSIGNED READING:

Review the elements of easements.

Are easements assignable?

What is an easement's scope? What is the remedy for violating the scope of an easement?

How can one terminate an easement?

Name something you do not understand about this week's material.

SHORT OUTLINE:

Covenants at law and in equity are use rights the owner grants by *promise*, not ownership interests in land.
Nature and type: **covenants** promise to permit grantees to use and enjoy the grantor's land as promised.
   Covenants at law, or **real covenants**, are *contract obligations* enforceable in damages action for breach.
      Successor owners of the **dominant land** the covenant benefits may be able to enforce the covenant.
         Real covenants *run with the land* only with horizontal and vertical privity.
   Equitable servitudes, or **covenants in equity**, are promises enforceable through *specific performance*.
      Specific performance involves the court's order that the owner of the **servient land** comply with the burden.
      Equitable servitudes can *run with the land* without horizontal or vertical privity.
Creation: as contracts, **covenants** must meet the **statute of frauds** if granting rights for more than one year.
   To run with the land, a **real covenant** must be *in a writing* that expresses or implies the *intent that it run*.
      Parties intend a covenant to run when stating the covenant applies to successors, heirs, and assigns.
      For the benefit to run with the land, the covenant must *touch and concern* the **servient land**.
      For covenant to run, parties must form the covenant in **horizontal privity**, transferring servient-land interest.
      For a covenant to run, the owners must also have **vertical privity**, such as one conveying to the other.
         Adverse possession interrupts vertical privity.
      For a covenant to run, the burdened owner must have **notice**, typically recording but also constructive notice.
      Benefitted owners usually enforce covenants at law through monetary-damages actions.
   Equitable servitudes run with the land *without horizontal or vertical privity* if in signed running showing intent.
      For a servitude to run, it must touch and concern the land and provide notice to the burdened land's owner.
      Equitable servitudes may also arise **by implication**, through notice or constructive notice of a *common plan*.
Scope of covenants at law or in equity depends on the promise that creates them and the intent of the parties.
   Courts give plain meaning to plain terms while resolving ambiguities against the drafter.
   Courts will not generally impose terms to which the parties have not agreed.
   The scope of a covenant in equity arising by implication depends on the circumstances of the implication.
Termination of covenants at law and in equity, or equitable servitudes, occurs in several ways.
   If the document of grant includes a durational restriction, then the covenant terminates when its term **expires**.
   Covenants can also terminate if a single owner acquires the dominant and servient parcels, **merging** interests.
   A benefitted owner can also **abandon** a covenant by indicating that intent to give up the rights that it affords.

LONG OUTLINE:

Covenants at law and in equity

Covenants at law involve rights of use that the owner of land grants by *contract* to another that the other may enjoy, even when inconsistent with the owner's current wishes, subject to a damages action for breach. **Covenants in equity**, also called *equitable servitudes*, involve rights of use that the owner grants in a contract obligation, as to which equity grants enforcement by *specific performance*. As indicated above, covenants in land do *not* involve ownership in land, only the contract obligation, although a following section shows that covenants can *run with the land* like ownership interests. The following sections address the *nature* and *type* of these covenants, their *creation*, and their *scope*, *enforcement*, and *termination*.

Nature and type

A **real covenant** is the grantor's contract promise and related obligation to permit the grantee to use and enjoy the grantor's real property without creating a freehold estate in the grantee. Because covenants in land involve *contract obligations* rather than ownership interests in land, covenants typically arise out of *promises* enforceable in contract rather than, for example, easements by implication, necessity, or prior use, although the effect of a covenant is often the same as that of an easement. For example, a resident who lives and owns a home behind another home the property for which the city has just changed to a commercial district, may for consideration contract with the other homeowner not to build a commercial structure that would burden the resident's own home. The resident would then have a *covenant*, not an *easement*, although the resident could enforce the covenant to prevent construction of a commercial structure or for contract-breach damages. Real covenants, though, have a unique quality beyond the typical contract in that **successor owners** of the land that a covenant benefits, called the **dominant land**, may be able to enforce the covenant. The law holds that covenants that successor owners can enforce must *run with the land*, the requirements for which the next section addresses.

The law also recognizes **equitable servitudes**, also called **covenants in equity**. An equitable servitude or covenant in equity is an enforceable promise relating to the use of land that the benefitted promisee enforces through the equitable form of relief *specific performance*. Specific performance involves the court's order that the owner of the servient land comply with the burden to benefit the owner seeking that equitable relief. Unlike covenants at law, equitable servitudes can arise *and run with the land* without horizontal or vertical privity, as the next section addresses.

Creation

As indicated briefly above, because **covenants in land** involve *contract obligations* rather than ownership interests in land, covenants typically arise out of *promises* enforceable in contract rather than by implication, necessity, or prior use, although the effect of a covenant is often the same as that of an easement. To create a covenant in land, the parties must satisfy the **statute of frauds**, specifically if the restriction lasts for more than one year. The bigger question, though, is often whether the covenant's creation allows it to *run with the land*, meaning to benefit and burden subsequent owners of the dominant and servient parcels.

To run with the land, a covenant must have been *in a writing* that expresses or implies the *intent that it run*. The courts readily construe that the parties intended a covenant to run when the writing states that the covenant applies to successors, heirs, and assigns. Yet courts will also construe intent from the circumstances. The covenant must also *touch and concern* the **servient land**, meaning the burdened land, such as requiring payment of association maintenance fees. For a covenant's burden to run with the land, the parties must also have formed the covenant when in **horizontal privity**, meaning when sharing some interest in the servient land, such as the sale from one to the other or a lease from one to the other. Thus, in the above example, the neighbors who agreed to a covenant not to build commercial on one neighbor's land would *not* have horizontal privity, meaning that the covenant could *not* run with the land.

For a covenant's burden or benefit to run, the servient land's owner must also have **vertical privity** with the owner with whose activities on the land the covenant interferes, such as the original owner making the covenant conveying the land to the burdened owner. While successor owners will usually have vertical privity with the owner originally covenanting to burden the land, *adverse possession* interrupts vertical privity. Finally, the burdened owner must have had **notice** of the burden, typically through the covenant's recording against the land, although sometimes through constructive notice of the existing burden. Benefitted owners usually enforce covenants at law through monetary-damages actions.

103

A signed writing satisfying the statute of frauds will also create an equitable servitude or covenant in equity enforceable by specific performance. Unlike covenants at law, though, equitable servitudes can arise and run with the land *without horizontal or vertical privity.* An equitable servitude need only be in a signed writing showing the intent that it run with the land, touch and concern the land, and provide notice to the owner of the burdened land.

Scope

The **scope** of covenants at law or in equity depends primarily on the promise that creates them and the intent of the parties behind that promise. Rules like those that courts apply to any contract interpretation apply to the express promise of a covenant at law or in equity. The courts will give plain meaning to plain terms while resolving ambiguities against the drafter. The court will not generally impose terms to which the parties have not agreed. On the other hand, the scope of a covenant in equity arising by implication depends on the circumstances of the implication. Refer to the section below on the scope and construction of easements for more detailed rules also applicable to covenants at law or in equity.

Termination

The law recognizes the **termination** of covenants at law and in equity, or equitable servitudes, in several ways. If the document of grant includes a durational restriction, then the covenant terminates when its term **expires**. Covenants can also terminate if a single owner acquires the dominant and servient parcels, in which case the covenant **merges**. A benefitted owner can also **abandon** a covenant by indicating that intent to give up the rights that it affords. Covenants terminate as easements terminate, covered in greater detail in a following section.

Fluency Cards

Cover and uncover the response to each prompt until you fluently recall the exact response.

Real covenants	**Equitable servitude**
Land use promised in contracts. Successors benefit only with horizontal and vertical privity.	Land use promised in contract. Run with the land without horizontal and vertical privity.
Creating covenant	**Creating servitude**
Signed writing stating run, and touch and concern, the land. Notify constructively or by recording.	Signed writing stating that they run, and touch and concern, the land. Notify owner.

Covenant scope

Depends on promise or implication, and lasts as stated or until merger or abandonment.

Definitions Worksheet on Real Covenants

1. What is a real covenant?

    _____

    _____

2. What distinguishes a real covenant from an easement?

    _____

    _____

3. When does a real covenant's burden run with the land?

    _____

    _____

4. What are horizontal and vertical privity?

    _____

    _____

5. When does a real covenant's benefit run with the land?

    _____

    _____

6. What does touch and concern the land mean?

    _____

    _____

7. How may servient owners have notice?

    _____

    _____

8. What is an equitable servitude?

    _____

    _____

9. How does an equitable servitude differ from a real covenant?

    _____

    _____

Answers for Definitions Worksheet on Real Covenants

1.   ***What is a real covenant?*** Real covenants are contract rights and obligations relating to one landowner's use of another's land, enforced in law by damages action.

2.   ***What distinguishes a real covenant from an easement?*** Unlike easements, real covenants are not interests in land, although they may run with the land and otherwise operate like an easement.

3.   ***When does a real covenant's burden run with the land?*** The parties to an enforceable contract (statute of frauds, etc.) must intend the burden to run, the burden must touch and concern the land, the parties must have horizontal and vertical privity, and the servient land's successor must have notice.

4.   ***What are horizontal and vertical privity?*** Horizontal privity is grantor transfer to grantee at covenant creation. Vertical privity is successor acquiring entire estate.

5.   ***When does a real covenant's benefit run with the land?*** Same requirements as the burden running except that most jurisdictions do not require horizontal or vertical privity, and if requiring vertical privity, don't require whole conveyance.

6.   ***What does touch and concern the land mean?*** The real covenant increases use and enjoyment of one land while decreasing use and enjoyment of the other land.

7.   ***How may servient owners have notice?*** Notice may be actual, imputed, or by recording or inquiry.

8.   ***What is an equitable servitude?*** Equitable servitudes, or covenants in equity, are contracts rights and obligations relating to land, enforced in equity by specific performance.

9.   ***How does an equitable servitude differ from a real covenant?*** Law enforces real covenants with damages but equitable servitudes with injunctions. Law does not require horizontal and vertical privity for an equitable servitude.

Comprehensiveness Exercise on Real Covenants

Insert words at the ^ mark that would make for a more-accurate or more-detailed law statement.
Follow the italicized hints for help. Suggested answers are on the next page.

1.   The holder of an easement appurtenant may assign the easement if the grantor intended assignment ^ . *[One other condition?]*

2.   Real covenants are ^ rights and obligations relating to one landowner's use of another's land ^ . *[What kind of rights and obligations? And how enforced?]*

3.   Unlike easements, real covenants are not interests in land ^. *[Any similarities?]*

4.   The parties to an enforceable contract must intend the burden to run, the burden must touch and concern the land ^ ^ . *[Two other conditions?]*

5.   Horizontal privity is grantor transfer to grantee ^ . Vertical privity is successor acquiring ^ estate. *[When must the transfer take place? How much of the estate?]*

6.   Notice may be actual, imputed ^ ^ . *[Two other ways?]*

7.   Equitable servitudes are contracts rights and obligations relating to land, enforced ^ by specific performance. *[In which court (which form of action)?]*

Answers for Comprehensiveness Exercise on Real Covenants

1.   The holder of an easement appurtenant may assign the easement if the grantor intended assignment *and the servient estate is on notice*.

2.   Real covenants are *contract* rights and obligations relating to one landowner's use of another's land, *enforced in law by damages action*.

3.   Unlike easements, real covenants are not interests in land, *although they may run with the land and otherwise operate like an easement*.

4.   For a real covenant to exist, the parties to an enforceable contract must intend the burden to run, the burden must touch and concern the land, *the parties must have horizontal and vertical privity, and the servient land's successor must have notice*.

5.   Horizontal privity is grantor transfer to grantee *at covenant creation*. Vertical privity is successor acquiring *entire* estate.

6.   Notice may be actual, imputed, *or by recording or inquiry*.

7.   Equitable servitudes are contracts rights and obligations relating to land, enforced *in equity* by specific performance.

Application Exercise on Real Covenants

Sort the fact patterns into whether they show horizontal privity (H), vertical privity (V), or neither (N). Answers are below.

1. When dividing off a parcel to sell to a builder for another home, the owner restricted the parcel to residential.

2. The builder who bought the restricted parcel decided not to build but to sell to another builder for a spec home.

3. A homeowner bought ten feet of her neighbor's side yard so that she could add a greenhouse to her home.

4. The farmer who had sold a parcel restricted for farming or residential sold the whole farm to another farmer.

5. When the farmer divided and sold the parcel, the farmer restricted the parcel to farming or single-family homes.

6. An investor who bought the parcel restricted to farming or residential sold the entire parcel to another investor.

7. The investor who bought the parcel sold a divided portion of it to another investor, restricted to residential.

8. A rancher granted permission to a conservation group to enter the ranchlands to count wild species.

9. A developer who owned a divided parcel restricted to single-family-home development sold to a builder.

10. A builder who bought development property divided a portion to sell to a relative, restricted to a one-level home.

11. A homeowner residing on a subdivision lot restricted to brick, one-level homes sold to an executive.

Answers: 1H 2V 3N 4V 5H 6V 7H 8N 9V 10H 11V

Sort the fact patterns into whether the servient owner's notice is actual (A), imputed (I), by recording (R), or by inquiry (Q) or has no notice (N). Answers are below.

1. The home's seller told the buyer before sale that all homes in that subdivision had to be brick one-levels.

2. The buyer's agent heard before purchase that no structure on that lot could be higher than twelve feet.

3. No one told the buyer or buyer's agent about the lake-access rights across the lot, but the plat reflected it.

4. When the buyer viewed the lot, cars parked on it, and people were walking back and forth to the lake across it.

5. Neither the investor nor agent had any reason to suspect that the landowner had promised recreational access.

6. The buyer had noticed that all twenty homes in the development were white stucco with red-tile roof.

7. Although the marketing materials didn't mention it, the developer had recorded home-size minimums.

8. The seller's agent told the buyer's lawyer reviewing the sale contract that the premises had use restrictions.

9. The buyer had heard that the land had unrecorded conservation and timber-clearing restrictions.

10. The seller told the buyer's spouse at the open house that the lot had no-trailer and no-boat restrictions.

11. The buyer asked her lawyer why all the homes in the district were contemporary, low-roof style.

Answers: 1A 2I 3R 4Q 5N 6Q 7R 8I 9A 10I 11Q

Factors Exercise on Real Covenants

Whether a covenant *touches and concerns the land*, satisfying that requirement for enforcement, depends on factors including the parties' **intent** that it touch and concern, **advantage** to one landowner, **disadvantage** to the other landowner, **peculiar** to the landowners rather than **general** to the community, involves more than **money**, and is more than **personal**. For each scenario, choose a factor that would weigh heavily in favor or against finding that the covenant touches and concerns the land, and analyze that factor by filling in the blanks.

1.   **The lot owner had a right on the lot's purchase to join the country club for the usual membership fee and annual dues, available to other community members.**

The [_choose a factor_] favors the [_choose a party_] when [_state relevant facts_] because [_explain your reasoning_] .

2.   **The parcel owner had to maintain and not trim or otherwise disturb the three-hundred-year-old oak tree the branches of which shaded two other lots.**

The [_choose a factor_] favors the [_choose a party_] when [_state relevant facts_] because [_explain your reasoning_] .

3.   **The landowner's inability under the restriction to disturb the grasslands or wetlands meant that the property had a fraction of the value that it would have had without the restriction.**

The [_choose a factor_] favors the [_choose a party_] when [_state relevant facts_] because [_explain your reasoning_] .

4.   **The seller and buyer of the divided parcel agreed that the old homestead structures on the two parcels should remain in their original appearance, still looking like a single traditional homestead.**

The [_choose a factor_] favors the [_choose a party_] when [_state relevant facts_] because [_explain your reasoning_] .

5.   **The seller liked so much to watch and photograph the butterflies in the garden that when she sold the home she insisted that the garden remain for her to view from the adjacent public sidewalk.**

The [_choose a factor_] favors the [_choose a party_] when [_state relevant facts_] because [_explain your reasoning_] .

6.   **The sale included the buyer's agreement to pay the seller a commission on any apples, pears, peaches, or other fruit sold from the orchard that the seller had planted and long tended on the property.**

The [_choose a factor_] favors the [_choose a party_] when [_state relevant facts_] because [_explain your reasoning_] .

Discrimination Exercise on Real Covenants

Indicate whether each statement *overgeneralizes*, *undergeneralizes*, or *misconceives* the rule, explaining why. *Overgeneralizing* states the rule too broadly, capturing circumstances to which it does not apply. *Undergeneralizing* states the rule too narrowly, omitting circumstances to which it applies. *Misconceiving* states the rule incorrectly.

1. Real covenants are contract rights and obligations relating to one's use of another's land.

____OVER/____UNDER/____MIS/ Why? _____

_____

2. Like easements, real covenants are interests in land.

____OVER/____UNDER/____MIS/ Why? _____

_____

3. For an enforceable real covenant to exist, the parties must intend the burden to run and the servient land's successor must have notice.

____OVER/____UNDER/____MIS/ Why? _____

_____

4. Vertical privity is grantor transfer to grantee at covenant creation, while horizontal privity is successor acquiring entire estate.

____OVER/____UNDER/____MIS/ Why? _____

_____

5. Notice may be imputed or by recording.

____OVER/____UNDER/____MIS/ Why? _____

_____

6. Equitable servitudes are contracts rights and obligations, enforced by specific performance.

____OVER/____UNDER/____MIS/ Why? _____

_____

Answers for Discrimination Exercise on Real Covenants

1. The statement **OVERgeneralizes** the rule. Real covenants are contract rights and obligations relating to one *landowner's* use of another's land, *enforced in law by damages action*.

2. The statement **MISconceives** the rule. *Un*like easements, real covenants are *not* interests in land*, although they may run with the land and otherwise operate like an easement*.

3. The statement **OVERgeneralizes** the rule. For an enforceable real covenant to exist, the parties must intend the burden to run, *the burden must touch and concern the land, the parties must have horizontal and vertical privity,* and the servient land's successor must have notice.

4. The statement **MISconceives** the rule. *Horizontal* privity is grantor transfer to grantee at covenant creation, while *vertical* privity is successor acquiring entire estate.

5. The statement **UNDERgeneralizes** the rule. Notice may be *actual,* imputed, or by recording *or inquiry*.

6. The statement **OVERgeneralizes** the rule. Equitable servitudes are contracts rights and obligations *relating to land*, enforced *in equity* by specific performance.

Multiple-Choice Questions with Answer Explanations

23. The owner of a lake-view lot bought the adjacent vacant parcel closer to the lake to ensure that no one would build on it and obstruct the owner's lake view. The lake-view owner then substantially improved the home with the lake view. The lake-view owner later sold the vacant parcel to a family for picnicking and boating but with a deed restriction against building on it. The family recorded the deed with the building restriction. Years later, after both the lake-view owner and family members had died, an heir of the family members began constructing a cottage on the vacant parcel that would obstruct the adjacent home's lake view. What result if the heir to the lake-view owner sued to enjoin the construction?

A.   The court will enjoin because of common-law rights of lake view.
B.   The court will enjoin, enforcing the recorded building restriction.
C.   The court will not enjoin because a servitude does not survive the grantee's death.
D.   The court will not enjoin because a servitude does not survive the grantor's death.

Answer explanation: Option B is correct because a deeded and recorded servitude that touches and concerns both the dominant and servient lands remains enforceable by and against successors in interest who take with notice. Option A is incorrect because no common-law right of lake view arises without satisfying the intent conditions of an equitable servitude. The right here is contractual, not common law. Options C and D are incorrect because a deeded and recorded servitude does survive the grantor's and grantee's deaths.

24. Two neighbors, a business executive and a junk collector, lived on spacious lots side by side. The business executive, often entertaining corporate customers at the executive's mini-mansion home, grew concerned that the collector was hauling all manner of unsightly junk to his adjacent property. The executive paid the collector $25,000 for the collector to limit his junk collection to the back of his property hidden by hills and trees. Years later, the executive sold the mini-mansion to a gallery owner who likewise entertained corporate customers frequently at home. When the collector began accumulating junk in the front of his property again, the gallery owner demanded that the collector comply with the collector's promise to the executive, but the collector refused. Does the gallery owner have the right to enforce the promise?

A.   No because $25,000 is not enough to restrict the land in favor of adjacent successors.
B.   No as the executive and collector had no horizontal privity when making the promise.
C.   Yes but only if the collector signed a writing indicating intent that the successors benefit.
D.   Yes because the gallery owner took with notice relying on the promise when purchasing.

Answer explanation: Option B is correct because a real covenant is a promise that relates to the use of land, different from an easement because contractual only rather than ownership in land. Because relating to land, the promise must be in a signed writing for the promisee to enforce it against the promisor. To enforce against successors to the burdened land, the promise must touch and concern the land, the parties must have intended that the covenant run, both parties must have had some ownership or contractual (leasehold) interest in the burdened land (horizontal privity), and the owners must have transferred voluntarily (not by adverse possession) to the burdened and benefited successors (vertical privity), with notice to the burdened successor. Here, the executive had no interest in the collector's land, such as a co-owner with or purchaser from the collector, and so without that horizontal privity, the promise does not run. Option A is incorrect because the courts generally do not examine the amount of the consideration, although it could be evidence of whether the parties intended that the burden run. The real concern here is the lack of horizontal privity. Option C is incorrect because while a signed writing and intent that the burden run are both necessary, the gallery owner would also need to show horizontal privity between the collector and executive when they made the promise. Option D is incorrect because notice and reliance are not sufficient to make the burden run. The promisor and promisee must also have intended that the burden run and must also have had horizontal privity when making the promise.

25. A group of eight lakefront-cottage homeowners grew disgusted at their inability to keep their private secluded beachfront clean of the excrement of pets. They all agreed at once in a writing that all signed and that each recorded that no present or future owner of their eight cottage properties would bring any pets to the properties. The agreement worked as intended for several years. In later years, though, several owners sold to new owners who had not agreed to the pet restriction. One absentee owner lost his cottage to adverse possession by a vagrant relative. Pets once again fouled the beach. May objecting owners enforce the agreement?

A. No because the original owners did not have horizontal privity when promising.
B. No as to any of the new owners, but yes as to any original owner making the promise.
C. Yes as to any of the new owners taking by purchase, but no as to the adverse possessor.
D. Yes as all had actual or constructive notice, and equitable servitudes don't require privity.

Answer explanation: Option D is correct because an equitable servitude is a promise or implication about which a successor has notice, binding all lands in a common plot for their common benefit. Unlike real covenants, no horizontal or vertical privity need exist to bind successors to an equitable servitude. Option A is incorrect because only real covenants, not equitable servitudes, require privity. Option B is incorrect because the equitable servitude, recorded and thus giving record notice, would bind successors. Option C is incorrect because even one who is not in vertical privity, such as an adverse possessor, takes subject to an equitable servitude benefiting all the lands in common.

26. An executive owned two lots overlooking the ocean, one slightly higher and behind the other. The executive built a retirement home on the higher back lot. To fund the construction, he agreed orally to sell the lower ocean-side lot to a friend who wanted beach access provided that the friend never build on the lot so as to preserve the executive's view. The executive's deed to the friend, which only the executive signed, included the grantee's covenant that neither the grantee nor successors, heirs, or assigns would build on the lot, specifically to preserve the ocean view for the higher back lot's owner and successors, heirs, and assigns. The friend accepted and recorded the deed. Years later, the executive decided to retire somewhere else and so sold the back lot and its home to a sports agent. The friend then promptly sold the vacant lot to a developer who began construction of a fabulous ocean-front home. What result if the sports agent sues to enjoin the developer's construction?

A. Developer wins because the grantee friend never signed the executive's deed.
B. Developer wins because equitable servitudes do not survive promisor conveyance.
C. Sports agent wins because equitable servitudes run with the land binding on notice.
D. Sports agent wins because the executive built before the developer bought and began.

Answer explanation: Option C is correct because a valid equitable servitude arises when touching and concerning both the benefitted and burdened properties, the parties intend that it bind others, the servitude satisfies the statute of frauds such as here by poll deed, and owners of the burdened land take with notice such as here by recorded deed. The outcome makes no difference that the initial sale agreement was oral. Once the executive reduced the agreement to a poll deed and the friend accepted that deed, all terms of the oral agreement that the written deed later recorded, whether contrary or inconsistent to the deed, would have merged into the deed so that only the deed terms were enforceable by either party. Option A is incorrect because a poll deed, one signed only by the grantor, binds the grantee and successors if the grantee accepts and especially, as here, the grantee records the deed. Even though not signed by the grantee, a poll deed satisfies the statute of frauds under these conditions. Option B is incorrect because servitudes meeting the above conditions including that they indicate the intent to bind successors in interest run with the land. Option D is incorrect because who builds first would not matter unless the deed so indicated, which it clearly did not do so here.

Week 8
Implied Reciprocal Servitudes

QUESTIONS FOR THE ASSIGNED READING:

What are the elements of a real covenant? An equitable servitude? What are the differences between them?

What is horizontal privity? What is vertical privity?

Can a promise be both a real covenant and equitable servitude?

Do you agree with the Supreme Court's decision in *Shelly v. Kraemer*? The case received criticism as an inappropriate use of state action, that the federal government should involve itself in state law of private real estate. What do you think of that concern? Should law allow covenants to discriminate against certain groups of people? When they do, what remedy would you suggest?

What are common-interest communities? What standards do courts use to determine whether to enforce a common-interest community's rules and regulations against individual members?

Name something you do not understand about this week's material.

SHORT OUTLINE:

Equitable servitudes may also arise **by implication**, through notice or constructive notice of a *common plan*.
　　The developer must intend that the restriction run with the land.
　　The restriction must also touch and concern the land rather than be personal in nature.
　　The developer must either record the restriction, or lot owners must have constructive notice.
Common lot owners must enforce the implied restriction for the restriction to persist.
　　A court may refuse to enforce where lot owners abandon the restriction and enforcement would be unfair.
　　Unclean hands, estoppel, changed conditions, and hardships weighing against enforcement are also defenses.

LONG OUTLINE:

　　Equitable servitudes may also arise **by implication**, meaning through notice or constructive notice of a *common plan*. For example, if a landowner divides a large parcel to sell lots under a common plan for only single-family residences but mistakenly leaves the written covenant out of some of the later conveyed deeds, then the other written restrictions and construction of only single-family homes will have put on notice lot owners taking those later deeds. Forming an implied reciprocal servitude requires that the developer intend that the restriction run with the land, that it touch and concern the land rather than be personal in nature, and that the developer either record the writing expressing that intent or that the lot owners have constructive notice from the uniformity of conditions.

　　The common lot owners must enforce the implied restriction for the restriction to persist. If lot owners begin to vary and violate the restriction, then a court may hold that the lot owners abandoned the restriction and accordingly refuse to enforce it, especially where enforcement against one lot owner would be unfair with respect to other lot owners violating the restriction. Other equitable defenses to an implied reciprocal servitude can include unclean hands, estoppel, laches, changed conditions, and a balance of hardships weighing against enforcement.

Fluency Cards

Cover and uncover the response to each prompt until you fluently recall the exact response.

Reciprocal servitude	**Forming reciprocal servitude**
Uniform restrictions on subdivided lots according to common developer plan.	Requires intent to run, touch and concern land, and recorded or constructive notice.

Reciprocal servitude termination	**Reciprocal servitude defenses**
Abandoning or failing to enforce restrictions can lead to restrictions' termination.	Laches, unclean hands, estoppel, changed conditions, and balance of hardship.

Definitions Worksheet on Other Servitude Issues

1. What is an implied reciprocal servitude?

_____

_____

2. When does an implied reciprocal servitude arise?

_____

_____

3. What is the typical form of notice?

_____

_____

4. Must the restriction be the same for all lots?

_____

_____

5. How can implied reciprocal servitudes terminate?

_____

_____

6. How if at all does law limit reciprocal servitudes?

_____

_____

7. What defenses may an owner have to enforcement of a servitude?

_____

_____

Answers for Definitions Worksheet on Other Servitude Issues

1. ***What is an implied reciprocal servitude?*** An implied reciprocal servitude, also called a reciprocal negative easement, involves uniform restrictions on all subdivided lots according to common scheme or plan.

2. ***When does an implied reciprocal servitude arise?*** An enforceable implied reciprocal servitude arises when the developer dividing the land meets all requirements for an equitable servitude including intent to run with the land, the servitude touches and concerns the land, and successors to the land have notice of the servitude.

3. ***What is the typical form of notice for an implied reciprocal servitude?*** A developer wishing to impose a reciprocal servitude typically states the uniform restriction on a recorded plat map and in all, or at least most, of the lot deeds.

4. ***Must the restriction be the same for all lots for owners to enforce a reciprocal servitude?*** The plan imposing an implied reciprocal servitude must be uniform but may differentiate in restrictions among types of lots.

5. ***How can implied reciprocal servitudes terminate?*** If lot owners fail to enforce an implied reciprocal servitude's restriction or abandon it, then law holds them to have acquiesced in its termination.

6. ***How if at all does law limit reciprocal servitudes?*** Reciprocal servitudes must not unlawfully discriminate based on race or other protected class.

7. ***What defenses may an owner have to enforcement of a servitude?*** Owners may have equitable defenses to specific-performance actions including laches, unclean hands, estoppel, changed conditions, and balance of hardship.

Issue-Spotting Servitudes: Scope & Termination

<u>Scope of easement</u>: The scope of an easement determines both how parties may use it and the purpose for which they use it. Base scope on the parties' intent when they created the easement. If the parties define the scope, then the definition governs. If they do not define the scope, then law presumes the easement's use to include reasonable enjoyment of the property. Scope never extends to use of another piece of property. <u>Termination of easement</u>: Easements can terminate by abandonment, when the easement holder stops use *and* indicates the intent to abandon. Mere cessation of use is not enough.

For each example, indicate whether the homeowner is likely to face a challenge from the neighbor and, if so, whether the homeowner is likely to succeed. Each problem starts with this scenario:

> **Homeowner bought her property from Seller. Her deed noted that Homeowner and her heirs, successors, and assigns have the right to use Neighbor's driveway to get to Homeowner's property.**

1. Homeowner's property abuts a lake. Homeowner has a canoe that she stores in a shed a few miles from her home. When she wants to use it, she drives it on a truck across Neighbor's driveway.

2. Homeowner's property abuts a lake. Homeowner runs a business where she drops people in canoes on the lake opposite from where she lives. Homeowner then picks them up on her property's side of the lake. She drives the canoes and paying guests across Neighbor's driveway several times a day every day during the summer. After a week, Neighbor notifies Homeowner he wants her to stop using the driveway for commercial purposes.

3. Before Homeowner started the business, she asked Neighbor if she could use the driveway for this purpose. Neighbor said "yes" but never put it in writing. After Neighbor sold his property to Buyer, Buyer told Homeowner she had to stop using the easement for business purposes.

4. Homeowner built a second driveway to access her home. She stopped using Neighbor's driveway. After Homeowner died, her daughter inherited the place and started using Neighbor's driveway for personal use. Neighbor told her to stop because Homeowner abandoned the easement.

5. After Homeowner built the second driveway, Homeowner gave Friend permission to fish in her lake, assigned Friend use of Neighbor's driveway. Friend used it to drive onto Homeowner's property to fish. He used it mostly on weekends.

Issue-Spotting: Easement, Covenant, Equitable Servitude, and Implied Reciprocal Servitude

Determine whether each scenario describes an easement, covenant, equitable servitude, or implied reciprocal servitude:

1. Engineer bought her property from Teacher. Engineer's deed noted that she has the right to use Neighbor's driveway to get to Engineer's property.

2. When Owner sold half of her lot to Buyer, each party promised in the deed only residential use. Owner passed away, leaving Owner's Heir owning the lot. Heir builds a convenience store.

3. Daughter has a document between her mother, from whom she inherited her land, and Neighbor. The document states that Daughter's mother has the right to use a path across Neighbor's land to get to a beachside park.

4. Doctor and his neighbor Plumber each promised the other that each would build only residential housing on their respective properties. They reduced their promise to a signed and recorded writing. Doctor sold his land to Storekeeper. Plumber sold her land to Mechanic. Mechanic starts building a gas station.

5. Owner had a home on the north end of her lot. She then built a more modern home on the south end of her lot. She walked daily across a path to the north end to sit in her favorite, wooded spot. Owner sold the north half of her lot to Newbie. Owner didn't use the pathway very often after she sold the land. Niece inherited the south end of the lot from Owner when Owner died. Niece started using the pathway. Newbie erected a fence across the border of the lots that covered the path.

6. Barista bought a townhouse from Lawyer. At the time of purchase, Barista promised Lawyer she would not block Lawyer's view from his window, in his adjacent townhouse. Barista then sold her townhouse to Grocer.

7. Homemaker bought a house in a lake association. Her deed gave the right to use a common lake for recreational purposes.

8. Developer divided a 100-acre lot into 50 plats. He sold 25 plats to new owners, each deed containing a provision that only single-family homes could be built on the lots. Developer then sold 5 plats to new buyers but did not include the restriction in their deeds. One of the new owners wants to build a duplex on his lot.

9. Architect owned a large piece of land. He split the land into two parcels, a western half and an eastern half, and sold the eastern half to Remodeler. At the time of the sale, each promised the other to only have one residence on the property. The promise was in a written deed and recorded. Architect built a single-family home. Architect then sold his property to Businesswoman when the land was still vacant, making no mention of the promise in the deed. Remodeler sold her parcel to Newcomer, also making no mention of the promise in his deed. Newcomer built a single-family home on his parcel. Businesswoman began construction of a second home on her large parcel.

Answers: 1 easement 2 covenant 3 easement 4 equitable servitude 5 easement 6 negative easement
7 easement 8 implied reciprocal servitude 9 real covenant & equitable servitude

Comprehensiveness Exercise on Other Servitude Issues

Insert words at the ^ mark that would make for a more-accurate or more-detailed law statement.
Follow the italicized hints for help. Suggested answers are on the next page.

1.   An implied reciprocal servitude ^ involves ^ restrictions on ^ subdivided lots ^ . *[What's another name for it? What kind of restrictions? How many lots? On what condition?]*

2.   An enforceable implied reciprocal servitude arises when the developer dividing the land ^ intends the servitude to run with the land, ^ ^ . *[On what set of conditions? Can you name two other conditions?]*

3.   A developer wishing to impose a reciprocal servitude typically states the uniform restriction on a ^ plat map ^ . *[What kind of a plat map (what would the developer do with the map)? State the restriction where else?]*

4.   The plan imposing an implied reciprocal servitude must be uniform ^ . *[Except not necessarily in one way.]*

5.   Reciprocal servitudes must not ^ discriminate ^ . *[Discriminate in what way? Based on what?]*

6.   Owners may have equitable defenses to specific-performance actions of an implied reciprocal servitude, including laches, unclean hands, estoppel ^ ^ . *[Two other defenses?]*

Answers for Comprehensiveness Exercise on Servitude Issues

1.   An implied reciprocal servitude *or reciprocal negative easement* involves *uniform* restrictions on *all* subdivided lots *according to common scheme or plan*.

2.   An enforceable implied reciprocal servitude arises when the developer dividing the land *meets all requirements for an equitable servitude including the developer* intends the servitude to run with the land, *the servitude touches and concerns the land, and successors to the land have notice of the servitude*.

3.   A developer wishing to impose a reciprocal servitude typically states the uniform restriction on a *recorded* plat map *and in all, or at least most, of the lot deeds*.

4.   The plan imposing an implied reciprocal servitude must be uniform *but may differentiate in restrictions among types of lots*.

5.   Reciprocal servitudes must not *unlawfully* discriminate *on the basis of race or other protected classes*.

6.   Owners may have equitable defenses to specific-performance actions of an implied reciprocal servitude, including laches, unclean hands, estoppel, *changed conditions, and balance of hardship*.

Application Exercise on Other Servitude Issues

Sort the fact patterns into whether the implied reciprocal servitude is uniform to enforce (U) or not (N). Answers are below.

1. The master plat and all deeds included the same no-outbuildings and no-satellite disks restrictions.

2. The master plan restricted two-thirds of the lots to colonial style but left the rest unrestricted.

3. The plat map and all deeds restricted the one-acre lots to single-level residences but five-acre lots to two levels.

4. The plat map and nearly all deeds restricted the twenty industrial lots to buildings under 20,000 square feet.

5. A few deeds but not the plat map restricted lots to single-family homes of at least 3,000 square feet.

6. The plat map and all deeds restricted main-driveway lots to rear-facing garages and all lots to attached garages.

Answers: 1U 2N 3U 4U 5N 6U

Sort the fact patterns into whether the implied reciprocal servitude has terminated (T) or not (N).

1. None of the lot owners followed the architectural restrictions or objected to others not doing so.

2. As soon as the lot owner began building an unattached structure, other lot owners sued to enforce the restriction.

3. After the association approved the plans and the lot owner built the home, other lot owners sued to enforce.

4. Although the developer had restricted all residences to Spanish style, many were Colonial or contemporary.

5. The developer was unable to sell five of the twenty-five lots, although all other owners had built as required.

6. All eight lot owners executed a recordable instrument terminating the several architectural restrictions.

7. One of the five lot owners paid the other five lot owners two-thousand dollars each to waive the restriction.

Answers: 1T 2N 3T 4T 5N 6T 7T

Sort the fact patterns into whether the lot owner has a defense to enforcement of the implied reciprocal servitude (D) or not (N).

1. The developer approved that the first two buyers build smaller-than-allowed homes just to get something built.

2. The lot owner claimed he could not afford to build with the expensive materials that the restrictions required.

3. The other lot owners did nothing for fifteen years before finally suing to force the owner to re-site the garage.

4. The three commercial lot owners who sued to enforce the restriction against incineration all had incinerators.

5. The lot owner's association-approved drawings didn't show the restriction-violating third-story widow's watch.

6. In thirty years, the entire area had moved from owner-occupied to rentals, including several of the restricted lots.

7. The materials that the restriction specified were no longer available when the vacant-lot owner applied to build.

Answers: 1D 2N 3D 4D 5N 6D 7D

Factors Exercise on Other Servitude Issues

Whether an implied reciprocal servitude is unlawfully discriminatory may depend on factors including **express language** of a written restriction, **customary construction** of restrictions, **pattern** restrictions produce, **practice** of restriction's application, and expressed **animus** against the protected class. For each scenario, choose a factor that would weigh heavily in favor or against the servitude's lawfulness, and analyze that factor by filling in the blanks.

1.   **The Asian-American prospective buyers reported that the seller's agent had told their buyer's agent that the neighborhood had been off-limits to foreigners since first platted.**

The [_choose a factor_] favors the [_choose a party_] when [_state relevant facts_] because [_explain your reasoning_].

2.   **The hundred-year-old original deeds in the secluded enclave all included that no lot owner was to sell to any white person, defined as any person of Caucasian descent.**

The [_choose a factor_] favors the [_choose a party_] when [_state relevant facts_] because [_explain your reasoning_].

3.   **No Hispanic-Latino prospective buyer had succeeded in buying into the development despite that Hispanic-Latinos had recently comprised more than half of the buyer pool.**

The [_choose a factor_] favors the [_choose a party_] when [_state relevant facts_] because [_explain your reasoning_].

4.   **The sellers, themselves of minority ethnicity, although not the ethnicity of the prospective buyers, and the buyer and seller agents, all indicated that they would have welcomed a sale to the prospective buyers if they had offered the highest price.**

The [_choose a factor_] favors the [_choose a party_] when [_state relevant facts_] because [_explain your reasoning_].

5.   **Although the antiquated restrictions were vague about qualifying buyers, selling agents admitted that they knew selling owners expected them to steer _unconventional_ buyers away, such that few minority buyers presented offers.**

The [_choose a factor_] favors the [_choose a party_] when [_state relevant facts_] because [_explain your reasoning_].

6.   **While a few ancient deeds included the repugnant racially restrictive covenant, the neighborhood had more minority residents than the general population in the area.**

The [_choose a factor_] favors the [_choose a party_] when [_state relevant facts_] because [_explain your reasoning_].

Discrimination Exercise on Other Servitude Issues

Indicate whether each statement *overgeneralizes*, *undergeneralizes*, or *misconceives* the rule, explaining why. *Overgeneralizing* states the rule too broadly, *undergeneralizing* too narrowly, and *misconceiving* incorrectly.

1. An implied reciprocal servitude or reciprocal negative easement involves varying restrictions on various lots subdivided off over the years.

____OVER/____UNDER/____MIS/ Why? _____

_____

2. An enforceable implied reciprocal servitude arises when the developer dividing the land meets some of the requirements for an equitable servitude including the developer intends the servitude to run with the land and the servitude touches and concerns the land.

____OVER/____UNDER/____MIS/ Why? _____

_____

3. A developer wishing to impose a reciprocal servitude typically states the uniform restriction on a recorded plat map and in all of the lot deeds.

____OVER/____UNDER/____MIS/ Why? _____

_____

4. The plan imposing an implied reciprocal servitude must be uniform.

____OVER/____UNDER/____MIS/ Why? _____

_____

5. Reciprocal servitudes must not discriminate.

____OVER/____UNDER/____MIS/ Why? _____

_____

6. Owners may have equitable defenses to specific-performance actions of an implied reciprocal servitude, including estoppel, changed conditions, and balance of hardship.

____OVER/____UNDER/____MIS/ Why? _____

_____

Answers for Discrimination Exercise on Other Servitude Issues

1. The statement **MISconceives** the rule. An implied reciprocal servitude or reciprocal negative easement involves *uniform* restrictions on *all* subdivided lots *according to common scheme or plan*.

2. The statement **OVERgeneralizes** the rule. An enforceable implied reciprocal servitude arises when the developer dividing the land meets *all* requirements for an equitable servitude including the developer intends the servitude to run with the land, the servitude touches and concerns the land, *and successors to the land have notice of the servitude*.

3. The statement **UNDERgeneralizes** the rule. A developer wishing to impose a reciprocal servitude typically states the uniform restriction on a recorded plat map and in all, *or at least most,* of the lot deeds. *Most jurisdictions enforce as to all lots if a majority of deeds include the restriction.*

4. The statement **UNDERgeneralizes** the rule. The plan imposing an implied reciprocal servitude must be uniform *but may differentiate in restrictions among types of lots*.

5. The statement **OVERgeneralizes** the rule. Reciprocal servitudes must not *unlawfully* discriminate *based on race or other protected classes*.

6. The statement **UNDERgeneralizes** the rule. Owners may have equitable defenses to specific-performance actions of an implied reciprocal servitude, including *laches, unclean hands,* estoppel, changed conditions, and balance of hardship.

Multiple-Choice Questions with Answer Explanations

27.   A developer divided 200 acres of land into two parcels of 100 acres each. The developer then platted the first 100-acre parcel for residential subdivision of 50 lots and the second 100-acre parcel for office development, consistent with all land-use and zoning restrictions. The developer then sold all 50 residential lots under deeds with reciprocal residential-use restrictions as to grantees, heirs, and assigns. An investor bought the 100-acre office-development parcel. If the investor bought 10 of the adjacent residential lots from lot owners who didn't want to live next to an office development, may the investor develop those 10 lots for office use when developing the 100-acre office development?

A.   No, because of the reciprocal residential-use restrictions.
B.   No, because of the land-use and zoning restrictions.
C.   Yes, because the lot owners who sold didn't want to build residential.
D.   Yes, because of the unity of residential and office-development title.

Answer explanation: Option A is correct because any property owner subject to reciprocal servitudes may enforce those servitudes against any other property owner also restricted. Here, any of the remaining 40 lot owners could object and prevent the investor from developing offices on the residential lots. The reciprocal restrictions were for the benefit of all lot owners, not only those who conveyed away to the investor. Option B is incorrect because the facts give no direct indication that the residential lots were restricted against office development. The district may have permitted both residential and office development. Option C is incorrect because the lot owners who sold were not the only ones with reciprocal restrictions. The remaining 40 lot owners could also enforce the restriction. Option D is incorrect because the investor owning both the office parcel and the 10 residential lots does not remove the restriction on the 10 lots. Unifying title in a single owner does not give the owner power to avoid reciprocal restrictions favoring other lots that the owner does not own or control.

28.   Forty years ago, a landowner divided a large parcel of land in half, getting local-government approval to develop one half for residential housing and the other half for commercial use. The landowner duly recorded plats for each property that included the government-approved development plans, one development for commercial and one development for residential. The residential development contained over two-hundred individual lots that the landowner promptly sold under deeds that referenced the plat's single-family, residential restrictions as binding on grantees and their heirs and assigns. The express restrictions, though, were to last for only thirty years. Those thirty years passed. What result if an original homeowner in the residential development sued, seeking approval to convert to a commercial use?

A.   Homeowner wins because the deed restrictions expired but must comply with zoning.
B.   Homeowner wins because the deed restrictions expired and need not comply with zoning.
C.   Homeowner loses to residential lot owners asserting an implied reciprocal servitude.
D.   Homeowner loses because homeowner took the property while still restricted.

Answer explanation: Option C is correct because property owners may enforce an implied reciprocal servitude that existed expressly in prior deeds from a general plan, when the owner challenging the restriction has actual, constructive, or implied notice of the restriction. Option A is incorrect for the same reason because the law will imply a reciprocal servitude not expressly present in the deeds on the conditions just recited. Option B is incorrect for the same reason and also because even if no deed or implied reciprocal servitude restricted the owner, then the owner would still have to comply with zoning. Zoning restrictions do not depend on deed restrictions. Option D is incorrect because simply taking a restricted property would not continue to restrict the owner once the restriction expired. The restriction would continue only under an implied reciprocal servitude, not because the owner had taken while restricted. The restriction would, though, establish the owner's actual notice.

Week 9
Zoning

QUESTIONS FOR THE ASSIGNED READING:

What is Euclidean zoning? Name other zoning types. What standard of review do the courts apply when a local legislative body passes comprehensive zoning laws?

The first issue with zoning is whether government may constitutionally limit an owner's use of land. What test does *Euclid* articulate for determining that question?

If zoning statute is constitutional, then the question remains whether government must compensate an owner when limiting the land's use. Consider how the following factors affect this question: whether the land is developed or undeveloped; whether the landowner has made plans to develop or change the use of the land; whether the landowner can use the land for the permitted use; whether the landowner can use the land for a use that is now not permitted; how the zoning affects the land's value; whether the regulation affects some parts of the land but not others.

The Court in the *Sullivan* case wrote that "the distinction between an ordinance restricting future uses and one requiring the termination of present uses within a reasonable period of time is merely one of degree." Do you agree?

Name something you do not understand about real covenants and equitable servitudes.

Name something you do not understand about this week's material.

SHORT OUTLINE:

Zoning: local governments by authorization of state *enabling acts* pass **zoning** laws that regulate land uses.
Traditional exclusive-use zoning creates *residential, commercial, industrial, agricultural*, and other zones.
Exclusive zones may also create high-density versus low-density or single-family housing.
Zoning may also allow *mixed-use* areas and *planned unit developments* for officials to grant special uses.
Other locales follow *cumulative* zoning, allowing uses in an area that have less impact than the zoned maximum.

LONG OUTLINE:

Zoning (fundamentals other than regulatory taking)

Local governments, whether cities, villages, townships, or other units, may by authorization of state *enabling acts* pass **zoning** laws that regulate land uses within their borders. A typical exclusive-use zoning scheme regulates uses to *residential, commercial, industrial, agricultural*, and other areas, allowing only those uses in those areas. Mutually exclusive zones may also dictate gradations for such as high-density versus low-density or single-family housing. Exclusive-use zoning may also allow from some *mixed-use* areas and *planned unit developments* that enable zoning officials to negotiate with landowners for special mixed or non-compliant uses. Other locales follow *cumulative* zoning, allowing all uses in an area that have less impact than the zoned maximum use, from *highest* use to *lowest* use. Thus, a residential area would allow only residential, but a commercial area would allow both commercial and residential, and an industrial area would allow all uses. Some locales mix exclusive and cumulative zones.

Fluency Cards

Cover and uncover the response to each prompt until you fluently recall the exact response.

Zoning	**Cumulative zoning**
Creates use zones, mixed-use areas, and planned unit developments.	Permits lower-impact uses in higher-impact zones.
Zoning challenge	**Zoning variances**
Zoning must not exceed state enabling act.	For undue hardship, unanticipated use, beneficial use, or nonsensical restriction.
Non-compliant uses	**Phaseout of uses**
Zoning grandfathers existing non-compliant uses.	Zoning forces end of abandoned or destroyed non-compliant uses. Ten-percent limit to renovation.

Definitions Worksheet on Zoning

1.   What is the source and limit of zoning authority?

_____

_____

_____

2.   What are two typical forms of zoning scheme?

_____

_____

_____

3.   How does zoning treat existing non-compliant uses?

_____

_____

_____

4.   How does the Constitution limit zoning?

_____

_____

_____

5.   What relief may landowners find from zoning?

_____

_____

6.   What may local government regulate in addition to uses?

_____

_____

_____

Answers for Definitions Worksheet on Zoning

1.   ***What is the source and limit of zoning authority?*** Local governments may enact zoning schemes that regulate land uses within their borders if complying with state enabling acts. Landowners may challenge *ultra-vires* zoning laws.

2.   ***What are two typical forms of zoning scheme?*** *Exclusive-use* zoning regulates uses to residential, commercial, industrial, agricultural, and other areas, often including *mixed-use* areas and *planned unit developments*. *Cumulative* zoning allows all lesser uses in a zone that have less impact than the zoned maximum use.

3.   ***How does zoning treat existing non-compliant uses?*** Zoning *grandfathers* non-compliant uses to avoid a taking for which constitutions require just compensation, although forced phase-out and repair restrictions commonly amortize non-compliant uses.

4.   ***How does the Constitution limit zoning?*** Zoning must leave economically viable use, bear a rational relationship to the general welfare, and not regulate the content of speech unless the least-restrictive means to achieve a compelling interest.

5.   ***What relief may landowners find from zoning?*** Zoning boards hold authority to grant a *variance* from zoning laws under criteria including undue hardship, unique use, beneficial use serving in unusually important ways, or that the restriction makes no sense for the proposed use in the specific location.

6.   ***What may local government regulate in addition to uses?*** Local zoning and building schemes often restrict conditions like setbacks, parking, height, and even exterior finishes, window percentage, and other architectural concerns, to preserve or improve a zone's character.

Comprehensiveness Exercise on Zoning

Insert words at the $\wedge$ mark that would make for a more-accurate or more-detailed law statement.
Follow the italicized hints for help. Suggested answers are on the next page.

1. Local governments may enact zoning schemes that regulate land uses within their borders $\wedge$ $\wedge$. *[With what limits? And how challenged?]*

2. Exclusive-use zoning regulates uses to residential and commercial $\wedge$ $\wedge$ $\wedge$. *[Can you name a couple other zones? Any exceptions?]*

3. Cumulative zoning allows all $\wedge$ uses in a zone $\wedge$. *[All what kind of uses? Define those uses?]*

4. Zoning grandfathers non-compliant uses to avoid a taking for which constitutions require just compensation $\wedge$. *[Any other way zoning treats non-compliant uses?]*

5. Zoning must leave economically viable use $\wedge$ $\wedge$. *[What two other ways (with what two other tests) does the Constitution limit zoning?]*

6. Zoning boards hold authority to grant a variance from zoning laws under criteria including undue hardship $\wedge$ $\wedge$ or that the restriction makes no sense for the proposed use in the specific location. *[Can you name two other criteria?]*

7. Local zoning and building schemes often restrict conditions like setbacks, parking, and height, $\wedge$ $\wedge$ $\wedge$ to preserve or improve a zone's character. *[Can you name two other examples? Can you name the class of examples?]*

Answers for Comprehensiveness Exercise on Zoning

1.   Local governments may enact zoning schemes that regulate land uses within their borders *if complying with state enabling acts. Landowners may challenge ultra-vires zoning laws.*

2.   Exclusive-use zoning regulates uses to residential, commercial, *industrial, agricultural, and other areas, often including mixed-use areas and planned unit developments.*

3.   Cumulative zoning allows all *lesser* uses in a zone *that have less impact than the zoned maximum use.*

4.   Zoning grandfathers non-compliant uses to avoid a taking for which constitutions require just compensation, *although forced phase-out and repair restrictions commonly amortize non-compliant uses.*

5.   Zoning must leave economically viable use, *bear a rational relationship to the general welfare, and not regulate the content of speech unless the least-restrictive means to achieve a compelling interest.*

6.   Zoning boards hold authority to grant a variance from zoning laws under criteria including undue hardship, *unique use, beneficial use serving in unusually important ways*, or that the restriction makes no sense for the proposed use in the specific location.

7.   Local zoning and building schemes often restrict conditions like setbacks, parking, height, *exterior finishes, window percentage, and other architectural concerns*, to preserve or improve a zone's character.

Application Exercise on Zoning

Sort the fact patterns into whether the zoning permits the use (P) or does not permit the use (N). Answers are below.

1. A builder desires to construct multi-family housing in a commercial zone of a cumulative-zoning scheme.

2. A manufacturer desires to construct an industrial plant in a commercial zone of a cumulative-zoning scheme.

3. A lot owner desires to construct a residence in a commercial zone of an exclusive-zoning scheme.

4. A developer desires to construct an apartment complex in a residential zone of an exclusive-zoning scheme.

5. An investor desires to finance a mixed commercial/residential development as a planned unit development.

6. A bank considers lending for a commercial center in a residential zone of a cumulative-zoning scheme.

7. A downtown authority recruits for development of a mixed commercial/light-manufacturing zone as a PUD.

8. A twenty-story condominium tower applies for special-use approval of a heliport on the top of the tower.

9. A homeowner desires to operate a backyard vehicle-repair business in a residential zone of a cumulative scheme.

10. A sandwich shop starts a canning operation classified as industrial use in a cumulative commercial zone.

11. An accounting office desires to convert upstairs space to lease as an apartment in a cumulative commercial zone.

Answers: 1P 2N 3N 4P 5P 6N 7P 8P 9N 10N 11P

Choose the best variance criterion among undue hardship (H), unique use (U), unusually beneficial use (B), or the restriction makes no sense in the location for the proposed use (L). Answers are below.

1. A family requires an add-on suite for a disabled elderly parent, that would violate square-footage restriction.

2. A conservationist homeowner proposes a nonconforming nonprofit aviary-rescue use for a backyard garage.

3. An adult foster-care home proposes to add nonconforming medical-care services for foster-care residents.

4. An industrial plant bordering expanding downtown zone proposes repairs not meeting window percentages.

5. A hospital proposes to install a nonconforming aero-med helicopter landing site at its suburban location.

6. A bicycle-riders club proposes to purchase and renovate a clubhouse without meeting parking requirements.

7. A grandfathered hundred-year homestead in an industrial zone needs non-permitted repair of plumbing services.

8. A tree farmer proposes non-permitted tree-trimming equipment storage in an exclusive-zoning industrial zone.

9. A homeowner couple unexpectedly has quadruplets, exceeding permitted number of residents per square footage.

10. A homeowner with a permitted therapeutic-massage business asks to add nonconforming meditation services.

11. A skilled physician proposes to make urgent house calls using his home as a base, in a nonconforming use.

12. A local employer is unable to find a relocation site within the ten-year amortization of its grandfather location.

Answers: 1H 2U 3B 4L 5B 6U 7H 8L 9H 10U 11B 12H

Factors Exercise on Zoning

When determining whether a zoning scheme's forced phase-out of a noncompliant use is constitutional or a taking requiring just compensation, courts consider factors including **nature of present use, present character** of area, **foreseeable development** of area, **effect** of regulation, **length** of amortization period, **value** amortized, **benefit** to community of phase-out, and **harm** to landowner. For each scenario, choose a factor that would weigh heavily in favor of or against the phase-out scheme, and analyze that factor by filling in the blanks.

1.   The boarding-house owner could not locate another suitable facility for her business within the three-year phase-out that the new zoning ordinance imposed.

The [*choose a factor*] favors the [*choose a party*] when [*state relevant facts*] because [*explain your reasoning*].

2.   The smelter's forced phase-out over a ten-year amortization period would relieve the encroaching multi-family residences from the smelter's 24/7 noise, bright lights, smoke, and smell.

The [*choose a factor*] favors the [*choose a party*] when [*state relevant facts*] because [*explain your reasoning*].

3.   The village's forced phase-out applied to the couple's duplex, in half of which they lived and half of which they rented, although the duplex was in a dense residential neighborhood of mixed new-and-old character.

The [*choose a factor*] favors the [*choose a party*] when [*state relevant facts*] because [*explain your reasoning*].

4.   Although the city council had not known or intended, the new ordinance included a forced phase-out of a unique health spa combining exercise, therapeutic massage, acupuncture, mental-health counseling, and spiritual training.

The [*choose a factor*] favors the [*choose a party*] when [*state relevant facts*] because [*explain your reasoning*].

5.   The city council enacted the zoning ordinance including its eight-year forced phase-out provision under a master plan that confirmed the swift and extensive recent downtown-waterfront entertainment development and the voluntary relocation of all but one of the industrial businesses.

The [*choose a factor*] favors the [*choose a party*] when [*state relevant facts*] because [*explain your reasoning*].

6.   In the best-case scenario, application of the new forced phase-out provision to the medical facility and private school would cost each millions of dollars in relocation costs and lost income, and tens of millions in the worst case.

The [*choose a factor*] favors the [*choose a party*] when [*state relevant facts*] because [*explain your reasoning*].

Discrimination Exercise on Zoning

Indicate whether each statement **overgeneralizes**, **undergeneralizes**, or **misconceives** the rule, explaining why. *Overgeneralizing* states the rule too broadly, capturing circumstances to which it does not apply. *Undergeneralizing* states the rule too narrowly, omitting circumstances to which it applies. *Misconceiving* states the rule incorrectly.

1. Local governments may enact zoning schemes that regulate land uses within their borders.

_____OVER/_____UNDER/_____MIS/ Why? _____

_____

2. Cumulative zoning regulates uses to specific residential, commercial, industrial, agricultural, and other zones, including planned unit developments.

_____OVER/_____UNDER/_____MIS/ Why? _____

_____

3. Cumulative zoning allows all uses in a zone that have greater impact than the zoned minimum use.

_____OVER/_____UNDER/_____MIS/ Why? _____

_____

4. Grandfathered uses remain because zoning preserves non-compliant uses to avoid a taking, for which constitutions require just compensation.

_____OVER/_____UNDER/_____MIS/ Why? _____

_____

5. Zoning may restrict as long as it bears a rational relationship to the general welfare.

_____OVER/_____UNDER/_____MIS/ Why? _____

_____

6. Zoning boards may grant variances from zoning laws.

_____OVER/_____UNDER/_____MIS/ Why? _____

_____

7. Local zoning schemes limit uses based on zones.

_____OVER/_____UNDER/_____MIS/ Why? _____

_____

Answers for Discrimination Exercise on Zoning

1. The statement **OVERgeneralizes** the rule. Local governments may enact zoning schemes that regulate land uses within their borders *if complying with state enabling acts. Landowners may challenge ultra-vires zoning laws.*

2. The statement **MISconceives** the rule. *Exclusive-use* zoning, not cumulative zoning, regulates uses to specific residential, commercial, industrial, agricultural, and other zones, including planned unit developments.

3. The statement **MISconceives** the rule. Cumulative zoning allows all uses in a zone that have *less impact*, rather than greater impact, than the zoned *maximum*, rather than minimum, use.

4. The statement **OVERgeneralizes** the rule. While zoning grandfathers non-compliant uses to avoid a taking for which constitutions require just compensation, *forced phase-out periods and repair restrictions may amortize non-compliant uses*.

5. The statement **OVERgeneralizes** the rule. While zoning must bear a rational relationship to the general welfare, it must also *leave reasonable, economically viable use*.

6. The statement **OVERgeneralizes** the rule. Zoning boards hold authority to grant a variance from zoning laws *under criteria including undue hardship, unique use, beneficial use serving in unusually important ways, or that the restriction makes no sense for the proposed use in the specific location*.

7. The statement **UNDERgeneralizes** the rule. Local zoning schemes limit uses based on zones *but also often restrict conditions like setbacks, parking, height, exterior finishes, window percentage, and other architectural concerns, to preserve or improve a zone's character*.

Multiple-Choice Questions with Answer Explanations

29. A builder of apartment units located land for sale at a reasonable price in a district that the city zoned industrial. While the zone had one industrial use, land in the zone was otherwise vacant and had remained so for a long time. The builder desired to build an apartment house on the land for sale in the industrial zone, reasonably believing that the zone would not develop for industrial and that apartment use would be a safe and reasonable use of the land. Under which type of zoning scheme may the builder build the apartment house?

A. Only an exclusive-use zoning scheme.
B. Only as a planned-unit development.
C. Only a cumulative zoning scheme.
D. No zoning schemes.

Answer explanation. Option C is correct because a cumulative zoning scheme generally permits lower-impact uses in a higher-impact zoning district. A residential use is lower impact than an industrial use. Option A is incorrect because an exclusive-use scheme limits development to the specified use. The zone specified industrial use, meaning an exclusive-use zone would permit only industrial. Option B is incorrect because while planned-unit development can allow for nonconforming uses, a single apartment house would be an unusual planned-unit development, which typically involves multiple uses. Option D is incorrect because a cumulative zoning scheme would allow for residential use in industrial zone.

30. A state zoning enabling act permitted only exclusive-use zoning acts but allowed for clearly defined mixed-use zones within the exclusive-zone definitions. The zoning enabling act also required that any local zoning act permit planned-unit developments under reasonable criteria. A city within the state adopted an exclusive-use zoning scheme that did not provide for planned-unit developments. A developer wished to build a mixed condominium and retail development on a half city block zoned industrial. Which is the best approach for the developer to take to obtain zoning approval?

A. Apply for project approval as a lower-impact use in a higher-impact industrial zone.
B. Claim the city's zoning is ultra vires, and seek planned-unit-development approval.
C. Pursue rezoning of the half city block at the next planning commission and council meetings.
D. Seek a variance from the industrial zoning to pursue the condominium and retail project.

Answer explanation. Option B is correct because local governments, whether cities, villages, townships, or other units, may only pass zoning acts consistent with state enabling acts. The state act required planned-unit developments, which the city's act did not provide. The developer may show the city's act to be outside of the enabling act's authority. Option A is incorrect because exclusive-use zoning allows only those uses designated for that zone, not lower-impact inconsistent uses. Option C is incorrect because rezoning is a political question that provides the developer with no assurance of success, making that course a less-attractive option than showing that the act does not comply and seeking a planned-unit development as the state enabling act permits. Option D is incorrect because the city act is ultra vires, and seeking a variance from it should not be necessary and would be discretionary with planning and city officials.

Week 10
Zoning Issues

QUESTIONS FOR THE ASSIGNED READING:
Name something you do not understand about this week's material.

SHORT OUTLINE:
Zoning boards hold authority to grant a **variance** from zoning laws under granted criteria.

Criteria may include *undue hardship*, *unique unanticipated uses*, *beneficial use*, or nonsensical restriction.

Local law may also require *setbacks*, *parking*, *height limits*, *exterior finishes*, and *window percentage*.

Officials must not engage in unlawful *spot zoning* favoring individual landowners.

Also avoid unlawful *exclusionary zoning* prohibiting low-income housing and other unpopular uses.

Aesthetics restrictions must have reasonable standards to avoid arbitrary and capricious application.

Speech content restrictions must be the least-restrictive means of obtaining a compelling government interest.

Time, place, and manner restrictions must relate directly to achieving a substantial government interest.

No substantially burdening religion unless least-restrictive means to achieve a compelling government interest.

LONG OUTLINE:
Zoning boards typically hold authority to grant a **variance** from zoning laws under criteria that the zoning scheme establishes. Common criteria include *undue hardship*, *unique uses* that the zoning scheme did not anticipate, *beneficial uses* that serve the community in unique or important ways, or that the restriction does not make sense for the specific use in the specific location. Local zoning and building schemes often have other restrictions other than use restrictions, for conditions like *setbacks*, *parking*, *height*, and even *exterior finishes*, *window percentage*, and other architectural concerns, to preserve or improve a zone's character. Zoning and building officials may also consider variances for those restrictions, although local officials tend to strictly enforce zoning provisions.

In varying zoning restrictions, officials must take care not to engage in unlawful *spot zoning* favoring individual landowners. Local zoning must also avoid unlawful *exclusionary zoning* that prohibits foster-care facilities, low-income housing, and other potentially unpopular uses. If zoning restricts the aesthetics of building design, then the zoning must have reasonable standards so that officials cannot apply the restrictions arbitrarily and capriciously. Zoning that restricts speech content is lawful only if the least-restrictive means of obtaining a compelling government interest. Zoning that restricts the time, place, and manner of speech, but not its content, must show that it relates directly to achieving a substantial government interest. Federal law prohibits zoning from substantially burdening religious exercises unless the regulations are the least-restrictive means of furthering a compelling government interest.

Fluency Cards

Cover and uncover the response to each prompt until you fluently recall the exact response.

Special use

Zoning may cede to a board the power to allow non-compliant uses under specific criteria.

Spot zoning

Zoning must not create single-parcel exceptions as political favor.

Aesthetic zoning

Must have standards limiting arbitrary and capricious application.

Speech content

No regulating unless least-restrictive means toward compelling interest.

Exclusionary zoning

Zoning must not prohibit foster care or low-income families. Allow low-income housing.

Speech time and manner

No regulating time and manner unless directly related to substantial interest.

Definitions Worksheet on Zoning Issues

1.   What is a special use or special exception in a zoning scheme?

_____

_____

2.   What is spot zoning?

_____

_____

3.   What is aesthetic zoning? Aesthetic zoning attempts to make zones more visibly attractive.

_____

_____

_____

4.   How if at all does law limit aesthetic zoning?

_____

_____

_____

5.   What First Amendment protections do landowners have against zoning?

_____

_____

_____

6.   What protections do religious organizations have?

_____

_____

_____

7.   How does law limit exclusionary zoning?

_____

_____

_____

Answers for Definitions Worksheet on Zoning Issues

1. ***What is a special use or special exception in a zoning scheme?*** If the enabling act allows, a zoning scheme may cede to a designated board the authority to permit an otherwise impermissible use, under specific criteria establishing standards.

2. ***What is spot zoning?*** The legislative body must not amend a general zoning scheme to single out small zones to favor individual applicant owners, known as *spot zoning*, contrary to master plan and without benefit to the public interest.

3. ***What is aesthetic zoning?*** Aesthetic zoning attempts to make zones more visibly attractive.

4. ***How if at all does law limit aesthetic zoning?*** Where permitted, aesthetic zoning must have standards limiting arbitrary and capricious or privileged application.

5. ***What First Amendment protections do landowners have against zoning?*** Zoning must not regulate the content of speech unless the least-restrictive means to achieve a compelling governmental interest and must not burden the time and manner of speech unless directly related to achieving a substantial interest.

6. ***What protections do religious organizations have?*** Federal law prohibits zoning from substantially burdening religious exercises unless the regulations are the least-restrictive means of furthering a compelling government interest. Zoning must not treat religious organizations differently.

7. ***How does law limit exclusionary zoning?*** Zoning may restrict some housing to families but must not intrusively regulate the nature of families, prohibit group foster-care homes, or exclude low-income families. Municipalities must provide reasonable opportunities for low-income housing.

Issue-Spotting Exercise

Which of these doctrines is implicated: nonconforming use (NC), a variance (V), a special exception (SE), vested rights (VR), amortization (A), spot zoning (SZ), or implicit taking (IT). What type of process would take place for each?

1. Developer owns a lot zoned residential that is one foot too narrow for a residence.

_____

2. Hardware store has operated for thirty years in an area that local government has since rezoned residential. The ordinance gives store owner five years to change use to residential.

_____

3. A private non-profit wants to build a hospital in a town with Euclidean zoning.

_____

4. A contractor owns undeveloped land in an area zoned industrial use. She obtains permits, hires an architect, and pays a deposit on heavy equipment to begin building a factory. Local government rezones the land commercial.

_____

5. Corporation wants to put a private airport adjacent to its corporate headquarters.

_____

6. Landlord has an apartment building in a mixed-use neighborhood. Landlord was planning to add a restaurant on the second floor, when local government rezoned the area residential only.

_____

7. Computer company owns a chip factory in a previously never-zoned area. Local government zones the area for the first time, making the factory land retail or residential only.

_____

8. Landlord owns multiple apartment buildings. City passes a regulation stating that any building with occupants must have an emergency phone within 100 yards of the building. The only place to put the phones is on Landlord's property.

_____

9. Owner has a lot in a never-zoned area. The area is mostly residential. Owner believes a small convenience store would be ideal for the neighborhood. Local government then zones the area residential only. Owner could build a home on the lot but thinks a convenience store is a better idea.

_____

Issue-Spotting Exercise: Zoning Review

For each scenario, identify the issue and discuss relevant considerations.

1.   A town's zoning regulation states that no bookstores may exist within the town limits.

_____

2.   A town's zoning regulation states that all single-family homes in the town must be at least 3,000 square feet.

_____

3.   A town's zoning regulation states that all single-family homes in the town must be at least 3,000 square feet, unless the Zoning Administrator finds that a variance should be granted based on the town's overall health, safety, and general welfare.

_____

_____

4.   A zoning regulation enacts a Euclidean zoning scheme with: (a) an existing coffee shop now in a residential zone; (b) an undeveloped lot big enough to construct a residence, now in a residential zone; (c) an undeveloped lot not big enough to construct a residence, now in a residential zone; (d) an existing coffee shop now in a residential zone, given twenty years to convert to a conforming use; (e) an existing coffee shop now in a residential zone, the owner of which wanting to build a second-story bakery; (f) an existing coffee shop now in a residential zone, the owner having obtained a permit to build a second-story bakery; (g) an existing coffee shop now in a residential zone, the owner of which obtained a permit to build a second-story bakery, now partially constructed; (h) the prior scenario, plus the owner purchased and installed ovens and industrial mixers in the space; (i) a landowner having an undeveloped parcel in a now-residential zone, with a huge surplus of housing, and fair-market value fell from $75,000 to $50,000; (j) the prior scenario, except fair-market value fell from $75,000 to $5,000; (k) the prior scenario, except the owner cannot sell the parcel, on the market for two years since the ordinance passed.

_____

_____

_____

_____

_____

Answers to Issue-Spotting Exercise: Zoning Review

1.   The zoning violates constitutional free-speech guarantees. A town may regulate the time and place of speech but not prohibit it entirely. The town would have to show a compelling state interest and a regulation narrowly crafted – which this regulation is not.

2.   While someone with a smaller lot could seek a space variance, and someone with an existing smaller home may claim a nonconforming use, this regulation is likely a substantive due process violation because it address all homes in the town.

3.   This regulation improperly delegates power from the legislative to the executive branch. The legislature cannot delegate its police power without providing more-specific criteria.

4.   (a) The coffee shop is a nonconforming use as to which the town must allow continued use, amortize (if constitutional in this jurisdiction), or pay just compensation.

(b) This regulation is likely permissible and the owner without recourse. The owner could seek a variance but would not likely get it.

(c) This owner should seek a space variance. Depending on how big the lot is, the owner may get it. If the town denies the variance, then the town must compensate the owner.

(d) In a jurisdiction where amortization is lawful, twenty years is probably enough time to amortize a coffee shop, although one would need to weigh factors.

(e) Merely wanting to build does not create vested rights. If the coffee shop continues as a nonconforming use, the town need not permit the bakery because it expands the non-conforming commercial use.

(f) This scenario presents a better case for vested rights, although it still might not be enough.

(g) This scenario presents a much better case for vested rights, which the law would likely recognize.

(h) This scenario almost certainly involves vested rights. The law would treat the bakery the same as a coffee shop.

(i) This scenario is like the *Village of Euclid* case: no relief for owner, who must use the lot for residential.

(j) This scenario presents some case for compensation, based on implicit-takings tests, even though the lot retains some minimal value.

(k) This scenario presents strong evidence of zero value, making it a taking under *Lucas*.

Statutory-Interpretation Exercise

How are these two statutes different from each other? Why was one upheld and the other stricken?

Stoyanoff Statute

In determining whether to approve design and other aesthetic elements of proposed construction, the Architectural Board shall consider: (1) whether the proposed house meets the customary architectural requirements in appearance and design for a house of the particular type which is proposed (whether it be Colonial, Tudor English, French Provincial, or Modern); (2) whether the proposed house is in general conformity with the style and design of surrounding structures; and (3) whether the proposed house lends itself to the proper architectural development of the City; and that in applying said standards the Architectural Board and its Chair are to determine whether the proposed house will have an adverse effect on the stability of values in the surrounding area.

Anderson v City of Issaquah Statute

IMC 16.16.060(B). Relationship of Building and Site to Adjoining Area.   1. Buildings and structures shall be made compatible with adjacent buildings of conflicting architectural styles by such means as screens and site breaks, or other suitable methods and materials. 2. Harmony in texture, lines, and masses shall be encouraged....

IMC 16.16.060(D). Building Design.   1. Evaluation of a project shall be based on quality of its design and relationship to the natural setting of the valley and surrounding mountains. 2. Building components, such as windows, doors, eaves and parapets, shall have appropriate proportions and relationship to each other, expressing themselves as a part of the overall design. 3. Colors shall be harmonious, with bright or brilliant colors used only for minimal accent. 4. Design attention shall be given to screening from public view all mechanical equipment, including refuse enclosures, electrical transformer pads and vaults, communication equipment, and other utility hardware on roofs, grounds or buildings. 5. Exterior lighting shall be part of the architectural concept. Fixtures, standards and all exposed accessories shall be harmonious with the building design. 6. Monotony of design in single or multiple building projects shall be avoided. Efforts should be made to create an interesting project by use of complimentary details, functional orientation of buildings, parking and access provisions and relating the development to the site. In multiple building projects, variable siting of individual buildings, heights of buildings, or other methods shall be used to prevent a monotonous design.

Comprehensiveness Exercise on Zoning Issues

Insert words at the ^ mark that would make for a more-accurate or more-detailed law statement.
Follow the italicized hints for help. Suggested answers are on the next page.

1.   ^ A zoning scheme may ^ permit an otherwise impermissible use ^ . *[What must first exist for local government to zone? Who decides whether to permit an impermissible use? Any conditions to permission?]*

2.   The legislative body must not amend a general zoning scheme to single out small zones ^ ^ ^ ^. *[Small zones alone may be permissible but not if for a certain reason. What's that kind of zoning called? Can you name two conditions that might permit small-zone amendment?]*

3.   Aesthetic zoning, attempting to make zones more visibly attractive, must have standards ^ . *[What is the purpose of the standards (what evil do they address)?]*

4.   Zoning must not regulate ^ speech ^ ^ . *[Just speech generally or some part of speech? Can you name two constitutional tests under which zoning may regulate speech?]*

5.   Federal law prohibits zoning from ^ burdening religious exercises ^ . *[Any burden or just a certain kind of burden? With what exception (under what constitutional test)?]*

6.   Zoning may restrict some housing to families ^ ^ ^ . *[With what three restrictions?]*

Answers for Comprehensiveness Exercise on Zoning Issues

1.   *If the enabling act allows*, a zoning scheme may *cede to a designated board the authority to* permit an otherwise impermissible use, *under specific criteria establishing standards*.

2.   The legislative body must not amend a general zoning scheme to single out small zones *to favor individual applicant owners, known as spot zoning, contrary to master plan and without benefit to the public interest*.

3.   Aesthetic zoning, attempting to make zones more visibly attractive, must have standards *limiting arbitrary and capricious or privileged application*.

4.   Zoning must not regulate *the content of* speech *unless the least-restrictive means to achieve a compelling governmental interest and must not burden the time and manner of speech unless directly related to achieving a substantial interest*.

5.   Federal law prohibits zoning from *substantially* burdening religious exercises *unless the regulations are the least-restrictive means of furthering a compelling government interest*.

6.   Zoning may restrict some housing to families *but must not intrusively regulate the nature of families, prohibit group foster-care homes, or exclude low-income families. Municipalities must provide reasonable opportunities for low-income housing*.

Application Exercise on Zoning Issues

Sort the fact patterns into whether they show a lawful amendment (L) or unlawful spot zoning (S). Answers are below.

1. City council amended to provide for a transition zone between industrial and residential.

2. Village council amended to create a commercial lot for an ex-councilmember inside a residential zone.

3. Township board amended for a mixed-use zone at the intersection of resident and commercial zones.

4. City council amended for the mayor's brother to build an office tower in a downtown-retail zone.

5. Township board amended for the newspaper editor to divide his residential lot to sell a valuable parcel.

6. Village council amended for an entertainment district along its main thoroughfare.

7. City council amended to allow development of a failed industrial park for needed low-income housing.

8. City council amended for a wealthy investor who funded annual fireworks to add three stories to his residence.

9. Village council amended to prohibit big-box retail solely on the site just purchased for that use.

10. Township board amended to require any new big-box retail to pay for any necessary public improvements.

Answers: 1L 2S 3L 4S 5S 6L 7L 8S 9S 10L

Sort the fact patterns into whether the aesthetic zoning would likely survive (S) or fail (F). Answers are below.

1. The village's downtown-retail zone required seventy percent of building streetfront to be window.

2. All of the suburb's single-family-residential zones required homes of five-thousand square feet or more.

3. The city empowered its architectural-review board for commercial zones to approve only *attractive* structures.

4. The city restricted exteriors in its historic residential zone to brick, where the historic homes were all brick.

5. The township restricted satellite disks in residential zones to the rear of the lot behind constructed homes.

6. The city restricted all homes in any residential zone to white stucco with authentic, expensive red-tile roof.

7. The township required fifty-foot setbacks in residential construction on lots larger than one acre.

8. The village restricted housing to modern designs approved by a board of contemporary architects.

9. The city restricted construction in the district to plans approved within the discretion of the historic board.

10. The village restricted construction in the Old Town district to storefronts having similar period character.

Answers: 1S 2F 3F 4S 5S 6F 7S 8F 9F 10S

152

Factors Exercise on Zoning Issues

Whether a zoning regulation affecting speech survives First Amendment review, under strict or intermediate scrutiny, can depend on factors including whether the provision regulates speech *content*, is content *neutral*, regulates only *time, place, or manner*, singles out a particular *viewpoint* or prohibits *all speech*, relates only to a *restricted forum*, permits an *alternative forum*, and pursues a *legitimate end*. For each scenario, choose a factor that would weigh heavily in favor or against the provision's constitutionality, and analyze that factor by filling in the blanks.

1.   **The city council prohibited any expression of pro-life views in any form within one-thousand feet of the entry of any clinic providing abortion services.**

The [*choose a factor*] favors the [*choose a party*] when [*state relevant facts*] because [*explain your reasoning*] .

2.   **The village prohibited yard signs on any subject, political, social, personal, commercial, or otherwise, of any size larger than two feet tall and three feet wide, to prevent obstruction of the view of children running toward and into the street or to frustrate public-safety personnel in fighting fires or otherwise accessing residences.**

The [*choose a factor*] favors the [*choose a party*] when [*state relevant facts*] because [*explain your reasoning*] .

3.   **The township prohibited outdoor events creating noise louder than 90 decibels at the perimeter of the event lands, later than 9 p.m. on school weeknights or 11 p.m. on weekends.**

The [*choose a factor*] favors the [*choose a party*] when [*state relevant facts*] because [*explain your reasoning*] .

4.   **The city prohibited sound, whether music or messages, broadcast outdoors from any amplifying device, within five-hundred feet of any school when school is in session.**

The [*choose a factor*] favors the [*choose a party*] when [*state relevant facts*] because [*explain your reasoning*] .

5.   **The village prohibited amplified public speaking in its downtown retail district while permitting amplified public speaking in the public parks at the district's center and ends.**

The [*choose a factor*] favors the [*choose a party*] when [*state relevant facts*] because [*explain your reasoning*] .

6.   **The city prohibited outdoor political speech in any residential zone.**

The [*choose a factor*] favors the [*choose a party*] when [*state relevant facts*] because [*explain your reasoning*] .

Discrimination Exercise on Zoning Issues

Indicate whether each statement *overgeneralizes*, *undergeneralizes*, or *misconceives* the rule, explaining why. *Overgeneralizing* states the rule too broadly, capturing circumstances to which it does not apply. *Undergeneralizing* states the rule too narrowly, omitting circumstances to which it applies. *Misconceiving* states the rule incorrectly.

1. If an enabling act allows, a zoning scheme may cede to a designated board the authority to permit an otherwise impermissible use.

____OVER/____UNDER/____MIS/ Why? _____

_____

2. A legislative body may amend a general zoning scheme to single out small zones to favor individual applicant owners, known as spot zoning, contrary to master plan and without benefit to the public interest.

____OVER/____UNDER/____MIS/ Why? _____

_____

3. Aesthetic zoning may attempt to make zones more visibly attractive.

____OVER/____UNDER/____MIS/ Why? _____

_____

4. Zoning may regulate the time, place, and manner of speech but not the content of speech.

____OVER/____UNDER/____MIS/ Why? _____

_____

5. Federal law permits zoning to burden religious exercises only if the regulations are the least-restrictive means of furthering a compelling government interest.

____OVER/____UNDER/____MIS/ Why? _____

_____

6. Zoning may restrict some housing to families.

____OVER/____UNDER/____MIS/ Why? _____

_____

Answers for Discrimination Exercise on Zoning Issues

1. The statement **OVERgeneralizes** the rule. If an enabling act allows, a zoning scheme may cede to a designated board the authority to permit an otherwise impermissible use, *under specific criteria establishing standards*.

2. The statement **MISconceives** the rule. A legislative body must *not* amend a general zoning scheme to single out small zones *especially* to favor individual applicant owners, known as spot zoning, contrary to master plan and without benefit to the public interest.

3. The statement **OVERgeneralizes** the rule. Aesthetic zoning may attempt to make zones more visibly attractive *but must have standards limiting arbitrary and capricious or privileged application*.

4. The statement **OVERgeneralizes** the rule. Zoning may regulate the time, place, and manner of speech *if directly related to achieving a substantial government interest* but not the content of speech *unless the least-restrictive means to achieve a compelling governmental interest*.

5. The statement **UNDERgeneralizes** the rule. Federal law permits zoning to *substantially* burden religious exercises only if the regulations are the least-restrictive means of furthering a compelling government interest.

6. The statement **OVERgeneralizes** the rule. Zoning may restrict some housing to families *if not intrusively regulating the nature of families, prohibiting group foster-care homes, or excluding low-income families. Municipalities must provide reasonable opportunities for low-income housing*.

Multiple-Choice Questions with Answer Explanations

31. A city lawfully changed the zoning on one side of a street from mixed residential-and-business use to solely residential, attempting to preserve the primarily residential character of the neighborhood consistent with the master plan. The other side of the street remained mixed residential-and-business use consistent with the master plan for further business and commercial development in that area. A resident whose home was then in the residential-only district sought city approval to operate a business from her home. What action should the resident pursue?

A. Claim a non-conforming use.
B. Claim a change in circumstances.
C. Rely on the doctrine of amortization.
D. Seek a variance.

Answer explanation: Option D is correct because an owner seeking relief from lawfully enacted zoning to conduct a new use not permitted in the district does so by request for variance. The resident was seeking a new non-permitted use in a district under lawfully enacted zoning. Variance is her only choice. Option A is incorrect because the resident was proposing a new use rather than attempting to preserve a prior non-conforming use. Option B is incorrect because the resident has no change in circumstance to plead but is simply seeking a new use. Change in circumstance is not a zoning doctrine but a doctrine relating to servitudes. Option C is incorrect because the doctrine of amortization has to do with phasing out a prior non-conforming use, when here the resident had no prior non-conforming use.

32. A developer of low-income housing paid for a housing study showing substantial need for such housing in a city that had none. The developer arranged for bank financing for a low-income housing development based on the strongly favorable market study. The developer also found several suitable vacant lots for sale in the city at prices that made sound economic sense for development. However, no properties within the city, whether for sale or not, had zoning appropriate for low-income housing. All zones in the city's zoning act effectively prohibited economic development of low-income housing. Which is the best legal challenge that the developer can make against the city and its zoning?

A. Challenge the enactment as beyond the state enabling act.
B. Challenge the enactment as exclusionary zoning.
C. Challenge the enactment as spot zoning.
D. Challenge the enactment as an unlawful variance.

Answer explanation: Option B is correct because local zoning must avoid unlawful *exclusionary zoning* that prohibits foster-care facilities, low-income housing, and other potentially unpopular uses. Option A is incorrect because state enabling acts may authorize exclusive zones, and the facts give no contrary information as to this state's enabling act. Option C is incorrect because spot zoning involves creating small zones for individual property owners out of political favor, none of which was present here. Option D is incorrect because a variance involves positive regulatory relief from lawful zoning rather than, as here, legal relief from unlawful zoning.

Week 11

Eminent Domain

QUESTIONS FOR THE ASSIGNED READING:

Name something you do not understand about this week's material.

SHORT OUTLINE:

Eminent domain is when government condemns private property for public use, with just compensation.
    Government may clearly take private property for public property like a street or park.
        Government may also take for public-use functions like utilities and railways.
            The U.S. Constitution permits taking for legitimate public purpose such as to remove blight.
                Most states restrict eminent domain to public land or function.
    Government pays fair market value, what a willing buyer would pay a willing seller on the open market.
        Use the value for the land's highest and best use.
            Law may also require payment of relocation expenses and attorney's fees.

LONG OUTLINE:

Eminent Domain

Eminent domain is when government condemns private property to acquire it for public use, on payment of just compensation as state and federal constitutions require. Under state and federal constitutions, the government's exercise of eminent domain must be only for public use and with just compensation. Government may clearly take private property for public property like a street or park. Government may also take private property for public-use functions like utilities and railways. If government can articulate a legitimate public purpose to exercise eminent domain, such as to remove blight, correct unsanitary conditions, or provide housing or employment, then the U.S. Constitution permits it even if conveyed to private entity for private use. Most states restrict eminent domain to public land or function. Government must then pay fair market value, what a willing buyer would pay a willing seller on the open market at the time of eminent domain's exercise, for the land's highest and best use. Law may also require payment of relocation expenses and attorney's fees.

When might regulation result in a taking? The government may buy land, with just compensation, for a public purpose, in what law would label a *condemnation*. Zoning a previously un-zoned area, thus restricting use, is not a taking if the zoning leaves some reasonable use, although one might still need to analyze under implicit-taking tests. Re-zoning from one use to another is not a taking if the owner has no current use and no vested rights, or if current use is still allowed, although again, one might need to analyze under implicit-taking tests. If the re-zoning does not allow the current use, then the owner should seek to continue as a grandfathered nonconforming use. If the re-zoning allows the current use long enough to reasonably amortize its lost value, and the jurisdiction permits amortization, then the re-zoning may end the use after the amortization period. Otherwise, the government must compensate.

When a new enactment prohibits a future use, the owner must seek a variance. Traditional tests are strict, like undue hardship not of the owner's making, which generally means the owner cannot use the land for the zoned use. Space variances are easier to get than use variances. When government denies a variance, and the owner cannot use the land a viable economic use, government must pay compensation. Physical invasions, no matter how slight, require compensation. As to implicit takings, one also looks to the extent of the diminution in value, the extent of investment-backed expectations, and the nature of government action in the public interest.

Fluency Cards

Cover and uncover the response to each prompt until you fluently recall the exact response.

Eminent domain

Government condemns private property for public use, with just compensation.

Regulatory taking

Regulation frustrates economically viable use. Construed as condemnation requiring compensation.

Eminent domain just compensation

Fair market value. What a willing buyer would pay a willing seller.

Definitions Worksheet on Eminent Domain

1. What is eminent domain?

_____

_____

_____

2. How do constitutions limit eminent domain?

_____

_____

_____

3. Distinguish a regulatory taking from eminent domain.

_____

_____

_____

4. Name two non-controversial examples of eminent domain.

_____

_____

_____

5. When may government use eminent domain outside of public access?

_____

_____

_____

6. How does law measure just compensation?

_____

_____

_____

Answers for Definitions Worksheet on Eminent Domain

1.   ***What is eminent domain?*** Eminent domain is when government condemns private property to acquire it for public use, on payment of just compensation as state and federal constitutions require.

2.   ***How do constitutions limit eminent domain?*** The government's exercise of eminent domain must be only for public use and with just compensation.

3.   ***Distinguish a regulatory taking from eminent domain.*** While eminent domain is purposeful exercise of government authority to acquire private property for public use, a regulatory taking does not intend the property's acquisition, but law construes it as such for just compensation.

4.   ***Name two non-controversial examples of eminent domain.*** Government may clearly take private property for public property like a street or park. Government may also take private property for public-use functions like utilities and railways.

5.   ***When may government use eminent domain outside of public access?*** If government can articulate a legitimate public purpose to exercise eminent domain, such as to remove blight, correct unsanitary conditions, or provide housing or employment, then the U.S. Constitution permits it even if conveyed to private entity for private use. Most states restrict eminent domain to public land or function.

6.   ***How does law measure just compensation?*** Government must pay fair market value, defined as what a willing buyer would pay a willing seller on the open market at the time of eminent domain's exercise, for the land's highest and best use. Law may also require payment of relocation expenses and attorney's fees.

Issue-Spotting Exercise

Identify the implicit-takings issue. Discuss how the facts relate to the cases in this week's reading. Answers are on the next page.

1.   The city's zoning statute required that residential lots had to be ten square feet larger than lots not in a residential zone. The city refused to grant a variance to an under-sized-lot owner. The provision offered no amortization.

2.   The city agreed to grant a permit to expand a store only if the store agreed to put in a walkway. The city maintained with some basis that the expansion would make people walk out of their usual way, without the addition of a walkway.

3.   The city passed an ordinance stating that all businesses in the zone had to connect to a public walkway where the walkway crossed private property.

4.   The regional planning council passed a rule banning toxic waste dumps inside city limits. A toxic waste dump was already inside the city limits.

5.   The state passed an emergency bill to confiscate all medical masks to give to hospitals during the emergency.

6.   The city passed an ordinance that no downtown buildings could be taller than fourteen stories. The owner of a twelve-story office building, fully rented, was considering adding ten stories to rent lucrative office space during a population boom.

7.   Same facts as the prior scenario, but the owner had obtained several million dollars in investment to back the ten-story addition.

8.   Same facts as the prior scenario, but the owner had already begun construction when the city adopted the ordinance.

Answers to Issue-Spotting Exercise

1.   The zoning statute leaves the lot zero economic value, not big enough for its only valid zoned use (residential). If the city had granted a use variance, or if the statute had lawful amortization, then the statute would not have taken the lot. But without either provision, this scenario shows a taking under the *Lucas* test.

2.   This exaction question asks if the city may require an owner to spend money on its own property in exchange for a permit to proceed. The *Nollan* test requires an essential nexus, which probably exists here.

3.   This provision is a taking under the *Loretto* test. The regulation results in a physical occupation of private land and thus requires compensation.

4.   This scenario is like *Hadacheck*, as affirmed in *Lucas*. If the council could have accomplished the same thing by suing for nuisance, then no taking exists.

5.   Legislation depriving an owner of personal property is a taking requiring government to pay just compensation. This scenario is like the *Horne* case.

6.   This scenario requires a *Penn Central* or *Mahon* ad-hoc analysis. The provision diminishes value, but the existing building is lucrative, as would be adding an allowed two stories. The regulation is in the public interest and does not intrude on existing physical space. The owner has no investment-backed expectations.

7.   The additional facts arguably add investment-backed expectations. However, owners rarely win cases under this test. And, the owner has no evidence of being in a worse position if having to give the money back.

8.   The additional facts show a vested interest, nearly as if the owner had already built the additional stories. The city must either grandfather the new construction in, or allow for its amortization, or pay just compensation.

Comprehensiveness Exercise on Eminent Domain

Insert words at the ^ mark for a more-accurate law statement. Follow the italicized hints. Answers are on the next page.

1.   Eminent domain is when government condemns private property ^ , on payment of just compensation ^ . *[Acquire why? Why pay compensation?]*

2.   The government's exercise of eminent domain must be only ^ with just compensation. *[Why exercise eminent domain?]*

3.   While eminent domain is purposeful exercise of government authority to acquire private property for public use, a regulatory taking does not intend the property's acquisition ^ . *[Why determine a regulatory taking, then?]*

4.   Government may clearly take private property for public property like a street or park ^ . *[Can you name another non-controversial exercise of eminent domain?]*

5.   If government can articulate a legitimate public purpose to exercise eminent domain, ^ ^ ^ then the U.S. Constitution permits it even if conveyed to private entity for private use. ^ *[Can you give three examples of a public purpose? Do states treat the issue any differently?]*

6.   Government must pay ^ value, defined as what a willing buyer would pay a willing seller ^ ^ ^ . ^ . *[What kind of value? On what market? At what time? For what use of the land? Anything else law may compensate?]*

163

Answers for Comprehensiveness Exercise on Eminent Domain

1.   Eminent domain is when government condemns private property ***to acquire it for public use***, on payment of just compensation ***as state and federal constitutions require***.

2.   The government's exercise of eminent domain must be only ***for public use and*** with just compensation.

3.   While eminent domain is purposeful exercise of government authority to acquire private property for public use, a regulatory taking does not intend the property's acquisition, ***but law construes it as such for just compensation***.

4.   Government may clearly take private property for public property like a street or park ***and for public-use functions like utilities and railways***.

5.   If government can articulate a legitimate public purpose to exercise eminent domain, ***such as to remove blight, correct unsanitary conditions, or provide housing or employment***, then the U.S. Constitution permits it even if conveyed to private entity for private use. ***Most states restrict eminent domain to public land or function***.

6.   Government must pay ***fair market*** value, defined as what a willing buyer would pay a willing seller ***on the open market at the time of eminent domain's exercise, for the land's highest and best use. Law may also require payment of relocation expenses and attorney's fees***.

Application Exercise on Eminent Domain

Sort the fact patterns into whether the exercise of eminent domain is proper (P), improper (I), or close-call controversial (C). Answers are below.

1. The city condemned thirty feet of the homeowner's front yard to widen the street turnaround at the cul de sac.

2. The village considered using eminent domain to acquire the dilapidated residence for a new grocery store.

3. The county condemned riverfront industry to resell to resort developers pursuing an entertainment district.

4. The city threatened eminent domain to shudder the auto-repair facility so that it might sell to a resort developer.

5. The county sought eminent domain over the industrial site to expand the municipal power station for natural gas.

6. The city sought condemnation of a low-income housing district to clear for a huge Tesla battery plant.

7. The city pursued eminent domain over the adult bookstore and movie house to sell to a cleaner business.

8. The state pursued condemnation of light-manufacturing sites for more parking for a private downtown stadium.

9. The state used eminent domain to acquire the boarded-up homes for a new courthouse on the downtown site.

10. The township used eminent domain to acquire the farm field for the new fire and police station.

11. The state condemned the elderly couple's home to convey it to a major donor to the governor's re-election.

12. The city condemned a fully occupied old downtown office building to clear for a private parking structure.

13. The state condemned suburban lands to expand sorting facilities for overnight-air FedEx shipments.

14. The city condemned the business of the losing mayoral candidate to increase the available vacant-land stock.

15. The state sought eminent domain over a retail marketplace to convert to woo Amazon or another tech company.

16. The village condemned the shuddered retail shop for a new library funded in part by the successful millage.

17. The county exercised eminent domain over the nursery grounds for a new jail in the county's geographic center.

18. The city pursued eminent domain over two vehicle-dealership sites to reduce competition for the mayor's son.

19. The state exercised eminent domain over a blighted urban neighborhood to spur business redevelopment.

20. The state condemned one quarter of the industrial site to extend a railway switch for the new passenger terminal.

21. The city pursued eminent domain over the waterfront parcel for the new pumping station for water supply.

22. The city condemned downtown service-business sites for developers to build new hotel and retail towers.

23. The state sought to condemn the refinery of a magnate who opposed the governor's renewable-energy agenda.

24. The village condemned a controversial massage parlor for a little-used recycling center.

Answers: 1P 2I 3C 4I 5P 6C 7I 8C 9P 10P 11I 12C 13C 14I 15I 16P 17P 18I 19C 20P 21P 22C 23I 24C

Factors Exercise on Eminent Domain

Whether the government has paid just compensation for land condemned under the exercise of eminent domain can depend on several factors including recent **price paid** for the land or legitimate **offers** for the land, prices paid for **comparable land**, **appraised value**, capitalized value of **income** from the land, value under **alternative use** other than as presently used, and **condition** of the land and buildings on it. For each scenario, choose a factor that would weigh heavily in favor or against the government's compensation, and analyze that factor by filling in the blanks.

1.   **In its exercise of eminent domain to construct a bus terminal, the city offered $500,000 as compensation for the crumbling old but occupiable mansion, the last selling price for which was $1.5 million five years earlier.**

The [*choose a factor*] favors the [*choose a party*] when [*state relevant facts*   ] because [*explain your reasoning*   ] .

2.   **The county offered $2 million for the farmland that it was condemning to build a new jail, where farmland in that area was selling at approximately twice that value for subdivision development.**

The [*choose a factor*] favors the [*choose a party*] when [*state relevant facts*   ] because [*explain your reasoning*   ] .

3.   **An investor demanded $25 million for lots that the investor had accumulated in the location of the rumored downtown stadium the state would help build through a public authority, when the investor had paid just $2.5 million for those lots within the prior two years.**

The [*choose a factor*] favors the [*choose a party*] when [*state relevant facts*   ] because [*explain your reasoning*   ] .

4.   **Appraisers for both sides set the condemned building's value between $5 million and $6 million, when the county had offered just $3 million in compensation in the course of condemnation proceedings to build a new road commission site.**

The [*choose a factor*] favors the [*choose a party*] when [*state relevant facts*   ] because [*explain your reasoning*   ] .

5.   **The state offered $800,000 for the farmland to complete the freeway loop around the city, after the farmer showed offers from other farmers between $750,000 and $850,000 for the land's use for farming.**

The [*choose a factor*] favors the [*choose a party*] when [*state relevant facts*   ] because [*explain your reasoning*   ] .

6.   **Although unattractive relative to other waterfront properties undergoing tourism and entertainment development, the scrap yard and port site earned its owner about three times in profit every five years as the city was offering for the site.**

The [*choose a factor*] favors the [*choose a party*] when [*state relevant facts*   ] because [*explain your reasoning*   ] .

Discrimination Exercise on Eminent Domain

Indicate whether each statement *overgeneralizes*, *undergeneralizes*, or *misconceives* the rule, explaining why. *Overgeneralizing* states the rule too broadly, capturing circumstances to which it does not apply. *Undergeneralizing* states the rule too narrowly, omitting circumstances to which it applies. *Misconceiving* states the rule incorrectly.

1. Eminent domain is when government offers to buy private property for public use.

____OVER/ ____UNDER/ ____MIS/ Why? _____

_____

2. The government's exercise of eminent domain must be for public access to public facilities and with just compensation.

____OVER/ ____UNDER/ ____MIS/ Why? _____

_____

3. Law construes a government zoning or land-use regulation that deprives a landowner of all economically viable use of the land, as if the government had exercised eminent domain, compensating for the cost of relocation.

____OVER/ ____UNDER/ ____MIS/ Why? _____

_____

4. Government may clearly take private property for public property like a street or park.

____OVER/ ____UNDER/ ____MIS/ Why? _____

_____

5. If government can articulate a legitimate public purpose to exercise eminent domain, such as to remove blight, correct unsanitary conditions, or provide housing or employment, then law permits condemnation even if conveyed to private entity for private use.

____OVER/ ____UNDER/ ____MIS/ Why? _____

_____

6. Government must pay fair market value, defined as what a willing buyer would pay a willing seller on the open market at the time of eminent domain's exercise, for the owner's current use.

____OVER/ ____UNDER/ ____MIS/ Why? _____

_____

Answers for Discrimination Exercise on Eminent Domain

1. The statement **MISconceives** the rule. Eminent domain is when government *condemns* private property, rather than offers to buy it, to acquire it for public use, on payment of just compensation as state and federal constitutions require.

2. The statement **UNDERgeneralizes** the rule. The government's exercise of eminent domain must be *for public use* and with just compensation, not just for public access to public facilities.

3. The statement **UNDERgeneralizes** the rule. Law construes a government zoning or land-use regulation that deprives a landowner of all economically viable use of the land, as if the government had exercised eminent domain, *compensating for the land's fair market value,* not just the cost of relocation.

4. The statement **UNDERgeneralizes** the rule. Government may clearly take private property for public property like a street or park *and for public-use functions like utilities and railways*.

5. The statement **OVERgeneralizes** the rule. If government can articulate a legitimate public purpose to exercise eminent domain, such as to remove blight, correct unsanitary conditions, or provide housing or employment, then *the U.S. Constitution* permits condemnation even if conveyed to private entity for private use, *but most states restrict eminent domain to public land or function*.

6. The statement **MISconceives** the rule. Government must pay fair market value, defined as what a willing buyer would pay a willing seller on the open market at the time of eminent domain's exercise, *for the land's highest and best use*, not for the owner's current use at condemnation.

Multiple-Choice Questions with Answer Explanations

33. The county that you represent retained the services of a master planner to locate a new county building housing courts and county offices. The master planner recommended using a centrally located, county-owned lot but acquiring neighboring privately owned lands to complete the new government complex. No other suitable properties are available. Several of the private landowners have banded together to refuse to sell to the county. If the county must build at that location, how may it best proceed?

A. Condemn the property under power of eminent domain, with no compensation.
B. Condemn the property under power of eminent domain, with just compensation.
C. So heavily limit by regulation as to deprive the owner of use, with just compensation.
D. Pay whatever price it takes even if substantially more than fair market value.

Answer explanation: Option B is correct because eminent domain is government power to condemn private property for public use with just compensation, permissible under state and federal constitutions. Eminent domain to take for use as public land, such as government offices, is a core exercise of eminent domain. Option A is incorrect because the exercise of eminent domain requires just compensation at fair market value. Option C is incorrect because in a regulatory taking, government does not attempt to acquire the property, but the landowner claims the regulation is so extensive as to deprive the landowner of use, known as *inverse condemnation*. This taking is intentional for public use, not regulatory. Option D is incorrect because the government may exercise eminent domain, paying only just compensation, which is fair market value. Here, landowners may hold out for far more than the county would have to pay as fair market value.

34. The elected council of the city whom you represent has charged its planning commission to investigate the use of eminent domain powers to advance the city's development. The planning commission has expressed an interest in having more public greenways, more privately operated public transportation such as light rail, better transit facilities for ride-hailing, limousine, and shuttle services, and less blight from vacant industrial, commercial, and residential buildings. The commission has turned to you for advice on the limits of eminent domain. How would you properly advise the commission as to eminent domain law under the U.S. Constitution and prevalent state constitutions?

A. Government may take land only for public use, not public function, with just compensation.
B. Government may take land only for public use, including public function, with just compensation.
C. Government may take land for public use or private use with public purpose, with just compensation.
D. Government may not take land for public use, public function, or public purpose.

Answer explanation: Option B is correct. The government's exercise of eminent domain must be only for public use and with just compensation, but public use includes public functions like utilities and railways. Option A is incorrect because public use includes public function. Option C is incorrect because although the U.S. Constitutions permits taking for public purpose, the prevalent state pattern is to limit takings to public use, not public purpose. Option D is incorrect because state and federal constitutions authorize eminent domain.

Week 12
Regulatory Takings

QUESTIONS FOR THE ASSIGNED READING:
Name something you do not understand about this week's material.

SHORT OUTLINE:
Government does not intend the property's acquisition in a *regulatory taking*, also known as *inverse condemnation*.
  The property owner claims that the government regulation so heavily limits as to deprive of use.
Locales adopting zoning typically *grandfather* **non-compliant** existing uses to avoid regulatory taking.
  State and federal constitutions require *just compensation* for government takings including *regulatory takings*.
Grandfather provisions may include forced phase-out of non-compliant uses when destroyed or abandoned.
  Forced phase-outs also restrict to *ten percent* the extent to which the owner may repair, improve, or expand.
    Suspect phase-outs give owners years within which to terminate, depreciating non-compliant-use value.
Landowners may challenge **ultra-vires** zoning laws that exceed the state enabling act's authority.

LONG OUTLINE:
Regulatory Taking
Eminent domain is purposeful exercise of government authority to acquire private property for public use. By contrast, government does not intend the property's acquisition in a *regulatory taking*, but law construes it as such for just compensation, when the government regulation so heavily limits use as to deny the landowner of the land's use. Regulatory takings are also known as *inverse condemnation* because the property owner rather than the government claims that the government action constitutes a taking. Government must pay fair market value, defined as what a willing buyer would pay a willing seller on the open market at the time of eminent domain's exercise, for the land's highest and best use. Law may also require payment of relocation expenses and attorney's fees.

When a locale adopts zoning that creates **non-compliant** existing uses, the laws typically *grandfather* those non-compliant uses to avoid a government **taking**. State and federal constitutions require *just compensation* for government takings including *regulatory takings*, which grandfathering avoids. Grandfather provisions, though, typically include forced phase-out of non-compliant uses. If the non-compliant owner discontinues the use, or fire or other cause destroys the non-compliant structure, then the owner loses the grandfathered right to continue the non-compliant use. Forced phase-outs also typically restrict to figures such as *ten percent* of value the extent to which the owner may repair, improve, or expand a non-compliant. Constitutionally suspect forced phase-outs require the owner to desist the non-compliant use after a period such as five years, giving the owner a period within which to depreciate the value. Landowners may challenge **ultra-vires** zoning laws that exceed the state enabling act's authority, such as if a zoning law failed to grandfather non-compliant structures or sought to impose monetary fines or other penalties that the state act did not authorize.

Fluency Cards

Cover and uncover the response to each prompt until you fluently recall the exact response.

Inverse condemnation

Regulation so heavily limits land use as to effectively deprive owner of its use.

Inverse condemnation tests

Physical intrusion or eliminating economically viable use.

Intrusion condemnation

Must be continuous, permanent, and more-than-minimally interfere.

Definitions Worksheet on Regulatory Takings

1.   What is inverse condemnation?

_____

_____

_____

2.   Who claims inverse condemnation?

_____

_____

_____

3.   Name two categorical tests for inverse condemnation.

_____

_____

_____

4.   How much of a government intrusion is necessary?

_____

_____

_____

5.   To what extent may government regulate to protect the public?

_____

_____

6.   What factors determine whether a regulation goes too far?

_____

_____

_____

7.   What remedies are available to address regulatory takings?

_____

_____

Answers for Definitions Worksheet on Regulatory Takings

1.   ***What is inverse condemnation?*** Inverse condemnation is a regulatory taking in which government does not intend to acquire private land but so heavily regulates it as to effectively deprive its owner of the land's use.

2.   ***Who claims inverse condemnation?*** Usually the government exercises eminent domain to condemn private land for public use, but with inverse condemnation, the landowner claims that the government effectively condemned the property by regulating it so heavily, while the government denies doing so.

3.   ***Name two categorical tests for inverse condemnation.*** If government physically intrudes and occupies the land, or if government deprives all economically viable use of the land, then government has condemned the property despite not intending to acquire it.

4.   ***How much of a government intrusion is necessary?*** A government occupation that is continuous, permanent, and more than minimally interferes is a taking, while temporary or transient intrusions depend on balancing interests.

5.   ***To what extent may government regulate to protect the public?*** Government may regulate against a nuisance without taking, even if reducing the land's value, but would have taken if reducing all economically viable use.

6.   ***What factors determine whether a regulation goes too far?*** Law considers diminution in land value, owner's investment-backed expectations, extent of public interest, nature of public interest, whether regulation abates a nuisance, character of invasion, extent of invasion, remedial treatment of landowner, and alternative economically viable uses.

7.   ***What remedies are available to address regulatory takings?*** Law may remedy a regulatory taking by imposing damages in the form of just compensation and authorizing an injunction against the regulation until amended.

Issue-Spotting Exercise

For each example, state whether the scenario describes a taking such that the government must provide just compensation. Also, state why or why not.

1. The city passed a regulation stating that emergency call boxes had to be installed within so many feet on every block in the downtown business district. Many locations were on private property.

_____

2. The state regulated undeveloped land adjacent to a large state park. The land can be developed for single family homes, but wildlife must be protected following certain guidelines.

_____

3. The regional development council legislated that any new development in industrial areas had to keep noise levels below certain decibel measurements.

_____

4. The city passed an ordinance prohibiting the building of any new permanent structures within a certain proximity to high school sports arenas.

_____

5. The national government passed legislation that any land within ten miles of the border had to remain undeveloped or, if already developed, no new development could begin. The owner has fifty acres of land, forty of which are within ten miles of the border.

_____

6. The state passed a law that birth-control traps for an invasive species of rodent must be in all places having at least twenty-five acres of woods, whether publicly or privately owned. The program will last one year.

_____

7. A developer owned a four-story building in the city. She planned to raze the building and put up a fifty-story building. The city passed an ordinance limiting new buildings to twenty-five stories.

_____

8. A developer applied for a permit to build a subdivision. The city granted the permit, provided the developer agreed to build sidewalks and bicycle paths throughout.

_____

Answers: 1Yes 2No 3No 4Probably yes 5No 6No 7Probably no 8Probably no

Comprehensiveness Exercise on Regulatory Takings

Insert words at the ^ mark for a more-accurate law statement. Follow the italicized hints. Answers are on the next page.

1.   Inverse condemnation is a ^ taking in which government ^ so heavily regulates it as to effectively take it from its owner. *[What kind of taking? With what intent?]*

2.   While eminent domain involves government condemning the land, with inverse condemnation the landowner claims that the government effectively condemned the property ^ . *[How far must regulation go to condemn?]*

3.   If government physically intrudes and occupies the land, ^ , then government has condemned the property despite not intending to acquire it. *[Can you name a second test?]*

4.   A government occupation that is continuous, permanent, ^ is a taking, while temporary or transient intrusions depend on balancing interests. *[How much interference is too much?]*

5.   Government may regulate against a nuisance without taking, even if reducing the land's value ^ . *[What's the limit to regulation, though?]*

6.   In determining whether regulation went so far as to take the property, law considers factors including diminution in land value, owner's investment-backed expectations, extent of public interest, nature of public interest, ^ ^ ^ ^ , and alternative economically viable uses. *[Can you name some other factors?]*

7.   Law may remedy a regulatory taking by imposing damages in the form of just compensation ^ . *[One other remedy?]*

Answers for Comprehensiveness Exercise on Regulatory Takings

1. Inverse condemnation is a *regulatory* taking in which government *does not intend to acquire private land but* so heavily regulates it as to effectively take it from its owner.

2. While eminent domain involves government condemning the land, with inverse condemnation the landowner claims that the government effectively condemned the property *by regulating it so heavily, while the government denies doing so*.

3. If government physically intrudes and occupies the land, *or if government deprives all economically viable use of the land*, then government has condemned the property despite not intending to acquire it.

4. A government occupation that is continuous, permanent, *and more than minimally interferes*, is a taking, while temporary or transient intrusions depend on balancing interests.

5. Government may regulate against a nuisance without taking, even if reducing the land's value, *but would have taken if reducing all economically viable use*.

6. In determining whether regulation went so far as to take the property, law considers factors including diminution in land value, owner's investment-backed expectations, extent of public interest, nature of public interest, *whether regulation abates a nuisance, character of invasion, extent of invasion, remedial treatment of landowner*, and alternative economically viable uses.

7. Law may remedy a regulatory taking by imposing damages in the form of just compensation *and authorizing an injunction against the regulation until amended*.

Application Exercise on Regulatory Takings

Sort the fact patterns into whether the government has clearly taken the land (T), has clearly not taken the land (N), or the question is a close call (C). Answers are below.

1. The city prohibited improvements of any type within 100 feet of the riverfront, affecting six riverfront lots.

2. The village prevented construction of more than three-story buildings in the historic downtown district.

3. The city imposed a five-year sunset/amortization period on a grandfathered auto-repair facility.

4. The county road commission ordered for sight lines that the corner lot owner not erect any vertical structure.

5. The state required abating exposed asbestos including removing structures where abatement was not possible.

6. The city authorized inspectors to enter residential lands where probable cause existed for a code violation.

7. The village's new storm system directed runoff across the owner's vacant lot, inundating it with every rain.

8. The state restricted landowners along the new highway from planting any tree or bush that limited sight lines.

9. The city required six building owners to permit a wifi service to install signal equipment on their lands.

10. The township required removal of waste piles dumped on private lands, including the farmer's old tire stack.

11. The city constructed a retaining wall for the new riverscape on the owner's back lot, dividing the lot.

12. A wetlands regulation as the township applied it prevented the suburban lot owner from using most of the lot.

13. The state used the farmer's fallow land along the freeway to dump concrete removed during freeway repairs.

14. When extending the municipal-airport runway, the city cleared the family's land of all buildings and trees.

15. The city permitted a cable company to run cables on existing utility poles already on private lands.

16. New storm-water regulations would require a landowner to build a retention area covering half the land.

17. The state limited wetlands development by prohibiting disturbance of wild plants typical to wetlands.

18. Renewable-energy mandates required existing homeowners to install city-approved equipment on roofs.

19. The township's new ordinance prohibiting disturbance of dune grass covered the owner's entire dune-grass lot.

20. The new historic-preservation law against increasing a structure's height, prevented building on the vacant lot.

21. The state prohibited fracking anywhere within the state's borders, including on private lands ideal for fracking.

22. The city ordered the demolition of any residential structure older than eighty years, including the old home.

23. The village required that the business owner permit street-repair crews to erect scaffolds on the owner's premises.

24. The township parked fire trucks on a homeowner's lands for twenty-four hours while dousing a neighbor's fire.

Answers: 1T 2N 3C 4T 5C 6N 7T 8N 9C 10N 11T 12C 13T 14T 15N 16C 17N 18C 19T 20T 21N 22T 23C 24N

Factors Exercise on Regulatory Takings

Whether a regulation constitutes a taking can depend on several factors including ***diminution in land value, owner's investment-backed expectations, extent of public interest, nature of public interest***, whether regulation ***abates a nuisance, character of invasion, extent of invasion, remedial treatment of landowner***, and ***alternative economically viable uses***. For each scenario, choose a factor that would weigh heavily in favor or against finding a covenant, and analyze that factor by filling in the blanks.

1. **After township health officials determined that the private landowner's dump constituted a public health and safety hazard, zoning officials ordered the dump closed.**

    The [*choose a factor*] favors the [*choose a party*] when [*state relevant facts*] because [*explain your reasoning*].

2. **The developer showed that the new height restrictions covering the downtown district reduced by ninety percent the capitalized value of rents that the developer's planned new office structure could earn.**

    The [*choose a factor*] favors the [*choose a party*] when [*state relevant facts*] because [*explain your reasoning*].

3. **In resolving that the homeowner must remove them, the city council acted on public outcry over the unsightly nature of the homeowner's outdoor sculptures, although the sculptures presented no health or safety risk.**

    The [*choose a factor*] favors the [*choose a party*] when [*state relevant facts*] because [*explain your reasoning*].

4. **Although the new historic-preservation scheme likely decreased significantly the value of lots and buildings within the district, the scheme offered development credits that largely offset the apparent decrease.**

    The [*choose a factor*] favors the [*choose a party*] when [*state relevant facts*] because [*explain your reasoning*].

5. **Although the owner had long used the site as a cement plant, the new ordinance prohibiting that use and requiring its sunset within five years did not prohibit converting the site to manufacturing, retail, or even multi-family residential, all of which appeared to offer equal or greater returns.**

    The [*choose a factor*] favors the [*choose a party*] when [*state relevant facts*] because [*explain your reasoning*].

6. **Officials had acted to close the business as arguably outside of the permitted use in that zone, on the complaint of only one citizen, while the business showed broad public support for the value of its services.**

    The [*choose a factor*] favors the [*choose a party*] when [*state relevant facts*] because [*explain your reasoning*].

Discrimination Exercise on Regulatory Takings

Indicate whether each statement *overgeneralizes*, *undergeneralizes*, or *misconceives* the rule, explaining why. *Overgeneralizing* states the rule too broadly, capturing circumstances to which it does not apply. *Undergeneralizing* states the rule too narrowly, omitting circumstances to which it applies. *Misconceiving* states the rule incorrectly.

1. Inverse condemnation is a regulatory taking in which government intends to acquire private land.

____OVER/ ____UNDER/ ____MIS/ Why? _____

_____

2. Usually the government exercises eminent domain to condemn private land for public use, but with inverse condemnation, the government claims that the government effectively condemned the property by regulating it so heavily, while the landowner denies so.

____OVER/ ____UNDER/ ____MIS/ Why? _____

_____

3. If government deprives all economically viable use of the land, then government has condemned the property despite not intending to acquire it.

____OVER/ ____UNDER/ ____MIS/ Why? _____

_____

4. A government occupation that is more than minimally interferes is a taking.

____OVER/ ____UNDER/ ____MIS/ Why? _____

_____

5. Government may regulate against a nuisance without taking, if not reducing the land's value, but would have taken if eliminating all economically viable use.

____OVER/ ____UNDER/ ____MIS/ Why? _____

_____

6. Law may remedy a regulatory taking by authorizing an injunction against the regulation until amended.

____OVER/ ____UNDER/ ____MIS/ Why? _____

_____

Answers for Discrimination Exercise on Regulatory Takings

1. The statement **MISconceives** the rule. Inverse condemnation is a regulatory taking in which government does *not* intend to acquire private land *but so heavily regulates it as to effectively take it from its owner*.

2. The statement **MISconceives** the rule. Usually the government exercises eminent domain to condemn private land for public use, but with inverse condemnation, the *landowner* claims that the government effectively condemned the property by regulating it so heavily, while the government *denies doing so*.

3. The statement **UNDERgeneralizes** the rule. If *government physically intrudes and occupies the land, or if* government deprives all economically viable use of the land, then government has condemned the property despite not intending to acquire it.

4. The statement **OVERgeneralizes** the rule. A government occupation that is *continuous, permanent, and* more than minimally interferes is a taking, *while temporary or transient intrusions depend on balancing interests*.

5. The statement **UNDERgeneralizes** the rule. Government may regulate against a nuisance without taking, *even if reducing the land's value,* but would have taken if eliminating all economically viable use.

6. The statement **UNDERgeneralizes** the rule. Law may remedy a regulatory taking by *imposing damages in the form of just compensation and* authorizing an injunction against the regulation until amended.

Multiple-Choice Questions with Answer Explanations

35. A landowner owned a vacant lot in a city district zoned commercial. The lot had previously held a commercial building used at different times for retail and services businesses, until the building's deterioration had required that the landowner demolish it. The landowner wished to rebuild for commercial use permissible within the zone, but the zoning's new setback, height, lot-size, and aesthetic restrictions effectively prevented any construction. Without zoning relief, the land must remain idle. If the city refuses any relief, then what is the landowner's best argument for relief in the form of just compensation?

A. Unreasonable seizure.
B. Condemnation by eminent domain.
C. Inverse condemnation by physical intrusion.
D. Inverse condemnation by regulatory taking.

Answer explanation: Option D is correct because inverse condemnation is a regulatory taking in which government does not intend to acquire private land but so heavily regulates it as to effectively deprive its owner of its use. Here, the regulation deprived the owner of effective use. Option A is incorrect because it refers to a Fourth and Fourteenth Amendment personal right, not a property-protection right protected by federal and state takings clauses. Option B is incorrect because although the government has the positive power of eminent domain, which is to take private property for public use with just compensation, here the government did not seek to acquire the landowner's property. Option C is incorrect because although government's physical intrusion onto land is one test for inverse condemnation, here the government did not physically intrude.

36. A landowner owned industrial land next to a county road-commission facility. The county facility needed to expand its vehicle-maintenance garage, and so the county dug footings to extend the garage onto the landowner's adjacent land. The county construction cut off the landowner's driveway to the back of the land where the landowner stored industrial equipment. The landowner protested the construction and, when the county ignored the protests, sought counsel as to a takings claim. What is the best evaluation of the landowner's takings claim?

A. The intrusion is not a taking because it is continuous, permanent, and more than minimally interfering.
B. The intrusion is a taking because it is temporary, transient, and only minimally interfering.
C. The intrusion is a taking because continuous, permanent, and more than minimally interfering.
D. The intrusion is a taking because temporary, transient, and only minimally interfering.

Answer explanation: Option C is correct because a government occupation that is continuous, permanent, and more than minimally interferes is a taking, while temporary or transient intrusions depend on balancing interests. Construction of a garage on underground footings indicates continuous, permanent intrusion, while cutting off a driveway to equipment indicates a more-than-minimal interference. Option A is incorrect because a continuous, permanent, and more-than-minimally interfering intrusion would constitute a taking. Option B is incorrect because although temporary, transient, minimally interfering intrusions are not takings, here, the intrusion was continuous, permanent, and more than minimally interfering. Option D is incorrect because a temporary, transient intrusion that only minimally interferes would not constitute a taking.

Week 13
Other Takings Issues

QUESTIONS FOR THE ASSIGNED READING:
Name something you do not understand about this week's material.

SHORT OUTLINE:
The takings clause requires government to pay just compensation for depriving others of their *personal property*.
Requiring cash or personal-property contributions as a condition for engaging in commerce is a taking.
Different branches of government take real or personal property different ways.
Legislatures take property by acquisition, intrusion, or legislating away all viable use.
Administrators take by condemning, intruding, or regulating away viable use.
An **exaction** requires a landowner to pay money, give land, or provide services in exchange for project approval.
Government does not take if in rough proportion between the exaction and development.
Government may require payment for new roads and utility lines, and to grant easements.
Government may not require substantial monies paid into the general fund, unrelated to the development.

LONG OUTLINE:
Other Takings
The takings clause requires government to pay just compensation for depriving others of their *personal property,* as well as real property. When government requires a person to relinquish personal property, even when as a condition for engaging in commerce, the government has taken the property and must pay just compensation. Different branches of government take real or personal property different ways. The legislative branch takes property, requiring just compensation, when its legislation acquires property, compels government intrusion, or deprives owners of all economically viable use. The administrative branch commits a taking by condemning, intruding, or regulating away economically viable use. In theory, a change in the common law that deprived an owner of property rights could constitute a judicial taking, under scant authority.

Exactions
An exaction requires a landowner to pay money, provide land, or provide for services in exchange for government approval of development. Government does not commit a taking if a roughly proportional connection exists between the exaction and the development. Government may, for instance, require developers to pay for new road entrances and utility lines, and to grant easements, to facilitate the development. Government would not be able to require developers to pay substantial monies into the general fund, unrelated to the development.

Fluency Cards

Cover and uncover the response to each prompt until you fluently recall the exact response.

Exaction	**Exaction limits**
Government requiring landowner to pay government for development.	Exaction and development must be roughly proportional.

Definitions Worksheet on Other Takings Issues

1. Does the takings clause protect personal property, too?

_____

_____

_____

2. What is the test for a personal-property taking?

_____

_____

_____

3. How does the legislative branch take property?

_____

_____

_____

4. How does the administrative branch take property?

_____

_____

_____

5. Can the judicial branch commit a taking?

_____

_____

6. What is an exaction?

_____

_____

7. When is an exaction lawful?

_____

_____

Answers for Definitions Worksheet on Other Takings Issues

1. ***Does the takings clause protect personal property, too?*** The takings clause requires government to pay just compensation for depriving others of their personal property, as well as real property.

2. ***What is the test for a personal-property taking?*** When government requires a person to relinquish personal property, even when as a condition for engaging in commerce, the government has taken the property and must pay just compensation.

3. ***How does the legislative branch take property?*** The legislative branch takes property, requiring just compensation, when its legislation acquires property, compels government intrusion, or deprives owners of all economically viable use.

4. ***How does the administrative branch take property?*** The administrative branch commits a taking by condemning, intruding, or regulating away economically viable use.

5. ***Can the judicial branch commit a taking?*** In theory, a change in the common law that deprived an owner of property rights could constitute a taking, under scant authority.

6. ***What is an exaction?*** An exaction requires a landowner to pay money, provide land, or provide for services in exchange for government approval of development.

7. ***When is an exaction lawful?*** Government does not commit a taking if a roughly proportional connection exists between the exaction and the development.

Comprehensiveness Exercise on Other Takings Issues

Insert words at the ^ mark for a more-accurate law statement. Follow the italicized hints. Answers are on the next page.

1. The takings clause requires government to pay just compensation for depriving others of their ^ real property. *[Just real property?]*

2. When government requires a person to relinquish personal property, ^ the government has taken the property ^ . *[Even as a condition for something? What's the consequence of a taking?]*

3. The legislative branch takes, property requiring just compensation, when its legislation acquires property ^ or deprives owners of all economically viable use. *[Can you think of another way?]*

4. The administrative branch commits a taking by condemning or intruding ^ . *[Can you think of a third way?]*

5. A change in the common law that deprived an owner of property rights could constitute a taking ^ . *[How strong is the authority for this theory?]*

6. An exaction requires a landowner to pay money ^ ^ in exchange for government approval of development. *[Two other forms of exaction?]*

7. Government does not commit a taking if a ^ connection exists between the exaction and the development. *[What kind of connection?]*

Answers for Comprehensiveness Exercise on Takings Issues

1. The takings clause requires government to pay just compensation for depriving others of their ***personal property, as well as*** real property.

2. When government requires a person to relinquish personal property, ***even when as a condition for engaging in commerce,*** the government has taken the property ***and must pay just compensation***.

3. The legislative branch takes property, requiring just compensation, when its legislation acquires property, ***compels government intrusion,*** or deprives owners of all economically viable use.

4. The administrative branch commits a taking by condemning, intruding, ***or regulating away economically viable use***.

5. ***In theory***, a change in the common law that deprived an owner of property rights could constitute a taking, ***under scant authority***.

6. An exaction requires a landowner to pay money, ***provide land, or provide for services*** in exchange for government approval of development.

7. Government does not commit a taking if a ***roughly proportional*** connection exists between the exaction and the development.

Application Exercise on Other Takings Issues

Sort the fact patterns into whether the taking is of personal property (P) or real property (R). Answers are below.

1. The city condemned a portion of the property at the intersection to expand the intersection for a left-turn lane.

2. The township commandeered the company's trucks and equipment to deploy in the flood emergency.

3. The state condemned the dairyman's entire herd, although healthy, to avoid the mad-cow-disease risk.

4. The village exercised eminent domain over the dilapidated residence for a public park and fountain.

5. The state took a hundred of the farmer's straw bales, thirty pallets, and two-hundred cinder blocks in the storm.

6. The city required that the office tower's owner relinquish the tower's first floor for city social services.

7. The state's wetland regulations kept the lot owner from making any use whatsoever of the lot.

8. State environmental officials interpreted the regulations to require that the farmer donate the entire crop.

Answers: 1R 2P 3P 4R 5P 6R 7R 8P

Sort the fact patterns into whether the taking is by the legislative (L), executive (E), or judicial (J) branch. Answers are below.

1. The township council resolved to acquire the corner parcel for a new fire station and recycling center.

2. The village building inspector ruled that the lot was too small for any structure to meet regulations.

3. The county commission went forward with the proposal to fund a new jail at the old plant's shuttered site.

4. The fire department destroyed the vacant but livable and valuable private home in their training exercise.

5. The mayor ordered the artist's outdoor sculptures confiscated and destroyed to promote the area as clean.

6. The city council amended the zoning ordinance to shutter the chemical plant immediately as nonconforming.

7. Reversing precedent, the appellate court held that common law granted the state the entire farm and its livestock.

8. The village board decided that the area was attracting tourists and so changed the zoning to close a tannery.

Answers: 1L 2E 3L 4E 5E 6L 7J 8L

Sort the fact patterns into whether the exaction is probably a taking (T) or not (N). Answers are below.

1. The county demanded the developer hand over the entire shoreline in exchange for any development.

2. The city required the homeowners to hook up to the new sewer line when renovating their home.

3. The township required the rancher to pay $100,000 for permission to build a new barn and corrals.

4. The state required the stadium developers to pay for police services in the surrounding neighborhoods.

5. The city required the apartment-complex developer to pay for installation of new streetlights at the complex.

Answers: 1T 2N 3T 4T 5N 5N 7T 8N

Factors Exercise on Other Takings Issues

Whether an exaction constitutes a taking can depend on several factors including the **closeness of the connection** between the exaction and development, the **proportionality** of the exaction to the development, the **nature of the exaction**, the **nature of the development**, the **uniformity** of the exaction across developments, **benefit to the public** from the exaction, and whether the exaction **frustrates development**. For each scenario, choose a factor that would weigh heavily in favor or against finding a covenant, and analyze that factor by filling in the blanks.

1.   The city required the subdivision developer to pay for the city to install a traffic light and create right-and-left turn lanes into the development, to accommodate the traffic to the development's two-hundred residences.

The [_choose a factor_] favors the [_choose a party_] when [_state relevant facts_] because [_explain your reasoning_] .

2.   The county required the ocean-front property owner to construct and maintain stairs down the bluff to the beach for public access, as a condition of approving the owner's request to reserve a street parking spot in front of the property for handicapped parking.

The [_choose a factor_] favors the [_choose a party_] when [_state relevant facts_] because [_explain your reasoning_] .

3.   The village required the vacant lot owner to pay for antique street lamps in front of the retail space that the owner proposed, like the street lamps that the village had required other retail-store owners to install throughout the shopping district.

The [_choose a factor_] favors the [_choose a party_] when [_state relevant facts_] because [_explain your reasoning_] .

4.   The township demanded that the lakefront property owner pay a $50,000 development fee to construct any structure on the vacant lakefront lot, in addition to paying for any necessary township services.

The [_choose a factor_] favors the [_choose a party_] when [_state relevant facts_] because [_explain your reasoning_] .

5.   The investors balked at relinquishing one third of the urban development's land to the city for public facilities of the city's design and choice because the significant reduction in the project's footprint meant that the project would not be able to produce a reasonable return on investment.

The [_choose a factor_] favors the [_choose a party_] when [_state relevant facts_] because [_explain your reasoning_] .

6.   The county required that the farmer grant a perpetual conservation easement across half the farmland in exchange for permission to construct a second residence on the land for the farmer's daughter.

The [_choose a factor_] favors the [_choose a party_] when [_state relevant facts_] because [_explain your reasoning_] .

189

Discrimination Exercise on Other Takings Issues

Indicate whether each statement *overgeneralizes*, *undergeneralizes*, or *misconceives* the rule, explaining why. *Overgeneralizing* states the rule too broadly, *undergeneralizing* too narrowly, and *misconceiving* incorrectly.

1. The takings clause requires government to pay just compensation for depriving others of their real property.

____OVER/ ____UNDER/ ____MIS/ Why? _____

_____

2. When government requires a person to relinquish personal property, the government has taken the property and must pay just compensation.

____OVER/ ____UNDER/ ____MIS/ Why? _____

_____

3. The legislative branch takes property, requiring just compensation, when its legislation acquires property or compels government intrusion.

____OVER/ ____UNDER/ ____MIS/ Why? _____

_____

4. The administrative branch cannot commit a taking, only the legislative branch.

____OVER/ ____UNDER/ ____MIS/ Why? _____

_____

5. The judicial branch cannot commit a taking.

____OVER/ ____UNDER/ ____MIS/ Why? _____

_____

6. An exaction requires a landowner to pay in exchange for government approval of development.

____OVER/ ____UNDER/ ____MIS/ Why? _____

_____

7. Government does not commit a taking if a connection exists between an exaction and development.

____OVER/ ____UNDER/ ____MIS/ Why? _____

_____

Answers for Discrimination Exercise on Other Takings Issues

1. The statement **UNDERgeneralizes** the rule. The takings clause requires government to pay just compensation for depriving others of their real *or personal* property.

2. The statement **UNDERgeneralizes** the rule. When government requires a person to relinquish personal property, *even as a condition for engaging in commerce,* the government has taken the property and must pay just compensation.

3. The statement **UNDERgeneralizes** the rule. The legislative branch takes property, requiring just compensation, when its legislation acquires property, compels government intrusion, *or deprives owners of all economically viable use*.

4. The statement **MISconceives** the rule. The administrative branch *commits a taking by condemning, intruding, or regulating away economically viable use*.

5. The statement **MISconceives** the rule. *Although scant authority for it exists, in theory, a change in the common law that deprived an owner of property rights could theoretically constitute a taking*.

6. The statement **UNDERgeneralizes** the rule. An exaction requires a landowner to pay, *provide land, or provide for services* in exchange for government approval of development.

7. The statement **OVERgeneralizes** the rule. Government does not commit a taking if a *roughly proportional* connection exists between the exaction and the development.

Multiple-Choice Questions with Answer Explanations

37. A city suffered a mass shooting incident in which the perpetrators used assault-style weaponry. In response, the city council considered enacting an ordinance requiring owners of assault-style guns and similar weaponry to turn it in to law-enforcement officials for destruction. Setting aside the question of the proposed ordinance's constitutionality under the Second Amendment's right to bear arms, what other constitutional hurdle would the ordinance most-likely face?

A. A taking requiring just compensation.
B. A seizure requiring probable cause.
C. An undue burden on the right of association.
D. An interference with interstate commerce.

Answer explanation: Option A is correct because the takings clause requires government to pay just compensation for depriving others not only of real property but also of personal property. Option B is incorrect because Fourth Amendment rights against unreasonable search and seizure protect personal privacy and liberty, not personal-property rights. Option C is incorrect because the First Amendment right of association protects liberty and expression, not personal-property rights. Option D is incorrect because local confiscation of certain weaponry does not likely interfere with Congress's exclusive right to regulate interstate commerce.

38. A developer purchased forty acres of vacant land along a busy township highway, to develop for single-family residences. The township had already zoned the land for the developer's planned use. The developer then applied to the township for site-plan approval and building permits. In the approval process, the township indicated to the developer that it would approve the plan only if the developer contributed a strip of land along the highway for a highway turn lane and paid half the cost of both widening the highway for safe entrance to the development and extending larger water and sewer lines to the property to facilitate the development. If the developer challenges those requirements, what is the most-likely outcome?

A. Prohibit as an unconstitutional taking.
B. Prohibit as an interference with interstate commerce.
C. Permit as a health-and-welfare regulation.
D. Permit as a roughly proportional exaction.

Answer explanation: Option D is correct because an exaction may require a landowner to pay money, provide land, or provide for services in exchange for government approval of development, if roughly proportional to the development. Here, the township's requirements related directly to the cost of access to the development and its benefit. Option A is incorrect because government may requirement payments and land contributions roughly proportional to landowner development without them being a taking. Option B is incorrect because a local exaction for development does not unduly interfere with Congress's exclusive right to regulate interstate commerce. Option C is incorrect because although local government may enact health-and-welfare regulations, an exaction related to land development is not a health-and-welfare regulation.

Core Concepts

Below are the core concepts for this course. Be sure in your studies and outlining that you can recall the definitions and applications for each of the concepts below. Use your fluency cards, class notes, prior outlines, class exercises, video reviews, reading notes, and multiple-choice answers to hone your use of these concepts.

Types of Tenancies
Term of Years [define]
Period Tenancy [define]
Tenancy at Will [define]
Tenancy at Sufferance [define]
American Rule [define]
English Rule [define]

Discrimination in Landlord/Tenant Relationships
Federal Fair Housing Act [define]
14th Amendment [define]
Civil Rights Act [define]

When Tenant Breaches
Surrender [define]
Abandonment [define]

When Landlord Breaches
Quiet Enjoyment [define]
Implied Warranty of Habitability [define]
Retaliatory Eviction [define]
Constructive Eviction [define]

Assignment & Sublease
Assignment [define]
Sublease [define]
Privity of contract [define]
Privity of estate [define]
Permission [define]

Nuisance
Nuisance [define]
Unreasonable [define]
Intentional [define]
Threshold Test [define]
Balancing Test [define]
Utilitarian Test [define]

Servitudes
Dominant estate [define]
Servient estate [define]

License [define]
Actual notice [define]
Constructive notice [define]
Inquiry notice [define]
Imputed notice [define]

Easements
Easement [define]
Scope [define]
Assignment [define]
Express easement [define]
Implied easement [define]
Prior use [define]
Necessity [define]
Appurtenant easement [define]
In gross easement [define]
Negative easement [define]
Easement by prescription [define]
Easement by estoppel [define]
Termination [define each way]
What is the remedy?

Covenants & Equitable Servitudes
Real covenant [define]
Equitable servitude [define]
How are real covenant and equitable servitude the same and how are they different? [define]
Implied reciprocal servitude [define]
Termination [define each way]
What is the remedy?
Horizontal privity [define]
Vertical privity [define]
Touch & concern the land [define]
Intend to bind successors [define]
In writing [define]
Notice [define]
Burden runs with the land [define]
Benefit runs with the land [define]

Zoning
Euclidean Zoning [define]
Model Zoning Act [discuss structure and separation fo powers issues]
Police power [define]
Rational Relationship Test [define]
Amortization [define]
Non-conforming use [define]
Variance [define]
Unnecessary hardship [define]
Substantial justice [define]
Aesthetic Zoning [define]

Exclusionary Zoning Issues [define]
Vested rights [define]
Strict scrutiny [define and identify when to use]
Intermediate scrutiny [define and identify when to use]

Eminent Domain & Takings
Eminent domain [define]
Regulatory taking [define]
Public Purpose Test [define]
Fair market value [define]
Inverse condemnation [define]
Implicit taking [define]
Categorical Tests x2 [define]
Mahon Factors [define]
Conceptual severance [define]
Penn Central Factors [define]
Hadacheck Test [define]
Exaction [define]

Multistate Bar Examination Property-Law Topics Table

Here is the Multistate Bar Examination's topics table for real-property topics, keyed to the questions that follow for Property II topics. The struck-through topics are within the Property I course description, not addressed in Property II:

Real Property

NOTE: Approximately one-fifth of the Real Property questions on the MBE will be based on each of the categories I through V.

I. **Ownership**
   ~~A. Present estates~~
      ~~1. Fees simple~~
      ~~2. Defeasible fees simple~~
      ~~3. Life estates~~
   ~~B. Future interests~~
      ~~1. Reversions~~
      ~~2. Remainders, vested and contingent~~
      ~~3. Executory interests~~
      ~~4. Possibilities of reverter, powers of termination~~
      ~~5. Rules affecting these interests~~
   ~~C. Co-tenancy~~
      ~~1. Types~~
         ~~a. Tenancy in common~~
         ~~b. Joint tenancy~~
      ~~2. Severance~~
      ~~3. Partition~~
      ~~4. Relations among cotenants~~
      ~~5. Alienability, descendibility, devisability~~
   D. The law of landlord and tenant
      1. Types of holdings[1,5,632]: creation[1,5,8] and termination[1,5,7]
         a. Terms for years[1,5,8]
         b. Tenancies at will[1,8]
         c. Holdovers[1,5,7] and other tenancies at sufferance[1,5,8]
         d. Periodic tenancies[1,5,8]
      2. Possession[1,7] and rent[5,8]
      3. Assignment[4] and subletting[4,6]
      4. Termination (surrender,[7,8] mitigation of damages,[9] and anticipatory breach[9])
      5. Habitability[10,9] and suitability[10,9]
   ~~E. Special problems~~
      ~~1. Rule Against Perpetuities: common law and as modified~~
      ~~2. Alienability, descendibility, and devisability~~
      ~~3. Fair housing/discrimination~~
II. **Rights in land**[626]
   A. Covenants at law[24,18] and in equity[25,26]
      1. Nature[24,18] and type[24,25,26]
      2. Creation[24,25,26]
      3. Scope[27,18]
      4. Termination[24,25,26]

B. Easements,[14,16,22] profits,[17,20] and licenses[13,21]
    1. Nature and type[16,17]
    2. Methods of creation[23,16,17]
        a. Express[15,17]
        b. Implied[16,22,28]
            i. Quasi-use[16,19]
            ii. Necessity[22,19]
            iii. Plat[25,28]
        c. Prescription[14,15]
    3. Scope[14,17]
    4. Termination[13,17]
C. Fixtures[604,646] (including relevant application of Article 9, UCC[604])
D. Zoning (fundamentals other than regulatory taking)[31,28]

III. ~~Contracts~~
    ~~A. Real estate brokerag~~
    ~~B. Creation and construction~~
        ~~1. Statute of frauds and exceptions~~
        ~~2. Essential terms~~
        ~~3. Time for performance~~
        ~~4. Remedies for breach~~
    ~~C. Marketability of title~~
    ~~D. Equitable conversion (including risk of loss)~~
    ~~E. Options and rights of first refusal~~
    ~~F. Fitness and suitability~~
    ~~G. Merger~~

IV. ~~Mortgages/security devices~~
    ~~A. Types of security devices~~
        ~~1. Mortgages (including deeds of trust)~~
            ~~a. In general~~
            ~~b. Purchase-money mortgages~~
            ~~c. Future-advance mortgages~~
        ~~2. Land contracts~~
        ~~3. Absolute deeds as security~~
    ~~B. Some security relationships~~
        ~~1. Necessity and nature of obligation~~
        ~~2. Theories: title, lien, and intermediate~~
        ~~3. Rights and duties prior to foreclosure~~
        ~~4. Right to redeem and clogging equity of redemption~~
    ~~C. Transfers by mortgagor~~
        ~~1. Distinguishing "subject to" and "assuming"~~
        ~~2. Rights and obligations of transferor~~
        ~~3. Application of subrogation and suretyship principles~~
        ~~4. Due-on-sale clauses~~
    ~~D. Transfers by mortgagee~~
    ~~E. Payment, discharges, and defenses~~
    ~~F. Foreclosure~~
        ~~1. Types~~
        ~~2. Rights of omitted parties~~
        ~~3. Deficiency and surplus~~

4. Redemption after foreclosure
5. Deed in lieu of foreclosure
V. **Titles**
A. Adverse possession
B. Transfer by deed
1. Warranty and non-warranty deeds (including covenants for title)
2. Necessity for a grantee and other deed requirements
3. Delivery (including escrows)
C. Transfer by operation of law and by will
1. In general
2. Ademption
3. Exoneration
4. Lapse
5. Abatement
D. Title assurance systems
1. Recording acts (race, notice, and race-notice)
a. Indexes
b. Chain of title
c. Protected parties
d. Priorities
e. Notice
2. Title insurance
E. Special problems
1. After-acquired title (including estoppel by deed)
2. Forged instruments and undelivered deeds
3. Purchase-money mortgages
4. Judgment and tax liens

All Multiple-Choice Questions with Answer Explanations

1.   A senior-living complex owner agreed to allow a new tenant to occupy one of the complex's units only until the complex owner completed a new wing of units then under construction, when the tenant would have to move into the new wing. The owner completed construction of the new wing but allowed the tenant to remain in her current unit without any communication to her of the construction's completion or new terms. What interest has the tenant held?

A.   A leasehold term of years followed now by a tenancy at will.
B.   A leasehold periodic tenancy followed now by a tenancy at sufferance.
C.   A defeasible fee terminable on the completion of construction.
D.   A life estate also conditioned on completion of construction.

Answer explanation: Option A is correct because the owner and circumstances plainly enough indicated intent to retain ownership while offering only a leasehold interest. A leasehold or non-freehold estate, constituting a right to control property owned by another, comes in the form of a term of years, periodic tenancy, or tenancy at will including a tenancy at sufferance. A term of years lasts for a specific period of time, not necessarily years but any period that the parties can calculate with certainty, such as here the completion of current construction. A tenancy at will is one that either party may terminate at any time for any reason, as here the tenant may leave or the owner move the tenant to the new wing at any time. Option B is incorrect because while a periodic tenancy lasts from period to period without having any definite duration longer than one period, here the initial leasehold had no specific period and so was not a periodic tenancy. Moreover, while a tenancy at sufferance, which is a form of tenancy at will, involves the tenant wrongfully overstaying before the landlord decides whether to hold the tenant over for a new term or to evict, here the tenant has not wrongfully overstayed, not yet having any notice of completion or request to move. Options C and D are incorrect because both suggest ownership rather than leasehold interests, when the owner and circumstances clearly enough indicate only intent to lease.

2.   Ralph, a third-generation American of Italian and Greek descent saw an ad for an apartment online. Ralph has dark, olive-colored skin. He e-mailed the landlord and asked to see the apartment. When he arrived, the landlord appeared taken aback and said to him, "What are you, a Muslim?" Ralph murmured "Why does it matter?" The landlord said, "I'm sorry, but something has come up and I am no longer able to rent the unit." Ralph went home. The next week, he discovered that a friend of his, Jenny Jones, a very light-skinned Muslim-American woman, had rented the unit. When he expressed surprise, Jenny said, "That landlord is kind of weird. The first thing he said to me was, "At least you're not a Muslim. I really liked the place so I didn't let him know he was wrong." Which is Ralph's strongest claim?

A.   A claim under the 14th Amendment to the U.S. Constitution.
B.   A claim under 42 U.S.C. § 1982.
C.   Ralph has no valid claim because he was a White person and not a Muslim.
D.   A claim under the Fair Housing Act.

Answer explanation: Option D. The Fair Housing Act prohibits discrimination in rental based on color, ethnicity, and religion, including based on perceived rather than actual characteristics. Even if the landlord was incorrect about Ralph's religion or ethnicity, basing his decision on that perception is discrimination. Also, Ralph's dark skin may have made the landlord think he was Muslim. Option A is incorrect because the 14th Amendment protects only against state action (government actors), and this matter involves a private landlord.

Option B is not the best answer because although the federal statute provides that all citizens have the same right to enjoy property as White citizens, it is unclear whether an Italian-Greek American would be considered non-white, even though Ralph's dark skin was likely a contributing factor to the denial of housing. The Fair Housing Act's inclusion of ethnicity, race, color, and religion make it a stronger claim. Option C is incorrect because the landlord's perception that the applicant is of a certain protected class is enough.

3.   Linda rented a commercial building to Terry for a term of years, ten years in length. After two years, Terry's business was suffering, and so he reached an agreement with Dennis where Dennis agreed to take over all of Terry's interests in the building for the duration of the lease. In that agreement, Dennis promised to assume all obligations under Terry's lease with Linda. After two more years passed, Dennis needed to take a medical leave of absence from his business and so entered an agreement with Joyce where Joyce would rent the entire premises for one year; at the end of the year, Dennis would resume possession. What best describes the relationship between Linda and each of the other parties?

A.   Privity of contract and privity of estate with both Terry and Dennis but not with Joyce.
B.   Privity of contract and privity of estate with Dennis but not with Terry or Joyce.
C.   Privity of contract with Terry and privity of contract and estate with Dennis but not with Joyce.
D.   Privity of contract with Terry and privity of estate with Dennis but not with Joyce.

Answer explanation: Option A. A lease of the full premises conveys privity of contract and estate. When Linda entered into the lease with Terry, she had privity of estate and privity of contract with Terry. A tenant's assignment of the full premises benefitting the landlord conveys privity of contract and estate. Terry's arrangement with Dennis was an assignment (Terry retained no current possessory interest nor any reversionary interest) benefitting Linda (when Dennis agreed to assume all lease obligations), so Terry remained in privity with Linda, but Dennis was now in privity of contract and estate with Linda. A conveyance of less than the full lease term is a sublease, not an assignment, creating neither privity of contract nor estate with the landlord. The agreement between Dennis and Joyce did not convey the full term and so is a sub-lease. Thus, Linda is neither in privity of contract or privity of estate with Joyce. Option B is incorrect because Linda retains privity with Terry. Option C is incorrect because Linda retains privity of estate with Terry. Option D is incorrect because Linda retains privity of estate with Terry and privity of contract with Dennis.

4.   A property owner leased an artist's studio to a sculptor for three years at $1,000 per month rent. The lease permitted sublease or assignment. After one year of paying the property owner rent, the sculptor subleased the studio to a painter for one year at the same rent. However, the painter moved out after six months without having paid any rent. When the sublease expired, the sculptor moved back in for the final year of the three-year lease but paid no rent. Who owes the property owner how much in rent?

A.   The sculptor owes $12,000 and the painter owes $12,000.
B.   The sculptor owes $18,000 and the painter owes $6,000.
C.   The sculptor owes the property owner $24,000 in rent.
D.   The sculptor owes the property owner $12,000 in rent.

Answer explanation: Option C is correct because a sublease is the lease of less than all of the property or for less than the full term, while an assignment is a lease of the entire property for the entire term. A sublease of less than the entire tenancy leaves only the tenant and not the subtenant liable to the property owner, while an assignment would make both tenant and subtenant liable unless the owner discharges the tenant. Here, the tenant remained liable for the last two unpaid years of rent. The subtenant would be liable only to the sculptor and only for the one unpaid year of rent. Option A is incorrect because the sculptor would owe both years of unpaid rent, not just the last year, and the subtenant would owe only the tenant, not the property owner. Option B is incorrect because the sculptor owes for the two full unpaid years, and the painter owes only the tenant and would owe $12,000, not $6,000. Option D is incorrect because the sculptor also owes for the unpaid sublet year, although the sculptor would have an action against the subtenant for that year.

5. A company sent a painting crew to paint a bridge, giving crew members housing stipends to find their own accommodations over the six- to nine-month expected duration of the project. One painter negotiated with a local homeowner to rent a carriage house above a detached garage. The painter and homeowner agreed in a signed writing that the painter was on a month-to-month lease with rent due in advance on the first day of the month. The painter paid timely on or before the first day of each month for the first seven months until the project looked near completion. The painter did not pay on the first day of the eighth month. The homeowner could tell that the bridge was nearly painted and suspected that the painter was going to stiff the homeowner for the last month's rent. What interest does the painter hold, giving the homeowner what if any recourse?

A. Periodic month-to-month tenancy, giving the homeowner only the right of suing for the month-eight rent but not to evict.
B. Tenancy at sufferance, giving the homeowner the option of holding the painter to another month's rent or evicting the painter.
C. Term of years for a total of nine months, giving the homeowner the right to sue for rent through the eighth and ninth months.
D. No interest, giving the homeowner the right to change the locks or otherwise take self-help to prevent the painter's trespass.

Answer explanation: Option B is correct because a tenancy at sufferance, which is a form of tenancy at will, involves the tenant wrongfully overstaying beyond the lease term, before the landlord decides whether to hold the tenant over for a new term equal to the original lease term (but no longer than one year and possibly shorter by statute) or to evict, which are the landlord's options. By failing to pay rent, the painter has breached the lease and is wrongfully overstaying, giving the landlord the right to evict or hold the painter to the full month even if the painter leaves before the month's end. Option A is incorrect because the periodic tenancy ended when the painter failed to pay rent and wrongfully overstayed, creating a tenancy at sufferance. Option C is incorrect because while the parties may have discussed that the painter would want to stay for as long as nine months (the expected longest duration of the project), they contracted instead for a month-to-month lease. If the homeowner wants to treat the painter as a holdover, then the holdover period would be another month (the periodic tenancy), not nine months. Option D is incorrect because landlord-tenant law discourages self-help and instead treats the wrongful holdover as a tenant at sufferance whom the owner can hold to another periodic term or file suit to evict.

6. A strip-mall owner leased storefront space to a discount shoe store for a four-year term. After two years, the discount shoe store, which wasn't making enough income to support the lease, subleased to a used sporting-goods reseller for the remaining two-year duration of the original lease. The sporting-goods reseller then made the shoe store's lease payments to the mall owner. After one year of subleasing, the sporting-goods reseller complained to the mall owner that the mall's sidewalks littered were and trash cans full, in insubstantial breach of the shoe store's original lease for clean premises. When the mall owner did nothing, the sporting-goods reseller quit the premises, leaving the storefront vacant for the last year of the four-year lease and two-year sublease. Who owes what obligations?

A.   The owner owes neither the shoe store nor the sporting-goods store clean premises, while neither store owes the owner rent.
B.   The owner owes both the shoe store and sporting-goods store clean premises, while both stores owe the owner rent.
C.   The owner owes only the shoe store clean premises, while only the shoe store owes the owner the last year's rent.
D.   The owner owes only the sporting-goods store clean premises, while only the sporting-goods store owes the owner the last year's rent.

Answer explanation: Option C is correct because a sublease is the lease of less than all of the property or for less than the full term, while an assignment is a lease of the entire property for the entire term. A sublease of less than the entire tenancy leaves only the tenant and not the subtenant liable to the owner, while an assignment would make both tenant and subtenant liable unless the owner discharges the tenant. While a tenant can enforce the owner's obligations, a subtenant on a sublease cannot. Option A is incorrect because the owner would owe the shoe store the lease obligation of clean premises, while the shoe store would owe the lease rent. Option B is incorrect because the owner owes the sporting-goods store no performance because not in privity of contract or estate, while only the shoe store owes the owner rent because the sporting-goods store has no contract with the owner. Option D is incorrect because the sporting-goods store only has a sublease with the shoe store, owing only the shoe store rent. Only the shoe store has a lease with the owner on which the shoe store owes rent. The reverse is also true that the owner owes the sporting-goods store nothing because the owner has no privity of contract or privity of estate with the sporting-goods store.

7.   A landlord agreed in writing to lease an apartment to a tenant for one year beginning on an upcoming date. When the date arrived, though, the tenant found a prior tenant still in the apartment and refusing to leave. The tenant notified the landlord who confirmed that the prior tenant's lease had expired just before the new tenant's occupancy date. What legal action would properly provide the new tenant with actual possession?

A.   Only an eviction action by the landlord to remove the prior tenant.
B.   An eviction action by either the landlord or new tenant to remove the prior tenant.
C.   Only an eviction action by the new tenant to remove the prior tenant.
D.   Nothing other than the new tenant's self-help because the prior tenant is a holdover.

Answer explanation: Option B is correct because any party with the lease right to possession may enforce that right. The landlord retains the right to terminate the prior lease while the new tenant has the right to actual possession that the new tenant may enforce under the new lease. Option A is incorrect because the new tenant also has a right under the new lease to actual possession. Option C is incorrect because the landlord retains a right to enforce the prior lease. Option D is incorrect because no circumstances suggest any right of the prior tenant to remain as a holdover.

8.   A landlord and tenant entered into a written, signed, and otherwise enforceable lease for an apartment unit near the university at which the tenant was a student. The lease term was for one year. The tenant stayed throughout the year, paying rent on time at the beginning of each month. The tenant had one year remaining at the university and so remained in the apartment at the end of the lease term. The tenant paid the landlord the next month's rent at the beginning of each of the next two months after the lease ended, consistent with the tenant's prior obligation and practice. At first, the landlord accepted the tenant's rent payments while tendering the next year's lease for the tenant's signature. The tenant did not sign, hoping that the landlord would accept

rent each month instead so that the tenant could leave without obligation when school ended after nine months. But the landlord instead served a notice to quit. The tenant paid another months' rent, which the landlord accepted despite the notice. If during that month for which the tenant paid rent the landlord sues to evict, then what is the tenant's status?

A. Tenant at will with a month-to-month lease because the landlord accepted rent.
B. Tenant at sufferance with no possessory rights because of the landlord's notice to quit.
C. Tenant on a periodic tenancy from year to year because of the prior one-year term.
D. Trespasser subject to both contract damages under the lease and tort damages.

Answer explanation: Option B is correct because although a tenant is at will month to month when the landlord accepts monthly rent after the lease term expires, the tenant is at sufferance with no possessory rights once the landlord protests the tenant's continued occupancy, such as by serving a notice to quit. Option A is incorrect because although the tenant was initially at will month to month when the landlord accepted rent and offered a lease, the tenant became at sufferance when the landlord served the notice to quit. Option C is incorrect because a periodic tenancy, one that adopts the prior lease's term, follows the rental payments (monthly, not yearly, here) rather than the full prior lease's term unless the lease specifies the same term for a tenant holding over after the original term. The lease term would be month to month, not year to year, but for the notice to quit making the tenancy at sufferance. Option D is incorrect because the tenant had consent for possession and the landlord has accepted rent although having served a notice to quit and filed suit to evict. The tenant would remain liable for lease damages but likely not damages in tort.

9. The owner of a small-town sandwich-shop business and the building housing the shop decided to rent the shop along with the apartment upstairs. The owner entered into a five-year written lease calling for the tenant, a youthful entrepreneur, to take possession in three months. Two months before the tenant took occupancy, the sandwich shop had a small fire the modest damage from which the owner took pains to clean up. At about the same time, the entrepreneur's inspection revealed some mold in the apartment upstairs. Thus, one month before the tenant was to take occupancy, the entrepreneur notified the owner that the entrepreneur was refusing to take occupancy but that he had a buddy who was interested in taking over the lease. The owner simultaneously discovered that the entrepreneur had joined the military and already left for training. If the owner sues the entrepreneur accelerating damages for the entire lease term, then what legal arguments should each side raise?

A. The entrepreneur the servicemembers' civil relief act, and the owner breach of the duty of occupancy and specific performance.
B. The entrepreneur the protection of the recording statute, and the owner breach of the warranty of habitability.
C. The owner breach of the duty of good faith and fair dealing, and the entrepreneur impossibility and impracticality, and the absence of any damage.
D. The owner anticipatory breach, and the entrepreneur breach of the warranties of habitability and suitability, and the obligation to mitigate damages.

Answer explanation: Option D is correct because a landlord may sue for anticipatory breach whenever a tenant refuses to perform a lease before the lease term begins or it reasonably appears that the tenant has made it impossible to perform the lease. On the other hand, a landlord owes a residential tenant a warranty that the apartment is habitable, a commercial tenant a warranty that the premises is suitable for the anticipated business, and owes a tenant a duty to mitigate damages. The facts implicate each of these legal theories. Option A is incorrect because although the servicemembers' civil relief act ordinarily holds immune from civil suit a servicemember whom authorities call up for active duty, here the entrepreneur apparently just voluntarily joined rather than received a call up. Even if the relief act applies, the law doesn't recognize a duty of occupancy or give the landlord a right of specific performance to force the tenant to occupy. Option B is incorrect because the recording act does not in any way apply, and the landlord doesn't have a claim against a tenant for breach of the warranty of habitability. It would be the other way around that the landlord owes the residential tenant that duty. Option C is incorrect because the landlord would sue for anticipatory breach, not breach of the duty of good faith and fair dealing. The entrepreneur would not defend on impossibility (the premises could with appropriate repair or cleaning still be occupied) or impracticality (the facts give no indication of occupancy being impractical other than the need to complete any clean up after the fire and remediate any dangerous mold). And the landlord hasn't found another tenant yet, even if the entrepreneur had an interested friend, so the landlord may well suffer damage.

10.   The owner of a mechanic's facility decided to retire but to keep the facility in case he needed or wanted to resume work. He leased the mechanic's shop to a young man who had just graduated from a vocational program. He separately leased a bungalow on the back of the property to a young woman who had just quit college to find herself. A city inspector tagged and closed the shop because it lacked the fire-suppression equipment mandated for commercial rentals. The inspector simultaneously tagged the bungalow as uninhabitable for not having a second means of egress in the event of fire. If the leases did not address such events, then what if any would be the owner's obligations to the young man running the shop and young woman living in the bungalow, and the tenants' remedies?

A.   Warranty of suitability owed the young man and warranty of habitability owed the young woman, requiring renovation and repair, or reduction in rent or lease termination.
B.   Duty of commercial care owed the young man and duty of ordinary care owed the young woman, requiring compensation for damages caused by unreasonable conditions.
C.   Obligation to hold harmless both the young man and young woman in the event of injury, property damage, or other loss, to the tenants and visiting third parties.
D.   No duties owed to either tenant because the leases did not address these eventualities, and the tenants have possession, leaving the tenants with no remedies.

Answer explanation: Option A is correct because a landlord owes a residential tenant a warranty that the apartment is habitable and owes a commercial tenant a warranty that the property is suitable for the anticipated business. If the breach is substantial, then a tenant may leave without lease liability, repair the breach and withhold rent in the cost of repairs, withhold rent representing the breach's reduction in the leasehold value, or sue for damages. Option B is incorrect because while tort law imposes duty of care, real-property law imposes warranties of suitability and habitability. Option C is incorrect because hold-harmless clauses might be appropriate if the tenants became liable to a non-party to the lease because of the owner's breach, but the concern as to the tenants is not their future loss but their present inability to use their premises. Option D is incorrect because the law imposes warranties of suitability for commercial use and habitability for residential use. Commercial leases may shift those obligations, but residential leases by law cannot.

11.   A resident lived in a posh development with the houses crowded closely together. A neighbor with teenage children moved in next door. The neighbor's teenagers frequently played amplified guitars, drums, and other rock-band instruments late into the night in the neighbor's garage. The resident called the police over the noise, who confirmed that the noise probably violated local ordinance but who also indicated that nothing would be done about it. The resident was fed up calling the police over the neighboring garage band's noise-

ordinance violations. Wondering whether there was anything else he could do to put a stop to the sleep-shattering racket, the resident consulted an attorney. What would be proper legal advice?

A.   The resident may be able to pursue a nuisance action to stop the ordinance violations.
B.   The resident may be able to pursue a trespass action to stop the ordinance violations.
C.   The resident may be able to pursue invasion of privacy claims to stop the teenagers.
D.   The resident has no tort remedy and can only hope the city enforces the ordinance.

Answer explanation: Option A is correct because intangible entries (noise, smell, light, etc.), while not a trespass, may be addressed through the tort of nuisance, which involves unreasonable interference with use and enjoyment rather than, as in trespass, interference with exclusive possession. The violation of law may provide a stronger basis on which to maintain that the noise was unreasonable. Option B is incorrect because there was no interference with exclusive possession (no entry). Option C is incorrect because there was no invasion of privacy (no exploitation, intrusion, false light, or public disclosure). Option D is incorrect because there may be a nuisance remedy.

12.   A farmer periodically watered his truck garden by opening and closing sluice gates to briefly flood the garden fields. Often, the sluicing of the fields would result in a pond forming across a public bike path and road running alongside the truck garden. The pond that formed across the bike path and road when the farmer sluiced his truck garden received more and more complaints from passersby using the bike path and road. The board of a nearby homeowner's association asked its legal counsel for an opinion on what could be done to correct the pond problem so that it no longer interfered with homeowner use of the bike path and road. What tort rights should counsel address in the opinion?

A.   The pond problem is just something to live with because the truck garden is productive.
B.   The pond problem may constitute a trespass to land to abate by damages action.
C.   The pond problem may constitute a private nuisance to discourage by damages action.
D.   The pond problem may constitute a public nuisance that could be abated by injunction.

Answer explanation: Option D is correct because a public nuisance is one that interferes with public enjoyment, while a private nuisance is one that substantially affects the use and enjoyment of private lands. Here, the pond may have interfered substantially enough with the use of the road and bike path so as to warrant a court action to abate the problem by injunction. Option A is incorrect because there may be a public-nuisance remedy. Option B is incorrect because no private land has been identified onto which the pond encroached as an entry. Option C is incorrect because there was no private nuisance, and no single individual would be likely to be able to prove sufficient damages to discourage the problem.

13.   A season-ticket holder to an outdoor summer commercial concert series brought intoxicating drinks and marijuana into the venue for the first several events. Each time, when other patrons called the season-ticket holder's rowdy behavior to security's attention, the event producer confiscated the drinks and marijuana, and warned the season-ticket holder not to do so again because it violated well-publicized event rules. If the conduct occurred yet again, may the producer revoke the holder's season tickets?

A.   Yes, because the producer has an obligation to comply with law.
B.   Yes, because the season-ticket holder had only a license.
C.   No, because the season-ticket holder had a contract right to attend.
D.   No, because the season-ticket holder would still have a right to comply.

Answer explanation: Option B is correct because tickets to a commercial event are a license revocable at the will of the licensor. Here, the producer may revoke the license for any reason or likely no reason but especially for violation of well-publicized rules. Option A is incorrect because the facts give no clear indication that either the producer or even the rowdy patron was violating the law, which would in any case not necessarily justify terminating the season tickets. Option C is incorrect because the law construes attending a commercial event as a revocable license notwithstanding the ticket purchase. The producer would have to pay damages if the revocation breached the purchase terms, but revocation would remain the producer's right. Option D is incorrect because the holder had several warnings, and even without warning the producer would have had a right to revoke the license.

14. A landowner granted a valid written driveway easement to a neighbor who in exchange agreed to pay for paving both adjacent parcels' driveways. The neighbor neglected to record the easement but did complete and regularly use the paved driveway on the landowner's land, sometimes even parking vehicles on the landowner's land. The landowner then granted a bank a deed of trust for a construction loan to build a house on the land. The bank promptly recorded the deed of trust. When the landowner failed to complete the house, the bank foreclosed on the trust deed and sought to sell the land free and clear of the neighbor's driveway easement. What right does the neighbor have, assuming that the jurisdiction has a conveyance statute that requires either recording or constructive notice?

A.   The neighbor retains the easement right because the bank received its trust deed later.
B.   The neighbor retains the easement right because of the bank's constructive notice.
C.   The neighbor loses the easement right for having failed to record the writing.
D.   The neighbor loses the easement right because trust deeds precede easements.

Answer explanation: Option B is correct because although trust deeds (a mortgage substitute used in some states in which the landowner grants a deed in the lender's favor for a trustee to hold and auction if the landowner defaults) are usually enforceable much like a mortgage, one taking an interest in land takes subject to easements over which one has constructive notice in a jurisdiction having a statute requiring recording or constructive notice. Here, the bank either would or should have seen the neighbor's paved driveway and driveway use, and known of the neighbor's easement interest, when loaning in exchange for a trust deed. The neighbor's completed easement thus has priority due to constructive notice. Option A is incorrect because the order of easement before trust deed is alone not enough without considering recording or constructive notice. Option C is incorrect because the neighbor does not lose the easement right over failure to record if as here the bank had constructive notice. The neighbor would have lost the right if the neighbor never built the driveway and the bank did not otherwise have notice. Option D is incorrect because no general rule places trust deeds ahead of easements. And by the way, the neighbor would likely not have the right to park vehicles on the landowner's land because the easement was for a driveway, driveways are generally for ingress and egress, and parking vehicles may be beyond the easement's scope.

604. An elderly man inherited an ornate heirloom fireplace mantel following the death of his parents. The elderly man still owed money on a business loan security for which he had granted to a bank, on all present and after-acquired personal property. The elderly man found that he could easily place the heirloom mantel over the existing fireplace mantel at his suburban home without damaging the permanent mantel. In doing so, the elderly man told his adult daughter that he wanted her to have the heirloom mantel for her own at his passing. The elderly man soon passed away, by will conveying everything to his adult daughter except deeding the home

to a suburban charity. The estate had plenty of cash assets to pay off the business loan. Who gets the heirloom mantel?

A.   The daughter.
B.   The bank.
C.   The charity.
D.   The charity, but it must pay the daughter its value.

604. Answer explanation: Option A is correct because the owner of a chattel who affixes the chattel to real property only temporarily, intending that the chattel not remain as a fixture, may bequeath the chattel apart from a deed or devise of the real property to which the chattel is affixed, if the chattel can be removed without damage to the real property. The doctrine of accession, in which a tenant or life estate holder affixes a chattel to the real property in a manner that law prohibits its removal such that it passes with the real property, does not apply. Option B is incorrect because although the bank has a security interest in the mantel, and UCC Article 9 authorizes security interests in fixtures, the estate has plenty of cash assets to pay off the loan, and so the bank would receive cash rather than the mantel. Option C is incorrect because the elderly man only affixed the mantel temporarily with the intent to convey it to the daughter. The mantel was not part of the real property for the charity to inherit. Option D is incorrect because the elderly man gave everything by will to his daughter other than the home, and the mantel was only temporarily affixed with the intent that the daughter receives it. The charity has no basis to claim the mantel whether it pays the value or not.

15.   In exchange for a few calves, a farmer executed a writing sufficient to convey an undescribed easement for a driveway for ingress and egress by a neighboring dairy herder and successors and assigns. The drive that the herder began using substantially improved the herder's access to the herder's own barns and lands even though not strictly necessary for access. The herder thereafter used the drive more and more consistently, even making small improvements such as lightly grading and filling the drive. In time, much longer than the jurisdiction's period for adverse possession, both the farmer and the herder conveyed their lands to adult children between whom a dispute arose as to the continued use of the undescribed drive. What are their respective rights?

A.   The farmer's children have the right to exclude the herder's children from any drive.
B.   The farmer's children must allow some drive but may designate a different drive.
C.   The herder's children still have the right to use the same drive.
D.   The herder's children have only the right to compensation for the lost drive.

Answer explanation: Option C is correct because a grantee may enforce an express written grant for value of an undescribed easement later defined by use and acquiescence. The farmer granted the easement, which the herder then defined and as to which the farmer acquiesced. Note that although the herder used the easement for much longer than the period for adverse possession, a prescriptive easement would not have arisen because the use was by the farmer's consent rather than hostile. Option A is incorrect because the farmer's children had no right to exclude the heirs who succeeded to the enforceable easement. Option B is incorrect because the farmer's children may not relocate an easement that the parties to the grant had defined by use and acquiescence. The easement then is as good as if described. Option D is incorrect because the herder's children may keep the easement and would not have a theory for compensation in relinquishing it.

16.   The owner of a home on a city lot discovered that his lot was large enough to divide front and back. The lot was between two city streets, one running along the lot's front and one running along the lot's back. The new back lot would have a new drive to the street in back, while the old front lot with the house would retain its drive to the street in front. The owner then sold the back lot to a buyer who constructed a house on the new back lot. When the buyer completed the new house and moved in, the buyer objected to the seller walking across the new back lot to a bus stop that the seller had used for twenty years to go to work. The deed to the new back lot said nothing about the bus stop and seller's use, but the buyer had known of and orally agreed to the use before buying. Does the seller have the right to continue to walk across the back lot to the bus stop?

A.   Yes because an easement by implication arose from prior use.
B.   Yes because the seller has a real covenant with the buyer to enforce.
C.   No because the seller failed to include the easement in the deed.
D.   No because by doing so, the seller would interfere with the buyer's privacy.

Answer explanation: Option A is correct because an easement is an interest in land allowing the holder to make or prevent use of another's property. Easements arise by grant expressly transferring the easement to another, reservation when transferring land to another, implication from circumstances showing that the parties must have intended the easement, and prescription through adverse possession. Easements by implication arise from either prior use or of necessity, when an owner divides and conveys parcels of land in ways that frustrate prior or necessary uses. Prior uses must be necessary, continuous, intended to continue, and apparent to the burdened purchaser. Option B is incorrect because the buyer made no promise to preserve the use, and so no real covenant arose to enforce. Option C is incorrect because easements by implication from prior use or necessity can arise without the easement in the deed or even in any other writing. Option D is incorrect because the facts do not indicate privacy interference, and moreover, even if the use affected some privacy, then the buyer would have known when taking the property subject to the use.

17.   A bay-side landowner enjoyed visiting his land to watch seabirds bathe, swim, fish, and dig for food in the land's ponds and tidal pools. While the landowner wanted the land unspoiled, the annual taxes burdened the landowner just enough to contract in a signed writing with a local for the local to remove frogs, crabs, and clams from the land's ponds and pools in exchange for an annual payment approximating the taxes. One day, the local built a campfire on the land and invited some buddies to join him for a few beers and steamed clams. The local shooed the landowner's visiting grandchildren away when they came over to the campfire to see what was going on. What right, if any, does the landowner have to discourage or prevent the local's activity?

A.   No right because the activity is reasonably incident to the easement in gross's purpose.
B.   Limited right not to renew the license for another year after the end of the current year.
C.   Full right to enforce the profit's limited scope and prevent other activity such as here.
D.   Absolute right to terminate the servitude at any time without reason or advance notice.

Answer explanation: Option C is correct because a profit a prendre is a right to take from the land, including the right to enter the land to do so, but is not an interest in the land itself. A profit arises by express agreement or by prescription, and can be either appurtenant to adjacent land or in gross, and transferable or nontransferable according to its terms. Profits terminate by voluntary release, merger of the benefitted lands, waste, or terms of the agreement. Here, the profit was to remove frogs, crabs, and clams, not to build fires, drink beer, and cook. Option A is incorrect because the interest here was only a profit, not an easement, and the profit had a much more-limited scope. Option B is incorrect because the interest is a profit, not a license, and because the landowner may at any time restrict the use to the profit's limited scope. Option D is incorrect because the interest is a profit, not a servitude, and termination would not be possible during a year for which the local had paid the profit's cost, the right being contractual.

18. A retailer owned land along a public highway. The owner of a salvage yard behind the retailer's land negotiated with the retailer for a right of way for ingress and egress across the retailer's land. The salvage yard had other access from a side street, but the right of way across the retailer's land was significantly more convenient. The salvage-yard owner duly recorded the retailer's deed that expressly granted the right of way to the salvage-yard owner "and successors, heirs, and assigns." The deed did not include a description of the right of way's specific location across the retailer's land. The retailer and salvage-yard owner agreed on a route that the salvage-yard owner then used for five years. The salvage-yard owner then sold the business and land to a new owner. The retailer also sold to an investor who demanded that the new salvage-yard owner move the right-of-way route to a different but reasonable alternative location on the investor's land. What result if the new salvage-yard owner refuses and the investor sues to either terminate or move the right of way?

A.   Investor loses because the deed granted the right of way, and use defined it.
B.   Investor loses because successive use fixed the right of way's location by prescription.
C.   Investor wins but only on moving the right of way to the proposed reasonable location.
D.   Investor wins and the right of way is extinguished for lack of its location description.

Answer explanation: Option A is correct because use can establish the location of a deeded but undescribed right-of-way easement, and once use establishes the location, the restriction at that location persists. Option B is incorrect because the facts suggest only five years of use, which would not meet the typical statute on prescriptive use for ten years or more, and here the use was not adverse and prescriptive but instead by grant, so that prescriptive-use rights would not arise. Option C is incorrect because once the grantor and grantee fix the granted and deeded easement's location, the easement remains fixed. The grantee need not move it whenever the grantor shows an alternative reasonable location. Option D is incorrect because a grantor and grantee may establish an easement's location in addition to by express description.

19. A husband and wife constructed a small home on one half of their own home's lot in which the wife's elderly mother then lived. When the mother passed away, the couple divided their lot and sold the small home to a college student. The couple later sold their own home to a surveyor. The surveyor promptly confirmed that the student's driveway to the small home was on the surveyor's main lot. The student pointed out that the surveyor's utility pole and line to the surveyor's house was on the student's lot. What rights if any do the surveyor and student have to continue their current uses on one another's lots?

A.   Neither gets to continue use of the other's lot unless the lot owner grants an easement.
B.   Neither gets to continue use of the other's lot unless able to prove necessity.
C.   Each gets to continue use of the other's lot under quasi easement implied by use.
D.   Each gets to continue use of the other's lot under implied reciprocal servitude.

Answer explanation: Option C is correct because apparent uses that existed when a landowner divides the land and that benefit the divided lots may exist as quasi easements implied by use even when not confirmed in the landowner's deed or other signed writing. Option A is incorrect because the law will imply a quasi easement by the evident use that existed at the time the owner divided the lots. Option B is incorrect because necessity is not a condition for an implied quasi easement by use to arise. Easements by necessity typically apply to landlocked lands. Here, the surveyor may be able to run utility lines or the student build a driveway on their own lots, but the evident use when the owner divided the lots is sufficient to establish the quasi easement. Option D is incorrect because the utility line and driveway are different uses rather than reciprocal (same, mutual) uses. Reciprocal servitudes typically arise by common plan, whereas here the two lots have different servitudes requiring different easements.

20.   Adjacent landowners hunted and fished on one another's wild lands at first by courtesy and later by express written agreement. Seeking to maximize the value of each land by this mutually beneficial agreement, the owners made their written agreement not only for the benefit of one another but for successors, heirs, and assigns. After years of mutual use, each landowner sold to other owners. One of those owners began to sell licenses to friends to come and hunt and fish on the both lands. The other owner protested and attempted to prohibit not only the other owner's friends but also the other owner from making any further use of the land. What result if the two owners seek a court declaration of their rights?

A.   Each owner may hunt and fish on the other's land by profit but not extend that right to others.
B.   Each owner must not hunt or fish on the other's land because any such right ceased on land transfer.
C.   The owner who sold licenses to friends to use the other's land has lost all right, and so has the other owner.
D.   The owner who sold licenses to friends must disgorge to the other owner half of the profits to retain the right.

Answer explanation: Option A is correct because a profit is a right to take from the land, including the right to enter the land to do so, but is not an interest in the land itself. A profit arises by express agreement or by prescription and can be either appurtenant to adjacent land or in gross and transferable. Profits terminate by voluntary release, merger of the benefitted lands, waste, or terms of the agreement. Here, the profits appear to be appurtenant and thus not transferable in gross but only on conveyance of the land. Option B is incorrect because the original profits by their terms were also for the benefit of successors, heirs, and assigns. The rights appurtenant to each land may run with the land where, as here, so provided. Option C is incorrect because although one could make an argument that the sale of licenses was a sufficient waste of the profit as to terminate it, depending on the damage to the fish and wildlife, the rest of the answer is incorrect because the other owner committed no waste and should have a continued right. Option D is incorrect because the profits were for the benefits of the landowners and their successors, heirs, and assigns, not the benefit of friends or for commercial licensing to friends. So disgorging half of the profits would not perfect such a right.

21.   A homeowner had long lived next to a vacant lot owned by a gardener who would visit her vacant lot to garden. The homeowner often allowed the gardener to use the home's restroom. The homeowner one day agreed to let the gardener's guests use the home's restroom at an upcoming garden party that the gardener planned. The homeowner helped the gardener erect a tent on the vacant land and with the invitations for the garden party, which included food and drink. Yet on the day of the garden party, the homeowner refused any guest the use of the restroom, frustrating and discomforting the guests, spoiling the event, and embarrassing the gardener. Did the homeowner violate a right of the gardener?

A.   Yes because the gardener acquired an irrevocable easement in gross for the usage.
B.   Yes because the gardener acquired a license that the homeowner is estopped to revoke.
C.   No because a grantor may revoke a license at any time and without reason or cause.
D.   No unless the gardener gave the homeowner valuable consideration for the usage.

Answer explanation: Option B is correct because the grantor of a license to use the grantor's property for a limited purpose may generally revoke the license at will except where the grantor expresses intent to make the license irrevocable for the license period or, in the case of estoppel, the license holder substantially and detrimentally relied and revocation would be unfair for a limited period. Here, revocation at the event was unfair, although the homeowner probably could have revoked the day before or a few days before giving the gardener time to rent a portable toilet. Option A is incorrect because the gardener's interest was a license, not an easement in gross. A license differs from an easement in gross in that the easement is an interest in the land rather than a contract promise and is of indefinite duration rather than limited in time. Option C is incorrect because, as explained above, circumstances may bar a grantor from revoking a license, particularly when the grantee substantially and detrimentally relies. Option D is incorrect because a license may arise without consideration, as here.

22.   A cabin owner had access to his land and cabin from a dirt road but wanted access instead to a paved road nearby, both for ease of use and to increase the cabin's value. The cabin owner negotiated with the neighbor for a driveway easement across the neighbor's land and out to the paved road. For valuable consideration, the neighbor signed and delivered to the cabin owner a written driveway easement, one that the cabin owner did not record. The cabin owner promptly completed the driveway. The neighbor then mortgaged his property to borrow money from a bank to construct his own cabin. The bank promptly recorded the neighbor's mortgage. Learning of the neighbor's plans, the cabin owner recorded the driveway easement. The neighbor decided not to build a cabin and instead defaulted on the loan and absconded with the loan money. The bank filed suit to foreclose on the mortgage to recover the defaulted loan from the sale of the neighbor's land, in doing so seeking to extinguish the cabin owner's easement. What would be the strongest grounds on which the court would preserve the easement?

A.   The bank had notice or constructive notice of the cabin owner's driveway use.
B.   The driveway easement was appurtenant and attached to the neighbor's land.
C.   The driveway easement was necessary for access to a paved public road.
D.   The cabin owner's recording before the foreclosure action protects the easement right.

Answer explanation: Option A is correct because a recording act ordinarily protects only bona fide purchasers who take and record without notice of superior rights. Purchasers who are or should be aware of the superior right, in this case the driveway easement, take subject to that right. Here, the cabin owner had a written easement but just hadn't recorded it. The bank knew or should have known of the easement because of the driveway's construction. Option B is incorrect because although an appurtenant easement, one pertaining to a particular benefitted parcel, ordinarily passes with the property, the question here is not whether the easement continues but which interest, mortgage or easement, is superior under the recording act. Because the bank took the mortgage with notice or constructive notice of the driveway, the bank does not get the protection of the recording act. Option C is incorrect because access to a paved road doesn't matter when the cabin owner already had access to a dirt road. Easements by necessity do not arise simply to improve access but rather to create access that doesn't exist. Option D is incorrect because recording before foreclosure would not matter. Recording before the bank recorded would matter, except that the bank had notice in any case.

23.   The owner of a lake-view lot bought the adjacent vacant parcel closer to the lake to ensure that no one would build on it and obstruct the owner's lake view. The lake-view owner then substantially improved the home with the lake view. The lake-view owner later sold the vacant parcel to a family for picnicking and boating but with a deed restriction against building on it. The family recorded the deed with the building restriction. Years later, after both the lake-view owner and family members had died, an heir of the family members began constructing a cottage on the vacant parcel that would obstruct the adjacent home's lake view. What result if the heir to the lake-view owner sued to enjoin the construction?

A.   The court will enjoin because of common-law rights of lake view.
B.   The court will enjoin, enforcing the recorded building restriction.

C.   The court will not enjoin because a servitude does not survive the grantee's death.
D.   The court will not enjoin because a servitude does not survive the grantor's death.

Answer explanation: Option B is correct because a deeded and recorded servitude that touches and concerns both the dominant and servient lands remains enforceable by and against successors in interest who take with notice. Option A is incorrect because no common-law right of lake view arises without satisfying the intent conditions of an equitable servitude. The right here is contractual, not common law. Options C and D are incorrect because a deeded and recorded servitude does survive the grantor's and grantee's deaths.

24.   Two neighbors, a business executive and a junk collector, lived on spacious lots side by side. The business executive, often entertaining corporate customers at the executive's mini-mansion home, grew concerned that the collector was hauling all manner of unsightly junk to his adjacent property. The executive paid the collector $25,000 for the collector to limit his junk collection to the back of his property hidden by hills and trees. Years later, the executive sold the mini-mansion to a gallery owner who likewise entertained corporate customers frequently at home. When the collector began accumulating junk in the front of his property again, the gallery owner demanded that the collector comply with the collector's promise to the executive, but the collector refused. Does the gallery owner have the right to enforce the promise?

A.   No because $25,000 is not enough to restrict the land in favor of adjacent successors.
B.   No as the executive and collector had no horizontal privity when making the promise.
C.   Yes but only if the collector signed a writing indicating intent that the successors benefit.
D.   Yes because the gallery owner took with notice relying on the promise when purchasing.

Answer explanation: Option B is correct because a real covenant is a promise that relates to the use of land, different from an easement because contractual only rather than ownership in land. Because relating to land, the promise must be in a signed writing for the promisee to enforce it against the promisor. To enforce against successors to the burdened land, the promise must touch and concern the land, the parties must have intended that the covenant run, both parties must have had some ownership or contractual (leasehold) interest in the burdened land (horizontal privity), and the owners must have transferred voluntarily (not by adverse possession) to the burdened and benefited successors (vertical privity), with notice to the burdened successor. Here, the executive had no interest in the collector's land, such as a co-owner with or purchaser from the collector, and so without that horizontal privity, the promise does not run. Option A is incorrect because the courts generally do not examine the amount of the consideration, although it could be evidence of whether the parties intended that the burden run. The real concern here is the lack of horizontal privity. Option C is incorrect because while a signed writing and intent that the burden run are both necessary, the gallery owner would also need to show horizontal privity between the collector and executive when they made the promise. Option D is incorrect because notice and reliance are not sufficient to make the burden run. The promisor and promisee must also have intended that the burden run and must also have had horizontal privity when making the promise.

25.   A group of eight lakefront-cottage homeowners grew disgusted at their inability to keep their private secluded beachfront clean of the excrement of pets. They all agreed at once in a writing that all signed and that each recorded that no present or future owner of their eight cottage properties would bring any pets to the properties. The agreement worked as intended for several years. In later years, though, several owners sold to new owners who had not agreed to the pet restriction. One absentee owner lost his cottage to adverse possession by a vagrant relative. Pets once again fouled the beach. May objecting owners enforce the agreement?

A.   No because the original owners did not have horizontal privity when promising.
B.   No as to any of the new owners, but yes as to any original owner making the promise.
C.   Yes as to any of the new owners taking by purchase, but no as to the adverse possessor.
D.   Yes as all had actual or constructive notice, and equitable servitudes don't require privity.

Answer explanation: Option D is correct because an equitable servitude is a promise or implication about which a successor has notice, binding all lands in a common plot for their common benefit. Unlike real covenants, no horizontal or vertical privity need exist to bind successors to an equitable servitude. Option A is incorrect because only real covenants, not equitable servitudes, require privity. Option B is incorrect because the equitable servitude, recorded and thus giving record notice, would bind successors. Option C is incorrect because even one who is not in vertical privity, such as an adverse possessor, takes subject to an equitable servitude benefiting all the lands in common.

26.   An executive owned two lots overlooking the ocean, one slightly higher and behind the other. The executive built a retirement home on the higher back lot. To fund the construction, he agreed orally to sell the lower ocean-side lot to a friend who wanted beach access provided that the friend never build on the lot so as to preserve the executive's view. The executive's deed to the friend, which only the executive signed, included the grantee's covenant that neither the grantee nor successors, heirs, or assigns would build on the lot, specifically to preserve the ocean view for the higher back lot's owner and successors, heirs, and assigns. The friend accepted and recorded the deed. Years later, the executive decided to retire somewhere else and so sold the back lot and its home to a sports agent. The friend then promptly sold the vacant lot to a developer who began construction of a fabulous ocean-front home. What result if the sports agent sues to enjoin the developer's construction?

A.   Developer wins because the grantee friend never signed the executive's deed.
B.   Developer wins because equitable servitudes do not survive promisor conveyance.
C.   Sports agent wins because equitable servitudes run with the land binding on notice.
D.   Sports agent wins because the executive built before the developer bought and began.

Answer explanation: Option C is correct because a valid equitable servitude arises when touching and concerning both the benefitted and burdened properties, the parties intend that it bind others, the servitude satisfies the statute of frauds such as here by poll deed, and owners of the burdened land take with notice such as here by recorded deed. The outcome makes no difference that the initial sale agreement was oral. Once the executive reduced the agreement to a poll deed and the friend accepted that deed, all terms of the oral agreement that the written deed later recorded, whether contrary or inconsistent to the deed, would have merged into the deed so that only the deed terms were enforceable by either party. Option A is incorrect because a poll deed, one signed only by the grantor, binds the grantee and successors if the grantee accepts and especially, as here, the grantee records the deed. Even though not signed by the grantee, a poll deed satisfies the statute of frauds under these conditions. Option B is incorrect because servitudes meeting the above conditions including that they indicate the intent to bind successors in interest run with the land. Option D is incorrect because who builds first would not matter unless the deed so indicated, which it clearly did not do so here.

27.   A developer divided 200 acres of land into two parcels of 100 acres each. The developer then platted the first 100-acre parcel for residential subdivision of 50 lots and the second 100-acre parcel for office development, consistent with all land-use and zoning restrictions. The developer then sold all 50 residential lots under deeds with reciprocal residential-use restrictions as to grantees, heirs, and assigns. An investor bought the 100-acre office-development parcel. If the investor bought 10 of the adjacent residential lots from lot

owners who didn't want to live next to an office development, may the investor develop those 10 lots for office use when developing the 100-acre office development?

A.   No, because of the reciprocal residential-use restrictions.
B.   No, because of the land-use and zoning restrictions.
C.   Yes, because the lot owners who sold didn't want to build residential.
D.   Yes, because of the unity of residential and office-development title.

Answer explanation: Option A is correct because any property owner subject to reciprocal servitudes may enforce those servitudes against any other property owner also restricted. Here, any of the remaining 40 lot owners could object and prevent the investor from developing offices on the residential lots. The reciprocal restrictions were for the benefit of all lot owners, not only those who conveyed away to the investor. Option B is incorrect because the facts give no direct indication that the residential lots were restricted against office development. The district may have permitted both residential and office development. Option C is incorrect because the lot owners who sold were not the only ones with reciprocal restrictions. The remaining 40 lot owners could also enforce the restriction. Option D is incorrect because the investor owning both the office parcel and the 10 residential lots does not remove the restriction on the 10 lots. Unifying title in a single owner does not give the owner power to avoid reciprocal restrictions favoring other lots that the owner does not own or control.

28.   Forty years ago, a landowner divided a large parcel of land in half, getting local-government approval to develop one half for residential housing and the other half for commercial use. The landowner duly recorded plats for each property that included the government-approved development plans, one development for commercial and one development for residential. The residential development contained over two-hundred individual lots that the landowner promptly sold under deeds that referenced the plat's single-family, residential restrictions as binding on grantees and their heirs and assigns. The express restrictions, though, were to last for only thirty years. Those thirty years passed. What result if an original homeowner in the residential development sued, seeking approval to convert to a commercial use?

A.   Homeowner wins because the deed restrictions expired but must comply with zoning.
B.   Homeowner wins because the deed restrictions expired and need not comply with zoning.
C.   Homeowner loses to residential lot owners asserting an implied reciprocal servitude.
D.   Homeowner loses because homeowner took the property while still restricted.

Answer explanation: Option C is correct because property owners may enforce an implied reciprocal servitude that existed expressly in prior deeds from a general plan, when the owner challenging the restriction has actual, constructive, or implied notice of the restriction. Option A is incorrect for the same reason because the law will imply a reciprocal servitude not expressly present in the deeds on the conditions just recited. Option B is incorrect for the same reason and also because even if no deed or implied reciprocal servitude restricted the owner, then the owner would still have to comply with zoning. Zoning restrictions do not depend on deed restrictions. Option D is incorrect because simply taking a restricted property would not continue to restrict the owner once the restriction expired. The restriction would continue only under an implied reciprocal servitude, not because the owner had taken while restricted. The restriction would, though, establish the owner's actual notice.

29.   A builder of apartment units located land for sale at a reasonable price in a district that the city zoned industrial. While the zone had one industrial use, land in the zone was otherwise vacant and had remained so for

a long time. The builder desired to build an apartment house on the land for sale in the industrial zone, reasonably believing that the zone would not develop for industrial and that apartment use would be a safe and reasonable use of the land. Under which type of zoning scheme may the builder build the apartment house?

A. Only an exclusive-use zoning scheme.
B. Only as a planned-unit development.
C. Only a cumulative zoning scheme.
D. No zoning schemes.

Answer explanation. Option C is correct because a cumulative zoning scheme generally permits lower-impact uses in a higher-impact zoning district. A residential use is lower impact than an industrial use. Option A is incorrect because an exclusive-use scheme limits development to the specified use. The zone specified industrial use, meaning an exclusive-use zone would permit only industrial. Option B is incorrect because while planned-unit development can allow for nonconforming uses, a single apartment house would be an unusual planned-unit development, which typically involves multiple uses. Option D is incorrect because a cumulative zoning scheme would allow for residential use in industrial zone.

30. A state zoning enabling act permitted only exclusive-use zoning acts but allowed for clearly defined mixed-use zones within the exclusive-zone definitions. The zoning enabling act also required that any local zoning act permit planned-unit developments under reasonable criteria. A city within the state adopted an exclusive-use zoning scheme that did not provide for planned-unit developments. A developer wished to build a mixed condominium and retail development on a half city block zoned industrial. Which is the best approach for the developer to take to obtain zoning approval?

A. Apply for project approval as a lower-impact use in a higher-impact industrial zone.
B. Claim the city's zoning is ultra vires, and seek planned-unit-development approval.
C. Pursue rezoning of the half city block at the next planning commission and council meetings.
D. Seek a variance from the industrial zoning to pursue the condominium and retail project.

Answer explanation. Option B is correct because local governments, whether cities, villages, townships, or other units, may only pass zoning acts consistent with state enabling acts. The state act required planned-unit developments, which the city's act did not provide. The developer may show the city's act to be outside of the enabling act's authority. Option A is incorrect because exclusive-use zoning allows only those uses designated for that zone, not lower-impact inconsistent uses. Option C is incorrect because rezoning is a political question that provides the developer with no assurance of success, making that course a less-attractive option than showing that the act does not comply and seeking a planned-unit development as the state enabling act permits. Option D is incorrect because the city act is ultra vires, and seeking a variance from it should not be necessary and would be discretionary with planning and city officials.

31. A city lawfully changed the zoning on one side of a street from mixed residential-and-business use to solely residential, attempting to preserve the primarily residential character of the neighborhood consistent with the master plan. The other side of the street remained mixed residential-and-business use consistent with the master plan for further business and commercial development in that area. A resident whose home was then in the residential-only district sought city approval to operate a business from her home. What action should the resident pursue?

A. Claim a non-conforming use.

215

B.   Claim a change in circumstances.
C.   Rely on the doctrine of amortization.
D.   Seek a variance.

Answer explanation: Option D is correct because an owner seeking relief from lawfully enacted zoning to conduct a new use not permitted in the district does so by request for variance. The resident was seeking a new non-permitted use in a district under lawfully enacted zoning. Variance is her only choice. Option A is incorrect because the resident was proposing a new use rather than attempting to preserve a prior non-conforming use. Option B is incorrect because the resident has no change in circumstance to plead but is simply seeking a new use. Change in circumstance is not a zoning doctrine but a doctrine relating to servitudes. Option C is incorrect because the doctrine of amortization has to do with phasing out a prior non-conforming use, when here the resident had no prior non-conforming use.

32.   A developer of low-income housing paid for a housing study showing substantial need for such housing in a city that had none. The developer arranged for bank financing for a low-income housing development based on the strongly favorable market study. The developer also found several suitable vacant lots for sale in the city at prices that made sound economic sense for development. However, no properties within the city, whether for sale or not, had zoning appropriate for low-income housing. All zones in the city's zoning act effectively prohibited economic development of low-income housing. Which is the best legal challenge that the developer can make against the city and its zoning?

A.   Challenge the enactment as beyond the state enabling act.
B.   Challenge the enactment as exclusionary zoning.
C.   Challenge the enactment as spot zoning.
D.   Challenge the enactment as an unlawful variance.

Answer explanation: Option B is correct because local zoning must avoid unlawful *exclusionary zoning* that prohibits foster-care facilities, low-income housing, and other potentially unpopular uses. Option A is incorrect because state enabling acts may authorize exclusive zones, and the facts give no contrary information as to this state's enabling act. Option C is incorrect because spot zoning involves creating small zones for individual property owners out of political favor, none of which was present here. Option D is incorrect because a variance involves positive regulatory relief from lawful zoning rather than, as here, legal relief from unlawful zoning.

33.   The county that you represent retained the services of a master planner to locate a new county building housing courts and county offices. The master planner recommended using a centrally located, county-owned lot but acquiring neighboring privately owned lands to complete the new government complex. No other suitable properties are available. Several of the private landowners have banded together to refuse to sell to the county. If the county must build at that location, how may it best proceed?

A.   Condemn the property under power of eminent domain, with no compensation.
B.   Condemn the property under power of eminent domain, with just compensation.
C.   So heavily limit by regulation as to deprive the owner of use, with just compensation.
D.   Pay whatever price it takes even if substantially more than fair market value.

Answer explanation: Option B is correct because eminent domain is government power to condemn private property for public use with just compensation, permissible under state and federal constitutions. Eminent domain to take for use as public land, such as government offices, is a core exercise of eminent domain. Option

A is incorrect because the exercise of eminent domain requires just compensation at fair market value. Option C is incorrect because in a regulatory taking, government does not attempt to acquire the property, but the landowner claims the regulation is so extensive as to deprive the landowner of use, known as *inverse condemnation*. This taking is intentional for public use, not regulatory. Option D is incorrect because the government may exercise eminent domain, paying only just compensation, which is fair market value. Here, landowners may hold out for far more than the county would have to pay as fair market value.

34. The elected council of the city whom you represent has charged its planning commission to investigate the use of eminent domain powers to advance the city's development. The planning commission has expressed an interest in having more public greenways, more privately operated public transportation such as light rail, better transit facilities for ride-hailing, limousine, and shuttle services, and less blight from vacant industrial, commercial, and residential buildings. The commission has turned to you for advice on the limits of eminent domain. How would you properly advise the commission as to eminent domain law under the U.S. Constitution and prevalent state constitutions?

A.   Government may take land only for public use, not public function, with just compensation.
B.   Government may take land only for public use, including public function, with just compensation.
C.   Government may take land for public use or private use with public purpose, with just compensation.
D.   Government may not take land for public use, public function, or public purpose.

Answer explanation: Option B is correct. The government's exercise of eminent domain must be only for public use and with just compensation, but public use includes public functions like utilities and railways. Option A is incorrect because public use includes public function. Option C is incorrect because although the U.S. Constitutions permits taking for public purpose, the prevalent state pattern is to limit takings to public use, not public purpose. Option D is incorrect because state and federal constitutions authorize eminent domain.

35. A landowner owned a vacant lot in a city district zoned commercial. The lot had previously held a commercial building used at different times for retail and services businesses, until the building's deterioration had required that the landowner demolish it. The landowner wished to rebuild for commercial use permissible within the zone, but the zoning's new setback, height, lot-size, and aesthetic restrictions effectively prevented any construction. Without zoning relief, the land must remain idle. If the city refuses any relief, then what is the landowner's best argument for relief in the form of just compensation?

A.   Unreasonable seizure.
B.   Condemnation by eminent domain.
C.   Inverse condemnation by physical intrusion.
D.   Inverse condemnation by regulatory taking.

Answer explanation: Option D is correct because inverse condemnation is a regulatory taking in which government does not intend to acquire private land but so heavily regulates it as to effectively deprive its owner of its use. Here, the regulation deprived the owner of effective use. Option A is incorrect because it refers to a Fourth and Fourteenth Amendment personal right, not a property-protection right protected by federal and state takings clauses. Option B is incorrect because although the government has the positive power of eminent domain, which is to take private property for public use with just compensation, here the government did not seek to acquire the landowner's property. Option C is incorrect because although government's physical intrusion onto land is one test for inverse condemnation, here the government did not physically intrude.

36. A landowner owned industrial land next to a county road-commission facility. The county facility needed to expand its vehicle-maintenance garage, and so the county dug footings to extend the garage onto the landowner's adjacent land. The county construction cut off the landowner's driveway to the back of the land where the landowner stored industrial equipment. The landowner protested the construction and, when the county ignored the protests, sought counsel as to a takings claim. What is the best evaluation of the landowner's takings claim?

A. The intrusion is not a taking because it is continuous, permanent, and more than minimally interfering.
B. The intrusion is a taking because it is temporary, transient, and only minimally interfering.
C. The intrusion is a taking because continuous, permanent, and more than minimally interfering.
D. The intrusion is a taking because temporary, transient, and only minimally interfering.

Answer explanation: Option C is correct because a government occupation that is continuous, permanent, and more than minimally interferes is a taking, while temporary or transient intrusions depend on balancing interests. Construction of a garage on underground footings indicates continuous, permanent intrusion, while cutting off a driveway to equipment indicates a more-than-minimal interference. Option A is incorrect because a continuous, permanent, and more-than-minimally interfering intrusion would constitute a taking. Option B is incorrect because although temporary, transient, minimally interfering intrusions are not takings, here, the intrusion was continuous, permanent, and more than minimally interfering. Option D is incorrect because a temporary, transient intrusion that only minimally interferes would not constitute a taking.

37. A city suffered a mass shooting incident in which the perpetrators used assault-style weaponry. In response, the city council considered enacting an ordinance requiring owners of assault-style guns and similar weaponry to turn it in to law-enforcement officials for destruction. Setting aside the question of the proposed ordinance's constitutionality under the Second Amendment's right to bear arms, what other constitutional hurdle would the ordinance most-likely face?

A. A taking requiring just compensation.
B. A seizure requiring probable cause.
C. An undue burden on the right of association.
D. An interference with interstate commerce.

Answer explanation: Option A is correct because the takings clause requires government to pay just compensation for depriving others not only of real property but also of personal property. Option B is incorrect because Fourth Amendment rights against unreasonable search and seizure protect personal privacy and liberty, not personal-property rights. Option C is incorrect because the First Amendment right of association protects liberty and expression, not personal-property rights. Option D is incorrect because local confiscation of certain weaponry does not likely interfere with Congress's exclusive right to regulate interstate commerce.

38. A developer purchased forty acres of vacant land along a busy township highway, to develop for single-family residences. The township had already zoned the land for the developer's planned use. The developer then applied to the township for site-plan approval and building permits. In the approval process, the township indicated to the developer that it would approve the plan only if the developer contributed a strip of land along the highway for a highway turn lane and paid half the cost of both widening the highway for safe entrance to the development and extending larger water and sewer lines to the property to facilitate the development. If the developer challenges those requirements, what is the most-likely outcome?

A.   Prohibit as an unconstitutional taking.
B.   Prohibit as an interference with interstate commerce.
C.   Permit as a health-and-welfare regulation.
D.   Permit as a roughly proportional exaction.

Answer explanation: Option D is correct because an exaction may require a landowner to pay money, provide land, or provide for services in exchange for government approval of development, if roughly proportional to the development. Here, the township's requirements related directly to the cost of access to the development and its benefit. Option A is incorrect because government may requirement payments and land contributions roughly proportional to landowner development without them being a taking. Option B is incorrect because a local exaction for development does not unduly interfere with Congress's exclusive right to regulate interstate commerce. Option C is incorrect because although local government may enact health-and-welfare regulations, an exaction related to land development is not a health-and-welfare regulation.

Complete Short Outline

This outline follows the Multistate Bar Examination's topics outline. It summarizes the law on all Multistate Bar Examination topics within the Property II course description. This outline omits topics within the Property I course description.

I. A.-C. [Omitted as within the Property I course description.]

D. The law of landlord and tenant involves the right of an owner to lease the real property.
    A non-freehold estate under **leasehold** or **lease** makes the occupant a **tenant** and the owner a **landlord**.
1. Types of holdings depend on **creation** and determine rights on **termination**.
    Landlords and tenants typically create the type of tenancy initially by forming a lease.
        Conditions for terminating a lease depend on type of tenancy that the lease and other circumstances create.
a. A terms for years is a leasehold that conveys the right to occupy and use the land *for a specific period*.
    Landlord and tenant may provide for a period of days, weeks, months, years, or any other specific period.
    Landlord and tenant need only know when the term will end.
        A term of years may be **determinable**, occurrence of a condition shortening and terminating the lease.
    A term of years terminates automatically, *without notice*, at the end of its term.
b. A tenancy at will is a leasehold that either party may terminate at any time, with or without reason.
    The common law does not require notice to terminate, but the modern rule/ statutes require *reasonable notice*.
    Landlords must not terminate in violation of **anti-discrimination laws** protecting many classes.
        Protected classes include race, color, national origin, sex, religion, age, disability, & family & marital status.
c. A holdover is a tenant who stays beyond lease termination by term of years or end of periodic tenancy.
    A holdover tenant has only a **tenancy at sufferance** where the landlord may evict or hold to a renewed term.
        The renewed term equals the original lease period, except some states make it monthly for residential leases.
        If the original lease was for more than one year, many states limit renewal term to one month or one year.
    The landlord must make the decision within a reasonable time whether to hold over or to evict.
d. Periodic tenancies renew automatically for the initial lease period or renewal period that the lease provides.
    A *month-to-month* lease is a periodic tenancy renewing for one month at a time while both agree.
    Landlord and tenant can have year-to-year periods or longer periods such as five years.
    Landlord or tenant may only terminate a periodic tenancy at the end of one of the periods.
        The lease may require notice a certain number of days before the end of a period.
2. Possession is the tenant's leasehold right while landlords have the right of **rent** and *duty to deliver possession*.
    Most states follow the English rule for the landlord to deliver *actual* possession, not just legal right.
        The tenant without actual possession could withhold rent for occupancy, void and sue for damages, or evict.
        If the landlord delivers only partial possession, the tenant could reduce rent for the lost portion or evict.
    Some states follow the American rule requiring landlords only to convey legal right, not actual possession.
        The tenant must then sue the holdover tenant to evict and take possession.
    Tenants must avoid **waste**, not destroying the property, allowing disrepair, or making significant changes.
        Tenants must also not deliberately destroy walls, floors, appliances, and mechanical systems.
    Tenants do *not* have a duty to renovate or remodel to address normal wear and tear.
    Tenants also have no duty to repair after catastrophic damage but must reasonably avoid such damage.
    Tenants must also avoid **illegal uses** such as prostitution, drug sales, and the like.
        A landlord discovering such uses may terminate the lease or seek to enjoin while enforcing the lease.
    Tenants must also not interfere with quiet use and enjoyment by *other tenants*.
Rent is the tenant's primary duty to the landlord, the lease stating the amount, absent infer *fair market value*.
    The lease also states when rent is *due*, absent rent is due on the last day of the term, monthly or otherwise.
    A landlord wishing to evict a non-paying tenant brings an action for **ejectment** also referred to as *eviction*.
    Frustration of purpose is a rent defense when the basis for forming the lease proves incorrect.

Illegal leases, such as for residence that fails to meeting housing codes, void the obligation to pay rent.

If the law changes, making use illegal, then the tenant may terminate if the tenant cannot use the premises.

3. **Assignment and subletting** involve transfer of the tenant's rights and obligations to a new tenant.

The law allows assignment or sublet of a leasehold unless the lease prohibits, which many leases do.

The rules for assignment and sublet implicate both *privity of contract* and *privity of estate*.

Assignment transfers the tenant's *entire* interest to a new tenant.

Assignment ends privity of estate between landlord and tenant but not privity of contract.

Assignment *creates* privity of estate between landlord and the tenant's assignee but *not* privity of contract.

Assignee owes landlord rent and enforces landlord's obligations. Landlord collects from tenant or assignee.

Sublet transfers *part* of the leasehold to a subtenant, the tenant keeping the remainder interest.

Sublease does *not* create privity of contract or estate between landlord and sublessee.

Tenant retains privity of contract/estate with landlord, and creates privity of contract/estate with sublessee.

Landlord collects rent from tenant, tenant from sublessee; tenant enforces lease, sublessee sublease.

4. **Termination** of a lease implicates other rights and obligations in addition to eviction and action for rent.

A landlord may sue for contract damages in **anticipatory breach** if a tenant unconditionally refuses possession.

A landlord may also pursue contract-breach damages if a tenant *abandons* a lease after having taken possession.

Landlords must **mitigate damages** promptly and diligently seeking to re-let the premises to another tenant.

Tenants may help mitigate, sending prospective tenants, later proving landlord's failure to mitigate.

A tenant may **surrender** a leasehold and landlord accept surrender with no rent, partial rent, or lease buyout.

Rather than *self-help eviction*, landlords often get *court order* after notice, hearing, and even jury-trial rights.

Landlords resorting to self-help may face civil liability and statutory or punitive damages.

States requiring judicial proceedings for eviction typically offer streamlined procedures.

5. **Habitability and suitability** warranties may grant tenants greater rights to use the premises as intended.

The common law imposes no landlord duty to maintain and repair, the tenant instead owing that duty.

Yet many states today require a *residential* landlord to maintain and repair the premises.

States also prohibit landlords from evicting tenants for reporting housing-code violations.

Some states also imply a *residential* landlords' **warranty of habitability** for safe and sanitary premises.

Where the warranty exists, a tenant has the option of deducting cost of necessary repairs from the rent.

Leases imply a **covenant of quiet enjoyment** for leasehold use, free of interfering actions and nuisances.

Nuisances that so badly disturb as to frustrate uses gives a tenant a right of **constructive eviction**.

Non-functioning heating, cooling, plumbing, and electricity are common constructive-eviction grounds.

Constructive eviction, a damages action and rent defense, requires the tenant to *leave the premises*.

The landlord must act so wrongfully or so neglect as to *substantially interfere* with tenant use.

The tenant must also *give notice* of interference, and landlord must fail to remedy.

States split whether landlord must prevent other interfering but hold landlords for common areas.

Landlords also breach by wrongfully locking out or allowing others to do so, from all or any part.

Common law also allows tenants to withhold rent for a landlord's breach of quiet enjoyment.

Commercial leases imply a landlord's warranty of **suitability** for the anticipated commercial use.

E. **[Omitted as within the Property I course description.]**

II. **Rights in land** extend beyond ownership estates to restricting and permitting land uses in favor of non-owners.

A. **Covenants at law and in equity** are use rights the owner grants by *promise*, not ownership interests in land.

1. **Nature and type**: **covenants** promise to permit grantees to use and enjoy the grantor's land as promised.

Covenants at law, or **real covenants**, are *contract obligations* enforceable in damages action for breach.

Successor owners of the **dominant land** the covenant benefits may be able to enforce the covenant.

Real covenants *run with the land* only with horizontal and vertical privity.

Equitable servitudes, or **covenants in equity**, are promises enforceable through *specific performance*.

Specific performance involves the court's order that the owner of the **servient land** comply with the burden.

Equitable servitudes can *run with the land* without horizontal or vertical privity.

2. **Creation**: as contracts, **covenants** must meet the **statute of frauds** if granting rights for more than one year.

To run with the land, a **real covenant** must be *in a writing* that expresses or implies the *intent that it run*.

Parties intend a covenant to run when stating the covenant applies to successors, heirs, and assigns.

For the benefit to run with the land, the covenant must *touch and concern* the **servient land**.

For a covenant to run, parties must have **horizontal privity**, transferring servient-land interest.

For a covenant to run, the owners must also have **vertical privity**, such as one conveying to the other.

Adverse possession interrupts vertical privity.

For a covenant to run, the burdened owner must have **notice**, typically recording or constructive notice.

Benefitted owners usually enforce covenants at law through monetary-damages actions.

Equitable servitudes run with land *without horizontal or vertical privity* if in signed writing showing intent.

For a servitude to run, it must touch and concern the land and provide notice to the burdened land's owner.

Equitable servitudes may also arise **by implication**, through notice or constructive notice of a *common plan*.

Equitable servitudes may also arise **by implication**, through notice or constructive notice of a *common plan*.

The developer must intend that the restriction run with the land.

The restriction must also touch and concern the land rather than be personal in nature.

The developer must either record the restriction, or lot owners must have constructive notice.

Common lot owners must enforce the implied restriction for the restriction to persist.

A court may refuse to enforce where lot owners abandon the restriction and enforcement would be unfair.

Unclean hands, estoppel, change, and hardships weighing against enforcement are also defenses.

3. Scope of covenants at law or in equity depends on the promise that creates them and the intent of the parties.

Courts give plain meaning to plain terms while resolving ambiguities against the drafter.

Courts will not generally impose terms to which the parties have not agreed.

The scope of a covenant in equity arising by implication depends on the circumstances of the implication.

4. Termination of covenants at law and in equity, or equitable servitudes, occurs in several ways.

If the document of grant includes a durational restriction, then the covenant terminates when its term **expires**.

Covenants can also terminate if a single owner acquires the dominant and servient parcels, **merging** interests.

A benefitted owner can also **abandon** a covenant by indicating that intent to give up the rights that it affords.

B. Easements involve ownership rights in land limited to use or restriction.

1. Nature and type of easements include **affirmative easements** entitling and **negative easements** restricting use.

Easements appurtenant are rights of a dominant-parcel owner over the servient parcel, running with the land.

Run with land means easement restrictions benefit and burden successors to dominant and servient parcels.

Easements in gross are rights over the servient parcel *not* attached to any dominant parcel, not running.

Beneficiaries in gross may *not* transfer rights unless parties agree or rights are for *commercial purpose*.

The servient land remains subject to an easement in gross on the servient land's conveyance.

Licenses in land involve right to use another's land for a *limited and temporary purpose*, not ownership.

Courts construe a license when parties are unclear what they intend but intend something temporary.

Licensors giving permission for limited use may generally revoke it at any time.

Estoppel prevents revocation if the grant so states *or* if the holder *substantially and detrimentally relies*.

Easement that fail the statute of frauds or otherwise may give rise to an **irrevocable license**.

Not all states recognize estoppel, and construed licenses last only as justice requires.

2. Methods of creating easements are numerous.

a. Express easements arise by **grant** of the servient land's owner in favor of the easement's grantee.

Easements also arise by **reservation** of an owner who transfers the servient land to another, reserving rights.

Law presumes easement by grant intends the easement to be permanent, unless expressly stated otherwise.

If the grant or reservation does not mention duration, then the court will construe as a permanent easement.

b. Implied easements arise from the circumstances of the conveyance, indicating easement intent.

i. Quasi-use easements involve owner dividing land into dominant and servient parcels reflecting prior use.

The owner or a purchaser of the dominant parcel get to continue the use after division.

A single owner must have owned dominant and servient lands, use must be reasonably necessary,

use must be continuous rather than sporadic, parties must intend the burden, and use must be apparent.

ii. Necessity easements arise when an owner divides land, leaving one parcel needing an easement.

Easements of necessity arise if not satisfying requirements for easement by implication or prescription.

The land division must deprive a parcel of a right that is *necessary* for the property's use.

Easements of necessity require *strict necessity*, not just convenience or other general benefit.

iii. Plat easements arise by implication from a recorded **plat**, a map of the owner's newly divided land.

Owners reference plat restrictions when granting deeds to lot buyers, including for express easements.

Law may imply plat easements omitted from deed, from the plat map and apparent uses of other parcels.

This rule of *beneficial enjoyment* depends on plat and use indicating the owner's intent.

c. Prescription: easements also arise by **prescription**, referring to *adverse possession* like for freehold estates.

The easement use must be open, notorious, continuous, hostile, and under claim of right, for the period.

The exclusive-use requirement of adverse possession is absent for a prescriptive easement.

An easement by prescription grants the holder only the earned adverse right, not greater rights.

3. Scope of an easement, meaning the use it affords, depends on how the easement arose.

Easements *by express grant or reservation* depend on the **terms of the express grant**.

The easement's holder must not use beyond the express grant, nor the servient owner restrict to less.

Right of use changes only when the parties creating the easement intended that it change.

Easements may limit use by quantity, such as for only a single person or residents of a single parcel.

Easements *by implication* look to the use from which the law implied the easement.

Quasi-use easements from prior use have the scope of the prior use.

Easements *by prescription* have the scope of the prescriptive use.

4. Termination of easements, typically *permanent* without ending date, can nonetheless occur in several ways.

Express easements, by grant or reservation, terminate per the *expressed* terms.

Easements appurtenant terminate by **merger** when the dominant land's owner acquires the servient land.

Easements in gross terminate by **merger** when the holder acquires the servient land.

Easements also terminate when the holder **releases** the servient land from the burden.

A release is effective only when satisfying the *statute of frauds*.

Easements terminate when the holder acts in ways that clearly express the holder's intent to **abandon**.

A holder simply not using an easement is *not* abandonment.

Easements terminate with **cessation of purpose**, but only if the easement was one *of necessity*.

Easements for facility use terminate when the facility suffers **destruction**, if *not* by the servient land's owner.

A servient land's owner may **adversely possess** and thereby terminate an easement.

The owner's possession must be open, notorious, continuous, hostile, and a claim of right, for the period.

C. Fixtures are things *permanently affixed* to real property such that removal *damage* would reduce property value.

Tenant vacating take only personal property, not what landlord or tenant affix permanently to the real property.

Unless the lease provides otherwise, tenants must generally leave behind **fixtures**.

Look to the parties' intent when constructing or improving the premises and removal damage.

A security interest in fixtures has *priority over the mortgage* if arising out of fixture purchase.

The fixture security interest also has priority if the lender perfected before the fixtures affixed.

D. Zoning: local governments by authorization of state *enabling acts* pass **zoning** laws that regulate land uses.

Traditional exclusive-use zoning creates *residential, commercial, industrial, agricultural*, and other zones.

Exclusive zones may also create high-density versus low-density or single-family housing.

Zoning may also allow *mixed-use* areas and *planned unit developments* for officials to grant special uses.

Other locales follow *cumulative* zoning, allowing uses that have less impact than the zoned maximum.

Locales adopting zoning typically *grandfather* **non-compliant** existing uses to avoid a government **taking**.

State and federal constitutions require *just compensation* for government takings including *regulatory takings*.

Grandfather provisions may include forced phase-out of non-compliant uses when destroyed or abandoned.

Forced phase-outs also restrict to *ten percent* the extent to which the owner may repair, improve, or expand.

Suspect phase-outs give owners years within which to terminate, depreciating non-compliant-use value.

Landowners may challenge **ultra-vires** zoning laws that exceed the state enabling act's authority.

Zoning boards hold authority to grant a **variance** from zoning laws under granted criteria.

Criteria may include *undue hardship, unique unanticipated uses, beneficial use*, or nonsensical restriction.

Local law may also require *setbacks, parking, height limits, exterior finishes*, and *window percentage*.

Officials must not engage in unlawful *spot zoning* favoring individual landowners.

Also avoid unlawful *exclusionary zoning* prohibiting low-income housing and other unpopular uses.

Aesthetics restrictions must have reasonable standards to avoid arbitrary and capricious application.

Speech content restrictions must be least-restrictive means of obtaining a compelling government interest.

Time, place, and manner restrictions must relate directly to achieving a substantial government interest.

No substantial burden on religion unless least-restrictive means to achieve compelling government interest.

III.-V. [Omitted as within the Property I course description.]

Nuisance claims protect those who own and use real property. Define nuisance as:
> *intentional, unreasonable, substantial, non-trespassory invasion of another's interest in using lands.*

    Private nuisance claims protect the individual interest of one who owns or controls private lands.
        Only those who own or control the private land have *standing to sue*.
    Public nuisance claims protect the general interest of all who may use public lands.
        Only public officials, private affected-class reps, and private persons with special injury may sue.
    Weigh these factors to determine whether nuisance exists:
        utility or value of the activity, how common the activity is, suitability to the locale,
        impracticality of avoiding invasion, and gravity of the harm that it produces.
    Nuisances are usually intentional but may include negligent or reckless conduct, in some states.
        Nuisance may also include conditions giving rise to strict liability as an abnormally dangerous activity.
        Other tort claims or law violations of law increases the likelihood of the conduct being a nuisance.
    The jury determines *nuisance in fact* based on the above factors.
        Some authority exists for a judge to determine a *nuisance in law* for conduct violating statute.
    Remedies include not only damages to those who prove harm but also a preliminary injunction.
        To enjoin, must show irreparable harm, substantial likelihood of success on the merits, and
        balance of hardships weighing in plaintiff's favor.

Eminent domain is when government condemns private property for public use, with just compensation.
    Government may clearly take private property for public property like a street or park.
    Government may also take for public-use functions like utilities and railways.
        The U.S. Constitution permits taking for legitimate public purpose such as to remove blight.
            Most states restrict eminent domain to public land or function.
    Government pays fair market value, what a willing buyer would pay a willing seller on the open market.
        Use the value for the land's highest and best use.
            Law may also require payment of relocation expenses and attorney's fees.
        The takings clause requires just compensation for depriving others of their *personal property*.
            Requiring cash or personal-property contributions as a condition for engaging in commerce is a taking.
        Different branches of government take real or personal property different ways.
            Legislatures take property by acquisition, intrusion, or legislating away all viable use.
            Administrators take by condemning, intruding, or regulating away viable use.
    An **exaction** requires a landowner to pay money or give land in exchange for project approval.
        Government does not take if in rough proportion between the exaction and development.
            Government may require payment for new roads and utility lines, and to grant easements.
            Government may not require payment into the general fund, unrelated to the development.

Complete Long Outline

This outline follows the Multistate Bar Examination's topics outline. It summarizes the law on all Multistate Bar Examination topics within the Property II course description. This outline omits topics within the Property I course description.

I. A.-C. [Omitted as within the Property I course description.]

D. The law of landlord and tenant

Owners of real property have rights to lease interests in the land. Those who wish to occupy land without an ownership interest may have the opportunity to form a non-freehold estate that the law recognizes as a **leasehold** or **lease**, making the occupant a **tenant**. Ownership thus needs to address the law of **landlord and tenant**, a landlord being the owner who leases occupancy to a tenant. Landlord/tenant law must address the *types* of leaseholds including how parties create and terminate them. Landlord/tenant law also must address tenant rights of *possession* versus landlord rights of *rent*. Landlords may *assign* their interest, while tenants may be able to *sublet*. The *termination* of tenancies is another subject as are issues of *habitability* and *suitability*, all addressed in the following sections.

1. Types of holdings: creation and termination

The law recognizes several different types of **tenancy**. The following sections address a *term of years*, which is a tenancy for a specific period whether or not measured in years, *tenancies at will*, terminable by either party, *holdovers* and other tenancies *at sufferance*, and *periodic tenancies*, typically measured by the period of the original lease. Landlords and tenants typically create the type of tenancy at least initially by entering into a lease. The conditions for terminating a lease depend on the type of tenancy that the lease or other circumstance has created.

a. Terms for years

A **term of years** is a common leasehold that conveys the right to occupy and use the land *for a specific period*. Although the law calls the leasehold a term of *years*, the landlord and tenant may provide for a period of days, weeks, months, years, or any other period, if the period is specific. The landlord and tenant need only know when the term will end. Thus, a lease that lasts *until the third full moon rises* is a term of years because the parties can calculate the date certain when the third full moon rises. A term of years may be **determinable**, meaning that although the lease provides for a specific period, the occurrence of a condition may shorten the period, terminating the lease. Thus, a lease *for one year, as long as tenant lives alone* is a determinable term of years. A term of years terminates automatically, meaning *without notice*, at the end of its term.

b. Tenancies at will

A **tenancy at will** is a leasehold that either party may terminate at any time, with or without reason. While the common law did not require notice to terminate, the modern rule and many state statutes require *reasonable notice*, particularly as to residential leases. Thus, a residential landlord may have to serve a thirty-day notice to quit. While a landlord may terminate a tenancy at will for any reason or no reason, a landlord must not terminate in violation of **anti-discrimination laws** protecting classes including race, color, national origin, sex, religion, age, disability, family status, meaning with or without children, and in some states marital status or other statuses, meaning with children.

c. Holdovers and other tenancies at sufferance

A **holdover** is a tenant who stays beyond the termination of the lease, whether the lease ends by term of years or at the end of a periodic tenancy. A holdover tenant has only a **tenancy at sufferance** during which the landlord may decide whether to evict the tenant or to hold the tenant to a renewed lease period equal to the original lease period. Thus, if the original lease was month-to-month, then the landlord could only hold the tenant over, meaning require the tenant to commit to and pay for, another month's lease. If, instead, the lease was year-to-year, many jurisdictions permit the landlord to hold the tenant to an additional year, although some states provide for only a month-to-month tenancy, particularly for *residential* leases. If the original lease was for more than one year, many jurisdictions would limit the landlord to holding the tenant over for a shorter period such as one month or one year. The landlord must make the decision within a reasonable time whether to hold over or to evict.

d. Periodic tenancies

A **periodic tenancy** is a tenancy that renews automatically for the initial lease period or other renewal period that the lease provides. Thus, for example, a *month-to-month* lease, providing that the tenant rents by the month, is a periodic tenancy that renews for one month as long as the landlord intends each month that the tenant stay and the tenant intends likewise. Landlord and tenant can also have longer periodic tenancy such as year-to-year or even providing for five-year renewal periods. The landlord or tenant may only terminate a periodic tenancy at the end of one of the periods. The lease may require notice a certain number of days before the end of a period.

2. Possession…

A lease grants the tenant the right of **possession** and the landlord the right of **rent**. A lease fundamentally includes the landlord's *duty to deliver* to the tenant the *legal right of possession*. Most jurisdictions hold to the English rule that the landlord also has a duty to deliver *actual* possession, not just the legal right to possess. Thus, in those cases, a landlord who grants legal right of possession to a tenant but leaves the premises occupied by a holdover tenant would have breached duty to deliver actual possession. The tenant's remedies would then be to either withhold rent until the tenant can occupy the premises or void the lease and sue the landlord for any damages due to the lost possession. If the landlord delivers only partial possession, though, the tenant has a right only to reduce the rent for the lost portion. The tenant may alternatively sue to evict the holdover tenant. Jurisdictions following the minority American rule do not require the landlord to deliver actual possession, instead requiring the tenant to sue the holdover to evict and take possession.

Tenants must avoid **waste**, meaning that they must not destroy the property, allow its collapse into disrepair, or make other significant changes to the property. For example, if a tenant discovers a significant plumbing leak, the tenant must act or notify the landlord promptly to do so, rather than ignore the problem as it causes growing damage. Tenants must also not deliberately destroy walls, floors, appliances, and mechanical systems. Tenants do *not*, though, have a duty to renovate or remodel to address normal wear and tear. Tenants also have no duty to repair after catastrophic damages, for instance from hurricane or flood, although they must try to avoid such damage when reasonably able to do so. Tenants must also avoid **illegal uses** such as prostitution, drug sales, and the like. A landlord discovering such uses may terminate the lease or seek to enjoin such uses while enforcing the lease. Tenants must also not interfere with quiet use and enjoyment by *other tenants*.

…and rent

While the landlord owes the duty to provide the tenant with legal and likely also actual possession, the tenant owes the landlord the duty to pay **rent**. While the traditional rule made the tenant's duty to pay rent independent of the landlord's duties, the above section and a following section on habitability and suitability show the widespread abandonment of the traditional rule. The lease states the rent amount, in the absence of which a court will infer a *fair market value*. The lease also states when rent is due, in the absence of which rent is due on the last day of the month in a month-to-month lease or the last day of the term for a tenancy in term of years. A landlord who wishes to eject a non-paying tenant brings an action for **ejectment** also referred to as *eviction*. **Frustration of purpose** can be a rent defense when the basis on which the landlord and tenant agreed to the lease proves incorrect. **Illegal** leases, such as for a residence that fails to meeting housing codes, void the obligation to pay rent. If the law changes, making the use illegal, then the tenant may terminate if the tenant cannot use the property legally. A section well below treats the question of the landlord's right to **fixtures** on the tenant vacating.

3. Assignment and subletting

A tenant may wish to **assign** the tenant's lease rights and obligations to a new tenant. An **assignment** transfers the tenant's *entire* interest to a new tenant. Tenants may also wish to **sublet** a part of the leasehold to a subtenant, keeping the remainder interest. A sublet refers to a conveyance of less than the tenant's full leasehold interest, such as to sublet for three months of a six-month lease. The law generally allows either assignment or sublet of a leasehold interest, unless the lease bars assignment or sublet, which many leases do. The rules for assignment and sublet implicate both *privity of contract*, referring to the agreement between landlord and tenant, and *privity of estate*, referring to the transfer of the leasehold estate from landlord to tenant.

Assignment ends the privity of estate between landlord and tenant but not privity of contract. The tenant continues to owe whatever obligation the lease calls for in the event of assignment, which is typically full right to enforce the lease against the tenant notwithstanding assignment. Assignment *creates* privity of estate between landlord and the tenant's assignee but *not* privity of contract. By contrast, sublease does *not* create any privity, whether of contract or estate, between landlord and the tenant's sublessee. The tenant retains both privity of contract and of estate with the landlord, while creating privity of contract and estate only between tenant and sublessee. The rules, then, are that a landlord can collect rent from anyone with whom the landlord is in privity of contract *or* estate, but a tenant can enforce obligations only of a landlord with whom the tenant is in privity of *estate*. So, in assignments, the landlord can collect rent from *either* the tenant or assignee, while only the assignee can enforce the landlord's obligations. Yet in subleases, the landlord can collect rent *only* from the tenant and the tenant from sublessee, while the tenant can enforce the landlord's obligations, and the sublessee can enforce the tenant's obligations.

4. Termination (surrender, mitigation of damages, and anticipatory breach)

The above sections on the types of tenancies address how each type terminates. The above section on **rent** addresses a landlord's action for ejectment or eviction for nonpayment of rent. The law strongly discourages *self-help evictions*, particularly for residential leases. Landlords must usually instead get a *court order* following appropriate procedures including notice, hearing, and in some cases even jury-trial rights. Landlords who resort to self-help such as changing locks and putting personal property out at the curb may have civil liability or criminal responsibility for those actions. On the other hand, states that require judicial proceedings for eviction typically offer streamlined procedures. A tenant may **surrender** a leasehold. The landlord may accept the tenant's surrender without pursuing unpaid rent, accepting partial payment of past due rent, or accepting a lease buyout of future unpaid rent.

A landlord may sue for contract damages in **anticipatory breach** if a tenant makes a positive and unconditional refusal to take possession and fulfill the lease, or becomes unable to perform. Likewise, if a tenant *abandons* a lease after having taken possession for part of the lease term, and does so without the landlord's agreement as to surrender terms, then the landlord may pursue a contract-breach action on the lease for past unpaid rent, future unpaid rent, and other damages as contract law allows. However, in the case of anticipatory breach or breach in abandonment of the lease, landlords have the same contract-law obligation to **mitigate damages** that others enforcing contracts owe. In the case of a lease, the landlord's duty to mitigate means that the landlord must ordinarily promptly and diligently seek to re-lease the premises to another tenant. In practice, tenants may attempt to help the landlord do so by sending prospective tenants to the landlord, which may also help the tenant prove the landlord's failure or refusal to mitigate as a defense to a rent action.

5. Habitability and suitability

The law implies in every lease a **covenant of quiet enjoyment**, not referring solely to peaceful premises but rather to use the property for the purpose that the lease intended including to be free of nuisances that interfere with that use. The common law, followed in most jurisdictions, allows the tenant to withhold rent if the landlord violates the covenant. Landlords can violate the covenant by either wrongfully locking out or evicting the tenant, or allowing another to do so, from all or any part of the premises. The landlord's doing so relieves the tenant of *all* liability to pay rent, unlike the forgoing rule for partial evictions in which the tenant must continue to pay partial rent.

In some jurisdictions, the law also implies in every *residential* lease a **warranty of habitability** that assures the tenant that the premises are fit for the tenant to inhabit the premises safely and sanitarily, even though the common law does not imply the warranty. Where the warranty exists, a tenant can add to the above remedies the option of deducting repairs from the rent. The common law, though, generally imposes no duty on the landlord's part to maintain and repair the premises, which instead becomes the tenant's responsibility on taking possession unless the lease provides otherwise. Many jurisdictions today require a residential landlord to maintain and repair the premises, creating an obligation much like that of the warranty of habitability. Jurisdictions do prohibit landlords from evicting tenants for reporting housing-code violations. In commercial leases, the law implies a warranty of **suitability**, which is roughly equivalent to the residential warranty of habitability. Unless the lease provides otherwise, the commercial premises must be suitable for the anticipated commercial use.

A tenant, whose possession nuisances so badly disturb as to frustrate or destroy those uses, has a right of **constructive eviction**. The landlord must have committed such wrongful actions or so neglected the premises as to *substantially interfere* with its uses. The tenant must also have *given notice* of the interference, and the landlord must have failed to remedy the interference. Constructive eviction also requires the tenant to *leave the premises*. Constructive eviction is both an action that the tenant may maintain for damages due to the interference *and* a defense to the landlord's rent action. Non-functioning mechanical systems for heating, cooling, plumbing, electricity, and access, often constitute grounds for constructive eviction. Jurisdictions split on whether landlords must prevent others from interfering if able to do so but do routinely hold landlords responsible for common areas.

E. [Omitted as within the Property I course description.]

II. Rights in land

Real-property law addresses and provides for other **rights in land** beyond the ownership estates that the above sections address. Those other rights in land include *covenants at law and in equity*, restricting and controlling the use of land, and *easements*, *profits*, and *licenses*, creating rights in others than the owners of the land to use the land, even if inconsistent with the owner's wishes. Covenants differ from easements in that covenants involve *contract* obligations while easements create *ownership* interests in the land. Keep that distinction in mind as you review the law of covenants and easements. Real-property issues also arise around *fixtures* permanently affixed to the land and *zoning* restrictions. The following sections address these other rights in land beyond the ownership issues addressed above.

A. Covenants at law and in equity

Covenants at law involve rights of use that the owner of land grants by *contract* to another that the other may enjoy, even when inconsistent with the owner's current wishes, subject to a damages action for breach. **Covenants in equity**, also called *equitable servitudes*, involve rights of use that the owner grants in a contract obligation, as to which equity grants enforcement by *specific performance*. As indicated above, covenants in land do *not* involve ownership in land, only the contract obligation, although a following section shows that covenants can *run with the land* like ownership interests. The following sections address the *nature* and *type* of these covenants, their *creation*, and their *scope, enforcement*, and *termination*.

1. Nature and type

A **real covenant** is the grantor's contract promise and related obligation to permit the grantee to use and enjoy the grantor's real property without creating a freehold estate in the grantee. Because covenants in land involve *contract obligations* rather than ownership interests in land, covenants typically arise out of *promises* enforceable in contract rather than, for example, easements by implication, necessity, or prior use, although the effect of a covenant is often the same as that of an easement. For example, a resident who lives and owns a home behind another home the property for which the city has just changed to a commercial district, may for consideration contract with the other homeowner not to build a commercial structure that would burden the resident's own home. The resident would then have a *covenant*, not an *easement*, although the resident could enforce the covenant to prevent construction of a commercial structure or for contract-breach damages. Real covenants, though, have a unique quality beyond the typical contract in that **successor owners** of the land that a covenant benefits, called the **dominant land**, may be able to enforce the covenant. The law holds that covenants that successor owners can enforce must *run with the land*, the requirements for which the next section addresses.

The law also recognizes **equitable servitudes**, also called **covenants in equity**. An equitable servitude or covenant in equity is an enforceable promise relating to the use of land that the benefitted promisee enforces through the equitable form of relief *specific performance*. Specific performance involves the court's order that the owner of the servient land comply with the burden to benefit the owner seeking that equitable relief. Unlike covenants at law, equitable servitudes can arise *and run with the land* without horizontal or vertical privity, as the next section addresses.

2. Creation

As indicated briefly above, because **covenants in land** involve *contract obligations* rather than ownership interests in land, covenants typically arise out of *promises* enforceable in contract rather than by implication, necessity, or prior use, although the effect of a covenant is often the same as that of an easement. To create a covenant in land, the parties must satisfy the **statute of frauds**, specifically if the restriction lasts for more than one year. The bigger question, though, is often whether the covenant's creation allows it to *run with the land*, meaning to benefit and burden subsequent owners of the dominant and servient parcels.

To run with the land, a covenant must have been *in a writing* that expresses or implies the *intent that it run*. The courts readily construe that the parties intended a covenant to run when the writing states that the covenant applies to successors, heirs, and assigns. Yet courts will also construe intent from the circumstances. The covenant must also *touch and concern* the **servient land**, meaning the burdened land, such as requiring payment of association maintenance fees. For a covenant's burden to run with the land, the parties must also have formed the covenant when in **horizontal privity**, meaning when sharing some interest in the servient land, such as the sale from one to the other or a lease from one to the other. Thus, in the above example, the neighbors who agreed to a covenant not to build commercial on one neighbor's land would *not* have horizontal privity, meaning that the covenant could *not* run with the land.

For a covenant's burden or benefit to run, the servient land's owner must also have **vertical privity** with the owner with whose activities on the land the covenant interferes, such as the original owner making the covenant conveying the land to the burdened owner. While successor owners will usually have vertical privity with the owner originally covenanting to burden the land, *adverse possession* interrupts vertical privity. Finally, the burdened owner must have had **notice** of the burden, typically through the covenant's recording against the land, although sometimes through constructive notice of the existing burden. Benefitted owners usually enforce covenants at law through monetary-damages actions.

A signed writing satisfying the statute of frauds will also create an equitable servitude or covenant in equity enforceable by specific performance. Unlike covenants at law, though, equitable servitudes can arise and run with the land *without horizontal or vertical privity*. An equitable servitude need only be in a signed writing showing the intent that it run with the land, touch and concern the land, and provide notice to the owner of the burdened land.

Equitable servitudes may also arise **by implication**, meaning through notice or constructive notice of a *common plan*. For example, if a landowner divides a large parcel to sell lots under a common plan for only single-family residences but mistakenly leaves the written covenant out of some of the later conveyed deeds, then the other written restrictions and construction of only single-family homes will have put on notice lot owners taking those later deeds. Forming an implied reciprocal servitude requires that the developer intend that the restriction run with the land, that it touch and concern the land rather than be personal in nature, and that the developer either record the writing expressing that intent or that the lot owners have constructive notice from the uniformity of conditions.

The common lot owners must enforce the implied restriction for the restriction to persist. If lot owners begin to vary and violate the restriction, then a court may hold that the lot owners abandoned the restriction and accordingly refuse to enforce it, especially where enforcement against one lot owner would be unfair with respect to other lot owners violating the restriction. Other equitable defenses to an implied reciprocal servitude can include unclean hands, estoppel, laches, changed conditions, and a balance of hardships weighing against enforcement.

3. Scope

The **scope** of covenants at law or in equity depends primarily on the promise that creates them and the intent of the parties behind that promise. Rules like those that courts apply to any contract interpretation apply to the express promise of a covenant at law or in equity. The courts will give plain meaning to plain terms while resolving ambiguities against the drafter. The court will not generally impose terms to which the parties have not agreed. On the other hand, the scope of a covenant in equity arising by implication depends on the circumstances of the implication. Refer to the section below on the scope and construction of easements for more detailed rules also applicable to covenants at law or in equity.

4. Termination

The law recognizes the **termination** of covenants at law and in equity, or equitable servitudes, in several ways. If the document of grant includes a durational restriction, then the covenant terminates when its term **expires**. Covenants can also terminate if a single owner acquires the dominant and servient parcels, in which case the covenant **merges**. A benefitted owner can also **abandon** a covenant by indicating that intent to give up the rights that it affords. Covenants terminate as easements terminate, covered in greater detail in a following section.

B. Easements, profits, and licenses

An **easement** involves an ownership right in land limited to its use or restriction, in contrast to the freehold estates described in sections above that reflect ownership interests in the full bundle of ownership rights. Easements function like *covenants at law or in equity*, addressed above, except again that an easement is an ownership interest rather than, as in the case of a covenant at law or in equity, only a contract interest. Consider the *nature* and *types* of easements in the following section, followed by sections on their *creation*, *scope*, and *termination*.

1. Nature and type

The law first distinguishes between **affirmative easements**, entitling the holder to use of the servient land, and **negative easements**, *restricting* the *owner* from some use. For example, an easement that permits one neighbor to use the driveway of another neighbor has an *affirmative* easement, while an easement that prohibits one neighbor from building a structure on a portion of that neighbor's *own* land, for the benefit of the other neighbor, is a *negative* easement. The law also distinguishes between **easements appurtenant**, referring to rights that owners of a dominant parcel have relative to the servient parcel, and **easement in gross**, referring to rights that owners hold relative to the servient parcel but *not* attached to any dominant parcel. For example, both above examples involve easements *appurtenant* because they both benefit a specific neighboring parcel of land. By contrast, an easement *in gross* would entail a person's right to enter another's land to, for example, put one's boat in the water, without that person's right benefitting any specific land. The law also labels types of easement by their manner of creation, as the next section addresses.

Easements appurtenant *run with the land*, while easements in gross do *not* run with the land. As indicated above in the sections on covenants at law and in equity, to run with the land means that the easement's restriction benefits the successors in interest to the dominant parcel while burdening successors in interest to the servient parcel. For example, the right to put one's boat in the water in the above example, being merely in gross, would *not* run with the land, while the other rights to driveway use or prevent building of structures, being appurtenant, *would* run with the land. Beneficiaries of easements in gross may *not* generally transfer their rights unless the parties so agree or the rights are for a *commercial purpose*, such as when a company buys the right to maintain a billboard on an owner's servient land. However, the servient land remains subject to an easement in gross on the servient land's conveyance.

The law also recognizes **licenses** in land. A license involves the right to use another's land for a *limited purpose*, such as if a landowner permits a friend to temporarily park the friend's motor home on the landowner's land. Unlike an easement, a license is *not* an interest in land. When the parties are not clear whether they intend a license or an easement in gross, the courts tend to construe a *license* unless the parties clearly intend the restriction to be more than temporary. The grantor of a license who gives oral or written permission to the limited use may generally revoke it at any time. However, under the **doctrine of estoppel**, the grantor must *not* revoke if the grant specifically stated that it would be irrevocable *or* if the license's holder has *substantially and detrimentally relied* on the license, although some jurisdictions refuse to recognize estoppel. Thus, in the above example, if the friend *had* to park the motor home on the owner's land overnight or for another short period to avoid a fine or fee that the friend would incur for having relied on the owner's license, then estoppel could prevent the landowner from objecting. Indeed, an easement that fails due to the statute of frauds or other reason may give rise to an **irrevocable license** of this type. However, an irrevocable license, while like a permanent easement in gross, lasts only until it no longer prevents an injustice.

2. Methods of creation

Parties create easements in several ways, each addressed in the following sections. Easements arise most easily and obviously by express **grant** of the owner of the servient land. Yet easements also arise by **reservation** of the owner who transfers the then-servient land to another. Easements also arise by **implication** from the circumstances of the conveyance, indicating transferor and transferee intent to recognize an easement. Easements also arise of **necessity** when an owner divides land and leaves one parcel needing an easement across the other to make use of the land. Finally, easements also arise by **prescription**, referring to *adverse possession*, in the manner that freehold estates arise by adverse possession.

a. Express

Parties create easements by **grant**, in which the servient land's owner transfers the right to the easement's grantee, and by **reservation**, in which the owner transfers land to another while reserving the easement right to the transferring owner. The law presumes that an easement by grant intends the easement to be permanent, unless the grant expressly states otherwise. For example, if a landowner agrees in exchange for a neighbor's consideration that the neighbor and successors to the neighbor's land may cross the landowner's property to reach a nearby beach, the landowner may grant the neighbor an easement that the neighbor can record to document the right. Alternatively, if the landowner decided to sell half of the land but reserve a path across the sold portion for the landowner and successors to reach the beach, the landowner could *reserve* the easement in the deed conveying the sold half. If the grant or reservation does not mention duration, then the court will construe the path as a permanent easement.

b. Implied

The law recognizes three types of **implied easement**, each treated in the following sections. Implied easements arise from the circumstances rather than by express grant. The first type of implied easement is a *quasi-use* easement that begins with an owner using the land in an apparent way that, when the owner later divides the land into dominant and servient parcels reflecting the prior use, allows the owner or a purchaser of the dominant parcel to continue the use. A second type of implied easement is an easement *of necessity* that the law implies to ensure that the dominant parcel would not otherwise be without use. A third type of implied covenant arises from the owner recording a *plat* on the land's division, burdening the platted lots with the initial restrictions.

i. Quasi-use

Parties can create an implied easement of **quasi-use** when a landowner begins with a single parcel on which the landowner conducts an apparent use, such as maintaining a driveway or providing for utilities. The owner's uses at that time are not easements, only *quasi* easements, because the owner holds the whole of the land. When the landowner then divides the land into two or more parcels at least one of which requires an easement to *continue the apparent use*, then an easement can arise by implication as necessary to continue the use. For example, if an owner maintains a driveway that the owner's land division subsequently interrupts, and the driveway is necessary to the owner's continued use of the parcel that the owner retains, then an easement by prescription will burden the parcel that the owner sells. Easements by implication, though, require that a single owner have owned the dominant and servient lands, that the use is reasonably necessary to the dominant land, that the use was continuous rather than sporadic before division, that the owner and successor have intended the burden of the continued use, and that the use was apparent to the successor when taking.

ii. Necessity

Easements **of necessity** can arise even when the circumstances do not satisfy all requirements for an easement by implication or prescription. An easement of necessity requires that the land division have deprived a parcel of a right that is *necessary* for the property's use, such as access to a public roadway. Thus, for example, if a landowner divides a property front to back rather than side to side, leaving the back parcel landlocked without public-road access, the law will recognize an easement of necessity even if prior use had not established the access, access use was not apparent, or the parties had not intended access, as a quasi-use easement would have required. Because easements of necessity do not satisfy the conditions for a quasi-use easement or easement by prescription, easements of necessity require *strict necessity*, not just convenience or other general benefit to the dominant land.

iii. Plat

Easements can also arise by implication from a recorded **plat**. A plat is a map of the owner's land divided into new parcels. The plat map may include descriptions of and restrictions on the land's use when divided, such as for single-family housing only. A master deed, master agreement, plat map, or other document recorded or referenced in recordings may include other restrictions, such as subjecting the parcels to control of an association, payment of association fees, and the like, and other benefits, such as use of the land's private streets, parks, and beach or other access. Prudent owners reference plat restrictions when granting deeds to individual lot buyers, including for express easements. However, when an owner neglects to include express easements in a deed, the law may imply those easements from the plat map and apparent uses of other parcels complying with the platted restrictions, under a rule of *beneficial enjoyment*. The plat and circumstances, though, must indicate the owner's intent to create the easement. Just because an easement would benefit all owners does not authorize the court to imply it.

c. Prescription

An easement by **prescription** can arise when a person adversely possesses the easement right. The use must be open and notorious, continuous, hostile to the owner's use, and under a claim of right, for longer than the state's statutory period for **adverse possession**. Notice that only the exclusive-use requirement of adverse possession is absent among the requirements for a prescriptive easement. When not creating a freehold estate because of the limited nature of the use or the absence of *exclusive* use, the use can give rise instead to an easement by prescription. Thus, for example, if neighbors cross an owner's land to reach a beach satisfying each of the above conditions and do so for the statutory period, then the neighbors acquire an easement by prescription to continue beach access. An easement by prescription grants the holder only the earned adverse right, not greater rights. Thus, the neighbors acquiring the access right would have no right to burden the easement further by, for instance, widening and improving their path, and building a deck for a beach overlook.

3. Scope

An easement's **scope**, meaning what rights it affords and burdens it imposes, depends on how the easement arose. If the easement arose by *express grant or reservation*, then the easement's scope depends on the **terms of the express grant**. The easement's holder must not expand the scope of the grant, such as by widening an area of use, improving the easement beyond the grant, or making a different use than the grant expressed. Likewise, the owner of the servient land must not restrict the grant to less than the rights that it expresses, such as by denying vehicular ingress and egress as the grant expressed while permitting only foot traffic. An easement's right of use should change only when the parties creating the easement intended that it change, such as for vehicular travel rather than horse-and-buggy travel on the advent of the automobile. Easements may also limit or grant use by quantity, such as for only a single person or residents of a single parcel to pass or for residents of multiple parcels or even the public to pass.

If, by contrast, the easement arose *by implication*, then the court must look to the use from which the law implied the easement. *Quasi-use* easements, arising from prior use, would have the scope of the prior use. Thus, if an owner divided the land in a way that one parcel depended on an apparent utilities easement across the other parcel, the dominant parcel would have the right to continue the utilities use but *not* to construct a driveway or otherwise expand the use. The same rule holds for easements *by prescription* that the prescriptive use determines the easement's scope. Thus, if the prescriptive use was beach access, then the users creating the prescriptive easement would have that right but not the right to widen and improve the access, or increase the use to include building decks or other structures, or partying on the servient land.

4. Termination

Although easements are typically *permanent*, without ending date, easements can nonetheless **terminate** in several ways. An express easement, whether by grant or reservation, may terminate per the *expressed* terms. Thus, if the grant creates an easement across servient land for as long as the dominant land is within a certain family, or used as a vacation home but for no other use, then the easement would terminate on a change in either expressed condition. Easements can also terminate by **merger**, when the easement in gross's holder acquires the servient land or when the owner of the dominant land acquires title also to the servient land, even if the owner later re-divides the land. Easements can also terminate when the easement's holder **releases** the servient land from the burden, often after negotiation and for consideration. A release is effective, though, only when satisfying the *statute of frauds* insofar as the release reflects a transaction in an interest in land.

Easements can also terminate when the holder acts in a way that clearly expresses the holder's intent to **abandon** the easement, such as by building a fence across that part of the path on the holder's dominant land. A holder simply not using an easement is *not* abandonment. Easements can also terminate with

cessation of purpose, but only if the easement was one *of necessity*. Thus, a landlocked parcel that had an easement of necessity across another parcel would lose the easement if a new public road provided the formerly landlocked parcel with access. Easements for use of a facility may also terminate when the facility suffers **destruction**, if the destruction was *not* at the hands of the servient land's owner. Finally, a servient land's owner may **adversely possess** and thereby terminate an easement, if the owner's possession meets the open, notorious, continuous, hostile, and claim-of-right conditions for the statutory period.

C. Fixtures (including relevant application of Article 9, UCC)

Real-property law must also occasionally deal with the question of what constitutes *real* property versus *personal* property. Land and buildings are obviously real property. The issue arises when personal property such as materials, lighting or furnishings, appliances, and even equipment get incorporated into and affixed to the real property. Things *permanently affixed* to the real property, such that their removal would *damage* the real property, reducing its value, constitute **fixtures**. Fencing attached to posts dug into the ground would ordinarily be a fixture. Custom cabinetry integrated into a building's interior also may be so. Lights installed into ceilings and walls are fixtures, while lighting plugged into a socket is not. Appliances that one can remove without damage to cabinetry, such as a refrigerator on wheels, are generally not fixtures, but appliances built into the cabinetry, such as range hoods, some microwaves, and other cabinet-style refrigerators, are probably fixtures.

The question as to what is a fixture, and thus real property rather than personal property, becomes important in landlord/tenant law, when a tenant vacates and must take only personal property but not what landlord or tenant have affixed permanently to the real property. Tenants vacating the premises take their personal property with them. Unless the lease provides otherwise, tenants must generally leave behind **fixtures**, even if the tenant was the party who affixed them. In disputes over removal of affixed items, courts look to the parties' intent when constructing or improving the premises and the damage that removal will cause.

The question as to what is a fixture also becomes important when dealing with mortgages of the land and security interests in equipment. For example, a mortgage company may finance a buyer's purchase of commercial property secured by a purchase-money mortgage. A bank may then extend a line of credit secured by a security interest in the buyer's commercial equipment. If both lenders foreclose, then they may dispute whether the buyer has so permanently affixed items like built-in freezers, special sinks, shelving, and even industrial equipment to the real property that the mortgage company rather than the bank should have the benefit of the security. The Uniform Commercial Code's **Article 9** holds that a lender like the bank in the prior example may take a security interest in fixtures *with priority over the property's mortgage* if the security interest arose out of the fixtures' purchase or if the lender perfected the security interest before the borrower incorporated the fixtures into the real property.

D. Zoning (fundamentals other than regulatory taking)

Local governments, whether cities, villages, townships, or other units, may by authorization of state *enabling acts* pass **zoning** laws that regulate land uses within their borders. A typical exclusive-use zoning scheme regulates uses to *residential, commercial, industrial, agricultural*, and other areas, allowing only those uses in those areas. Mutually exclusive zones may also dictate gradations for such as high-density versus low-density or single-family housing. Exclusive-use zoning may also allow from some *mixed-use* areas and *planned unit developments* that enable zoning officials to negotiate with landowners for special mixed or non-compliant uses. Other locales follow *cumulative* zoning, allowing all uses in an area that have less impact than the zoned maximum use, from *highest* use to *lowest* use. Thus, a residential area would allow only residential, but a commercial area would allow both commercial and residential, and an industrial area would allow all uses. Some locales mix exclusive and cumulative zones.

Regulatory Taking

Eminent domain is purposeful exercise of government authority to acquire private property for public use. By contrast, government does not intend the property's acquisition in a *regulatory taking*, but law construes it as such for just compensation, when the government regulation so heavily limits use as to deny the landowner of the land's use. Regulatory takings are also known as *inverse condemnation* because the property owner rather than the government claims that the government action constitutes a taking. Government must pay fair market value, defined as what a willing buyer would pay a willing seller on the open market at the time of eminent domain's exercise, for the land's highest and best use. Law may also require payment of relocation expenses and attorney's fees.

When a locale adopts zoning that creates **non-compliant** existing uses, the laws typically *grandfather* those non-compliant uses to avoid a government **taking**. State and federal constitutions require *just compensation* for government takings including *regulatory takings*, which grandfathering avoids. Grandfather provisions, though, typically include forced phase-out of non-compliant uses. If the non-compliant owner discontinues the use, or fire or other cause destroys the non-compliant structure, then the owner loses the grandfathered right to continue the non-compliant use. Forced phase-outs also typically restrict to figures such as *ten percent* of value the extent to which the owner may repair, improve, or expand a non-compliant. Constitutionally suspect forced phase-outs require the owner to desist the non-compliant use after a period such as five years, giving the owner a period within which to depreciate the value. Landowners may challenge **ultra-vires** zoning laws that exceed the state enabling act's authority, such as if a zoning law failed to grandfather non-compliant structures or sought to impose monetary fines or other penalties that the state act did not authorize.

Zoning boards also typically hold authority to grant a **variance** from zoning laws under criteria that the zoning scheme establishes. Common criteria include *undue hardship, unique uses* that the zoning scheme did not anticipate, *beneficial uses* that serve the community in unique or important ways, or that the restriction does not make sense for the specific use in the specific location. Local zoning and building schemes often have other restrictions other than use restrictions, for conditions like *setbacks, parking, height*, and even *exterior finishes, window percentage*, and other architectural concerns, to preserve or improve a zone's character. Zoning and building officials may also consider variances for those restrictions, although local officials tend to strictly enforce zoning provisions.

Zoning boards typically hold authority to grant a **variance** from zoning laws under criteria that the zoning scheme establishes. Common criteria include *undue hardship, unique uses* that the zoning scheme did not anticipate, *beneficial uses* that serve the community in unique or important ways, or that the restriction does not make sense for the specific use in the specific location. Local zoning and building schemes often have other restrictions other than use restrictions, for conditions like *setbacks, parking, height*, and even *exterior finishes, window percentage*, and other architectural concerns, to preserve or improve a zone's character. Zoning and building officials may also consider variances for those restrictions, although local officials tend to strictly enforce zoning provisions.

In varying zoning restrictions, officials must take care not to engage in unlawful *spot zoning* favoring individual landowners. Local zoning must also avoid unlawful *exclusionary zoning* that prohibits foster-care facilities, low-income housing, and other potentially unpopular uses. If zoning restricts the aesthetics of building design, then the zoning must have reasonable standards so that officials cannot apply the restrictions arbitrarily and capriciously. Zoning that restricts speech content is lawful only if the least-restrictive means of obtaining a compelling government interest. Zoning that restricts the time, place, and manner of speech, but not its content, must show that it relates directly to achieving a substantial government interest. Federal law prohibits zoning from substantially burdening religious exercises unless the regulations are the least-restrictive means of furthering a compelling government interest.

III.-V. [Omitted as within the Property I course description.]

Nuisance

Nuisance is a tort claim protecting those who own and use real property. A nuisance is an *intentional, unreasonable, substantial non-trespassory invasion of another's interest in using lands*. A **private nuisance** claim protects the individual interest of one who owns or controls private lands, while a **public nuisance** claim protects the general interest of all who may use public lands. In the case of private nuisance, only those who own or control the private land have *standing to sue*. In the case of public nuisance, public officials or private representatives of the affected class, and private individuals who show special injury, have standing to sue.

Determining whether a nuisance exists depends on weighing factors. In general, one compares the utility or value of the activity, including how common the activity is, its suitability to the locale, and the impracticality of avoiding invasion, with the gravity of the harm that it produces. Nuisances do not always involve intentional conduct. Liability may exist for unintentional conduct that is negligent or reckless, or for conditions giving rise to strict liability as an abnormally dangerous activity. The existence of other tort claims or violations of law, rule, or regulation increases the likelihood of the conduct being a nuisance. As to who determines whether a nuisance exists, a jury determines *nuisance in fact* based on the factors mentioned above, while some authority exists for a judge to determine a *nuisance in law* when the conduct violates statutes and regulations. The remedies for a nuisance may include not only damages to those who prove harm but also a preliminary injunction on a showing of irreparable harm, substantial likelihood of success on the merits, and a balance of hardships weighing in plaintiff's favor.

Eminent Domain

Eminent domain is when government condemns private property to acquire it for public use, on payment of just compensation as state and federal constitutions require. Under state and federal constitutions, the government's exercise of eminent domain must be only for public use and with just compensation. Government may clearly take private property for public property like a street or park. Government may also take private property for public-use functions like utilities and railways. If government can articulate a legitimate public purpose to exercise eminent domain, such as to remove blight, correct unsanitary conditions, or provide housing or employment, then the U.S. Constitution permits it even if conveyed to private entity for private use. Most states restrict eminent domain to public land or function. Government must then pay fair market value, what a willing buyer would pay a willing seller on the open market at the time of eminent domain's exercise, for the land's highest and best use. Law may also require payment of relocation expenses and attorney's fees.

Other Takings

The takings clause requires government to pay just compensation for depriving others of their *personal property,* as well as real property. When government requires a person to relinquish personal property, even when as a condition for engaging in commerce, the government has taken the property and must pay just compensation. Different branches of government take real or personal property different ways. The legislative branch takes property, requiring just compensation, when its legislation acquires property, compels government intrusion, or deprives owners of all economically viable use. The administrative branch commits a taking by condemning, intruding, or regulating away economically viable use. In theory, a change in the common law that deprived an owner of property rights could constitute a judicial taking, under scant authority.

Exactions

An exaction requires a landowner to pay money, provide land, or provide for services in exchange for government approval of development. Government does not commit a taking if a roughly proportional connection exists between the exaction and the development. Government may, for instance, require developers to pay for new road entrances and utility lines, and to grant easements, to facilitate the development. Government would not be able to require developers to pay substantial monies into the general fund, unrelated to the development.

CPSIA information can be obtained
at www.ICGtesting.com
Printed in the USA
BVHW011933170520
579827BV00004B/17